What Others are Saying about
The Purple Curtain

There are not enough books written by Evangelical theologians on the intriguing subject of beauty. Brian Chan's contribution is a much-welcomed addition. Of Socrates' trinity: goodness, truth and beauty—it is beauty Dostoyevsky reminds us that "will save the world". From its pinnacles of perfection to its brokenness by sin—beauty pierces the heart, continually astonishing us at every turn. Chan's thorough investigation correctly challenges the reader to fully embrace a living theology with beauty at its core.

Barry Krammes
Professor of art at Biola University
& Editor of CIVA Seen Journal for
Christians in the Visual Arts

In this splendid book, Brian Chan challenges fuzzy, relativistic thinking about beauty with serious, biblical theology. He writes in an easy, engaging style, showing clearly what beauty is and why Christians should care. This book will make you think, increase your appreciation for all forms of art, and elevate your worship of the God of beauty. The church can thank God for creative young leaders like Brian Chan.

Garrett J. DeWeese
Professor of Philosophy and Philosophical Theology
Talbot School of Theology
Biola University

FOREWORD BY HOWARD G. HENDRICKS

THE
PURPLE
CURTAIN

Living Out Beauty
in Faith & Culture
from a Biblical Perspective

BRIAN S. CHAN

CrossHouse

Printed in the United States of America
by Lightning Source Inc.
Cover design by Dennis Davidson

Interior photographs/artwork are original works of Brian S. Chan and Ellen L. Chan

Library of Congress Control Number: 2011924847
ISBN: 978-1-61315-001-6

CrossHouse Publishing
PO Box 461592
Garland, TX 75046
1-877-212-0933

www.crosshousepublishing.org

Unless otherwise indicated, all Scripture taken from the Holy Bible,
New International Version, copyright 1973, 1978, 1984
by International Bible Society

FOREWORD

A dingy blur seems to have settled over our world, obscuring what is good or bad, right or wrong, ugly or beautiful. Occasionally a brilliant sunset or a moving melody enchants us, but it seems to vanish quickly. John Keats speaks poetically of a lovely autumn season that " dwells in beauty, beauty that must die." The 18th century poet Thomas Gray opined that power, wealth and beauty all await the grave.

Is there a roadmap for clear direction to what is valid, durable beauty? Artist and theologian Brian Chan's *The Purple Curtain* examines and defines true beauty, indestructible perfection that improves the soul, lifts the spirit and lives on eternally. Here is an eloquent treatment of an elusive concept—how to discern true exquisiteness through the eye of a creative craftsman who erases the smog for those who truly want to experience authentic beauty.

Howard G. Hendricks
Distinguished Professor Emeritus
Christian Education and Leadership
Dallas Theological Seminary

CONTENTS

What moves people? Passions move people. Without passions, the world would stand still. Passions are drawn from what we find beautiful, because the things we find beautiful attract, allure and excite us. Ah, the things people would do for beauty.

I remember noticing the magazine rack in the staff lunchroom. It was adorned with *Mademoiselle, Cosmopolitan, Vanity Fair, People, Elle* and many other magazines that catered to a female audience. There must've been 25 different titles. I saw one of the supervisors walk in and place another magazine on the rack. I said, "Are you adding to the collection?" She replied, "These are all mine. I brought them from home." As she sat across from me with a different magazine in hand, I watched her flip through pages of barely clothed female models. My ignorant, male curiosity was piqued. I interrupted her leisure reading and asked, "So, why do women like looking at images of other women?" It seemed like a sensible question. She answered, "Because women want to be them", as she pointed to the page, "and men want them". I found her comment very enlightening about our society's drive for beauty.

In the hype of the media industry of fashion, cosmetics and gossip, beauty is defined by what sells. It's no wonder our contemporary society perceives beauty to be fickle, superficial and relative. However we define beauty, the perception of it shapes our images, values, relationships, pursuits and loves. But there is more to beauty than mere luxury and decoration. There is an understanding of beauty that ought to be recovered because it does drive our perceptions, desires and loves.

In addition to having been an exhibiting artist in the San Francisco Bay Area and in Chicago, I embarked on a thesis research at Dallas Theological Seminary entitled, "The Beauty of God and the Art of Worship", that focused on a biblical perspective of beauty in relation to God. So what importance could beauty have on our spirituality? What if beauty is not an invention of culture but of God? What if beauty is not defined by commercialism but by God? What impact could beauty have on us then?

This is a book about a theology of beauty, to understand beauty from a biblical perspective and its effects on our relationship with God. Our biblical perception of beauty will inform our walk with God and our engagement with culture. If you're ready to unravel a biblical view of beauty defined by God, the beauty He makes and the beauty He delights in, then buckle in for a venture of transformation because God uses beauty to change broken people. What you should expect from this book is to discover more of the loveliness of God and the compelling to love Him more. Beauty in the end has one aim – to ravish our hearts with God's unfurled splendor, to arrest our souls and direct our pursuits. This is ultimately a book about discovering a greater love for God so that our love for Him becomes the one thing that orders our pursuits and mission in life.

When the beauty of God is core to living and our worldview, it is also a central reference point for how we interact with culture. Culture is a funny thing because it's shaped by society and people. Culture could in one way be described as the sum of a society's values, customs and principles that affect the individuals' identities, pursuits and tastes. So culture naturally evolves and changes. But while culture is fluid as it moves with the trends, there is also constancy within culture because God is both the creator and Lord of culture. We see God interacting within culture in biblical passages like the instructions for the Tabernacle's construction and usage. It's important to acknowledge that God has not stopped intervening with our cultures.

What's more, culture is still girded with God's common grace so that we can recognize truths in it that align with God's Word. This book finds that a theological view of beauty requires a two-way conversation with beauty in culture. One side of the conversation is about us learning the theology of beauty presented in Scriptures and to allow culture to enlighten our understanding of beauty as it aligns with Scriptural truths. This book interacts with cultural ideas about beauty from historical and contemporary philosophers, artists, writers, films, art and stories.

The end goal of discovering a biblical theology of beauty is to better embrace the greatest commandment of loving God out of our redeemed brokenness in a contemporary culture. If you're looking for what the purple curtain means, well, this book is about journey, story and discovery. So, you won't find out until you've taken the journey with me and arrived at the final chapter (and no cheating).

Chapter One

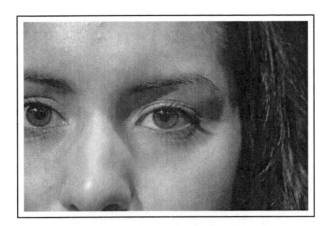

REALITY

C limbing 463 steps seems like an unnecessary activity unless your life depends on it. The promise of a beautiful, Italian cityscape seen from Florence's highest vista point motivated my wife Ellen and me to climb the steps of the Florentine Cathedral. But the journey tested our enthusiasm. The narrow corridor with the low ceiling would've made an excellent medieval torture chamber (ironic, I know, since it was a church). My knuckles grazed against the wall, allowing me to feel the cold, abrasive stone wall break my skin. The steps were uneven and often too small to offer a secure footing. By the 302nd step, my thighs burned, my ankles ached and the soles of my feet were numb. But there was no turning back from the hope of the experience awaiting us at the 463rd step.

At the top, the panoramic view of the Florentine cityscape was spectacular and yet poetically quieting. The red rooftops accented off the green hills in the background. The pieces of architecture masterfully interwove with each other as if it were one painting. Even the crisp air harmonized with the scene, giving life to the nostalgia of this city's historicity. From this bird's-eye view, I gained a perspective of Florence that wasn't available from the streets. It was ironic that the path to unspeakable beauty was a painful trek. Perhaps it was not too unlike our lives that are lined with various 463 steps that challenge our pursuits for the things of beauty, the things that capture us. These "things" may be a summit that reveals a scenery, a high-school crush that got our blood rushing, a lifestyle we dream of or the picture of heaven we yearn for. We shouldn't underestimate the attracting and motivating power of beauty.

Why should we understand beauty?

Why Beauty Matters

Beauty drives people. Augustine wrote, "Do we love anything unless it is beautiful? What, then, is beauty and in what does it consist? What is it that attracts us and wins us over to the things we love? Unless there were beauty and grace in them, they would be powerless to win our hearts."[1] Beauty triumphs the heart, driving us to climb any amount of steps in order to possess it. We want to have the things we perceive to be beautiful. Augustine was a man who grappled with the lusts of the flesh and a love for God.[2] He understood the ravishing powers of beauty while he wrestled between the lesser beauties of a sinful world and the greater beauties of God. Whether portrayed on the screen, in magazines or in stories, beauty is significant to life and culture because it compels and moves people towards a pursuit. The things of beauty are both tangible and intangible. You may recall seeing the image of a dream home or a car that symbolized a lifestyle and social status you desired to have. Or, perhaps you were struck by the virtue of a person, such as the extraordinary acts of Mother Teresa or the sacrificial bravery of a soldier, and thought to yourself, *I wish I could have that kind of compassion or courage*. Whether we desire tangible things or intangible qualities, the desire to possess what we deem beautiful sends us on a quest of pursuit.

Our pursuit for beauty in turn reveals our values, principles and philosophies about life, society and spirituality. What we find beautiful says a lot about who we are. When we ask the question, *Why is that beautiful to me?*, we unveil something of what we value and believe. In other words, our concept of beauty manifests our worldview.[3] It is of no surprise that throughout history society's definitions of beauty mirrored the prevailing philosophies, beliefs and social values of that time. Our perceptions of beauty are thus revelatory of our humanity, showing us who we are as a people.

But not only can our perception of beauty reveal who we are, beauty defined by God can reveal who He is, so that our understandings of beauty are closely related to our theology (beliefs about God). If God reveals to us His sense of beauty, it draws into question whether our perceptions are aligned with His — *are we attracted to the things He's attracted to?* If we dare ask this question, transformation begins to take place.

Transformation is akin to beauty. People don't want only to possess the things of beauty. People want to become it. We want to take qualities of beauty into ourselves. There is thus an incarnational effect of beauty. For many those 463 steps mark the amount of change they will endure in order to attain beauty within themselves. Our desire to have beauty and be beautiful reveals that we on some level realize we're imperfect and broken. But we are people who will not settle for brokenness. It is in our nature not only to have more but to be more. We will traverse the 463 steps and more to be transformed from our brokenness and imperfection into beauty and wholeness.

In light of these effects of beauty, possession, revelation and transformation, beauty ultimately evokes one response in us — *love.* As Augustine asked: would we love anything unless there was beauty in it? While living in Hollywood, I am reminded of the effect of beauty when I see thousands of people clambering to get a glimpse of certain celebrities as they scream, "I love you, _____." From a popular media perspective, the Angelina Jolies and Brad Pitts of western culture are seen as *the* beautiful people. The screaming crowds don't know these celebrities, but a social portrayal of beauty rests on them. And people love them for it. When I see the fans' passions for famous people, I can't help but wonder how often the fame and beauty of God arrests people, igniting a passion within them that is brewed from a relentless love for Him.

Love is the greatest driving force of all humanity. People will work, sacrifice, and die for love. Jacob's story of his willingness to work 14 years (that seemed like days to him) for the opportunity to marry the woman he loved and found beautiful illustrates the compelling power of love. It is no wonder that the greatest commandment in the Bible is to love God. Our 463 steps mark our journey in life. Every step takes us somewhere. And it's our love that defines the course of our steps, because where we place our love illustrates what we want to pursue and whom we want to be transformed into. In the end, the only question that remains of our lives is the same question that Augustine asked, "Where do your steps lead you?"[4] If the things you find beautiful do not evoke in you a love for God, then to where are your steps leading you? And, at the end of life's journey, where will you find yourself?

This book begins a journey of discovering a biblical perspective of beauty and beauty's impact on our spiritual and social lives as it influences our pursuits, love for God, engagement with the world and redemptive transformation from brokenness to beauty. But to appreciate the influences of beauty, we have to see that beauty is not merely an invention of social culture, even though social culture is significant in shaping people's perceptions of beauty. Rather, it is crucial to see that beauty is a reality created by God. People resonate with beauty, seek beauty and are naturally influenced by beauty because it is from God. To see this, we need to go to *the beginning.*

Nature of the Universe

The nature of the universe was determined at the beginning of creation when the stage was empty and no audience was present, where only the creative director was on set. The opening scene of Genesis showed God as *the* writer, composer and artist of creation. His act of creating was described with a unique Hebrew term, *bara*, meaning "to fashion" or "to shape" with the nuance of a craftsman.[5] The term implies creating out of nothing and the artist's free-

> "Belief in God, as deliberate, immediate Creator, allows us to appreciate the beauty of the world as intended..."[i]
>
> —David Thistlethwaite

dom and power to unfurl his imagination.[6] Revisit with me this account of God as the Maker of beauty.

It is difficult not to recognize the artistic process in God's creative activity. God hovered above a void like a painter standing before a blank canvas ready to transform it into His vision (Gen. 1:1-2). He spoke into the abyss to draw up broad compositions and forms (Gen. 1:3,9; Isa. 45:23). He brought forth light and dark, which determined contrast, and then He divided the expanse into thirds and established a horizon line (Gen. 1:3-7). He formed basic shapes in the background, like the land, sea and sky. There were moments when He actively molded the material and shaped the very objects Himself, as if He gathered the dirt from the ground to sculpt a mountain (Gen. 1:14-16, 20-21; Isa. 45:9, 66:1-2). He filled the background with detailed colors and hues through an array of plants, animals, birds and sea creatures (Gen. 1:12, 20-21, 24-25). One might hang a sign on Genesis 1 that reads: "A cosmic artist is at work."[7] I think John Calvin put it well when he wrote, "We must therefore admit in God's individual works but especially in them as a whole that God's powers are actually represented as in a painting."[8]

The act of creating out of nothing demonstrated God's supreme power, while the diversity He decorated the universe with exhibited His limitless imagination. Genesis 2:1 described God being pleased with creation's "vast array", where monotony and homogeneity are two qualities that did not characterize God's creativity. The world He visualized and brought forth was filled with luster and fullness of every shape, tone, color, hue and size, a world wrought with more variety than all our collective minds could conceive. Genesis 2:9

> "You cannot in one glance survey this most vast and beautiful system of the universe, in its wide expanse, without being completely overwhelmed by the boundless force of its brightness. The reason why the author of the Letter of Hebrews calls the universe the appearance of things invisible [Heb. 11:3] is that this skillful ordering of the universe is for us a sort of mirror in which we can contemplate God, who is otherwise invisible."[ii]
>
> —John Calvin

reads that God created "all kinds of trees" and Genesis 1:12 reads that God made seed-bearing plants and fruit-bearing plants of "all different kinds". He created plants, animals, sea creatures and birds according to their "kinds". Creation was a work of art caringly crafted (*bara*) out of an artistic process of forming and filling[9] and characterized with divine, imaginative variety. To all of this, God declared, "it was good", using a Hebrew term (*tob*) that expressed aesthetic delight (we'll expound on this term in the next chapter).

A Beautiful Waste

To a pure pragmatist, the variety would seem like an elaborate and unnecessary waste. But to someone who loves beauty, this excessive extravagance is the amalgamation of a masterpiece. Variety communicates creativity, originality and inventiveness. The world is a place of countless variety. It is a place where flowers have a million different shapes and scents, where new species are still being discovered and where no two human beings in all of history look exactly the same or have the same fingerprint. It is no understatement to say that God is the God of a "vast array" when we consider that there are more stars in space than grains of sand on all our beaches or that, according to data from the Hubble Telescope, more than 50 billion galaxies exist.[10] Or, we can observe on a microscale of "the things [that subhuman creatures] make—such as coral or honeycombs, spider webs or multicolored shells—are not their own conscious deliberate creation but an expression of God's thought."[11]

God unleashed His imagination, like a child with crayons, coloring the universe with as many different kinds of everything as He delighted. The

> "But upon His individual works He has engraved unmistakable marks of His glory, so clear and so prominent that even unlettered and stupid folk cannot plead the excuse of ignorance."[xiii]
>
> —John Calvin

vast array of creativity in the universe is a reflection of God's glory because He shows us the incalculable enormity of His thoughts and the power to create a limitless diversity that forms a single, visionary whole. But also, this vast array reveals His passion because He *chose* to create limitlessly. A purely pragmatic God might merely create a world that works effectively and efficiently without the excessive extravagance. A passionate God would choose to create what He envisioned to be beautiful and glorious according to His pleasure, a world that is both practical and pleasing.

God made the world to have two qualities – practicality and aestheticism. The second part of Genesis 2:9 reads that the trees were "pleasing to the eye" and "good for food". "Good for food" meant the plant life served as sustenance for other life forms (Gen. 1:29-30). "Pleasing to the eye" meant He intended for His creative variety to give

> *"...I learn that my feelings about art and my feelings about the Creator of the universe are inseparable."* [iv]
>
> —Madeleine L'Engle

pleasure to the soul when we looked upon them. Genesis 2:12 mentioned there being gold in the land and it was good. Andy Crouch observed that gold is not a practically useful material but its validation in Scripture was for its beauty. [12] In addition to the minerals, we see from this same verse the mentioning of "aromatic resin and onyx". Not only was the land adorned with visual brilliance, but it also smelled great! The land stimulated the senses, causing elation in one's spirit, and God made it all. He created a world where beauty had many shapes and expressions. We forget sometimes that the world was created not only to be good for sustaining the physical needs but also for enriching the soul. We forget that the world God designed was meant to be enjoyed, to entice our eyes and to touch our spirits.

Aesthetics, artistry and beauty were deliberately part of the nature of the universe. The world we live in is a world of beauty and aesthetics, laden with God's infinite imagination, and a representation of His delight. It is a world that He looked upon and found aesthetic satisfaction in when He pronounced it to be "very good."

Nature of Humanity

What about human beings? What in our human nature causes us to resonate with beauty? Identity is the most fundamental issue for understanding ourselves. Some begin with their names, birthplaces and childhood histories to find a sense of who they are, but we begin with God's design of us.

First, we are God's artwork when He molded us from the clay of the earth, like a potter sculpting a vase (Gen. 2:7). The Hebrew term used to indicate God's making of man in Genesis 2:7 was *yasar*, a term typically used to describe the artistic work of craftsmen.[13] The imagery of God forming man from the clay of the earth could not have more vividly portrayed Him as an artist. God's activity of making humans was not merely science but art. Being an artwork of the creative God versus a result of random chemical reactions should have profound implications on our identity as humans.

Second, as the artistic product of God's craftsmanship, the model He used for sculpting people was His own image (the *imago Dei*). For centuries, scholars and theologians pondered over this concept of the *imago Dei*, because this and the breath of God are the two elements that distinguish humans from the rest of creation. These two elements are essential to our identities. "The image of God in man is inclusive and descriptive of His entire being. It is the essence of what man is."[14] So what does being made in the image of God mean to us?

Genesis 1:26-27 reads,

> "Let us make man in our image, in our likeness, and let them rule over the fish of the sea and the birds of the air, over the livestock, over all the earth, and over all the creatures that move along the ground.
>
> "So God created man in His own image, in the image of God He created him; male and female He created them."

Some scholars argued that the *imago Dei* could not be isolated to one component of the human being, such as the intellect, rationalization, conscience or the spirit.[15] Rather than particularizing the image of God to one aspect of our identity, it is more accurate to understand His image as defining our overall human identity. Wayne Grudem wrote that, "The expression refers to every way in which man is like God."[16] To be an "image" of someone is to resemble the person but not be exactly that person. Perhaps being made in someone's image is similar to the expression, "like father, like son", as in Adam's case who had a son "in his likeness, in his own image" (Gen. 5:3). Since God is man's model, understanding the human identity requires understanding God, and we find an introduction of Him in the first twenty-five verses of Genesis during His grand, dramatic act on an empty stage.

The Creative Side of God and Us

Dorothy Sayers in her book *The Mind of the Maker* observed: "Looking at man, he sees in him something essentially divine, but when we turn back to see what he says about the original upon which the 'image' of God was modeled, we find only the single assertion, 'God created'."[17] Sometimes the most vivid explanations are provided not in propositional statements but in dramatic presentations. Before the creation of humans, we see God's power to shape, form and mold the universe and His delight in colors and light, all of which reflect His goodness and imaginativeness to create beauty and limitless diversity. Then at the height of His masterful venture, we arrive at "the climax of God's creative activity"[18] where He makes humans in His image, an image that was portrayed vividly and viscerally in the grand account of the creative drama we just read. I echo these words by Franky Schaeffer, "If from this world around us we can learn anything about God's character, surely it is that He is creative and diverse, a God whose interest in beauty and detail must be unquestioned when one looks at the world He has around us, and particularly people themselves as the result of His craftsmanship...."[19]

We even see God spout poetry at this climactic event of creating humans. The three lines (cola) in verse 27 about making man and woman in God's image resound a crescendo of excitement and accomplishment, where each line is meant to be read interdependently of each other and not separately. These lyrical lines are strung together by a rhythmic meter formed with the repeated word *bara* (create).[20] It is as if God broke out in song at the height of His creative expression!

Genesis introduces the image of a creative, passionate and inventive God who delights in beauty. At the core of our nature, like our Creator therefore, we hold the capacity to imagine, be creative and love what's beautiful. We can see this quality of God's image in individuals throughout the Bible. We find skilled artists like the ones who created the Tabernacle's elaborate artistry, which was crucial in theologically teaching Israel how to worship and relate to God (Exod. 31:1-11; more on this later). But it is also not unusual to find a prophetess like Miriam perform an impromptu dance (Exod. 15:1-20), a shepherd like David with the talent to compose music that was beautiful enough to soothe the tormented mind of a king (1 Sam. 16:14-23) and a father like Jacob who was capable of creating a beautiful robe of diverse colors that aroused the jealousy of others (Gen. 37:3).

It is inherent in us to not only resonate with beauty but long for it. We are like God, who desired not to leave the universe in a state of chaos but to fashion the cosmos out of it, when we choose to order our own lives and relationships. We are like Him, who filled the void with fullness, light, colors and diversity, when we surround ourselves with things that are good, true and beautiful. We are like Him, who delighted in making the parts come together to form a meaningful whole, when we want to find purpose in our lives that gives a sense of wholeness to all our activities and endeavors. While there are many other implications about the *imago Dei*, creativity and a love for beauty are among the ways in which we are like God. The fiber of our souls resonates with aesthetics and artistry where being creative is "to experience more fully the richness of being human".[21]

> "It is true that everybody is a 'maker', in the simplest meaning of the term. We spend our lives putting matter together in new patterns and so 'creating' forms which were not there before. This is so intimate and universal a function of nature that we scarcely ever think about it."
>
> —Dorothy L. Sayers

I love Peter Jackson's remake of the film "King Kong". When the giant monkey is first presented, we see a savage beast tearing through the jungle.

Until Kong gazes at the sunset with Ann Darrow on top of the Empire State Building and places his hand over his heart to silently gesture the word, "beautiful", we suddenly see more than a savage creature; we see a sentient life that grasps a distinct human ideal. Because he comprehended and loved beauty, Kong showed us a unique quality of a soulish being.

Makers of Beauty

God doesn't only endow humans with the capacity to know and love beauty but also expects them to participate in making beauty. We see first off that God blessed man with the privilege of ruling over the earth that God made (Gen. 1:28).[22] As the stewards of the earth people were expected to appreciate the beauty God made. When God put Adam in the Garden of Eden to "work it and take care of it" (Gen. 2:15), He called Adam to take up the task of cultivating His masterpiece. Adam had to work the ground with his hands in a similar imagery to God scooping up clay to form man. During his labor in the garden, Adam had the opportunity to experience the boundless beauty of creation in multi-sensory ways, as he padded the clay with his hands, listened to the birds sing, differentiated the colors of plants, and identified the scents of flowers. Adam and Eve had the freedom and calling to learn about this vast world, love it and dive into experiencing all of its extravagance as the benevolent rulers who cared for it as their own.

Second, God paraded all the animals and the birds He created in front of Adam and told him to name each one (Gen. 2:19). God created the creatures and invited Adam to complete the creativity by naming them, which was an incredible exercise of his imagination as he named each creature from the earthworm to the elephant and indulged in creative variety as God had done. In addition, the verse reads that God wanted to "see" what Adam would name each animal, not in a judging way where God might revoke Adam's choices in case He didn't like certain names. But since "whatever the man called each living creature, that was its name", God actually watched Adam exercise his creativity with approval. He encouraged Adam's creative thinking and imagination, which reflected the *imago Dei* back to God.

There is an artist within each of us that resonates with beauty because of the *imago Dei*. Genesis 2 reminds us that God intended for humans to act creatively, imaginatively and intuitively within a world of beauty. It reminds us to fashion beauty in our work-weeks and to find inspiration in our faith. We could name our newborn child, design a family day at the park, paint on a canvas, experiment with a culinary idea, or form mental images of being in heaven. When we do such creative things, we tap into a chord of our humanity that reflects God's image.

> "Creativity is a part of the distinction between man and non-man. All people are to some degree creative. Creativity is intrinsic to our mannishness."[vi]
>
> —Francis A. Schaeffer

We will continue to develop an aesthetic theology by defining beauty according to the Bible and by applying that understanding to our faith, discipleship and cultural engagements. We will also see that theological truths can be gleaned from the arts and media culture through God's common grace. Since not everything creative is glorifying to God or honoring to His image within us, we will address the moral concern. In the end, rediscovering a biblical perspective of beauty forges our love of God, challenges our spiritual formation and reframes our call to God's mission of redemption in our lives and in the world. Our next step then is to consider the question of, "what is beauty?"

Walk in Color

- In what ways have you been influenced or motivated by beauty?
- In what ways do you exercise creativity throughout your week?
- Revisit the creation account in Genesis 1. Outline the seven days of creation and note God's steps of creativity.

Notes: Chapter One

[1] Augustine, *Confessions*, transl. by R. S. Pine-Coffin (London: Penguin Group, 1961), 83.

[2] Augustine, *Confessions*, 80 & 83.

[3] A worldview is a composite of one's beliefs, particularly about reality, God, values, society and knowledge. J. P. Moreland, *Kingdom Triangle: Recover the Christian Mind, Renovate the Soul, Restore the Spirit's Power* (Grand Rapids: Zondervan, 2007), 33.

[4] Augustine, *Confessions*, 82.

[5] T.E.M., "bara," in *Theological Wordbook of the Old Testament*. 127.

[6] Gordon J. Wenham, *Word Biblical Commentary: Genesis 1-15*. ed. by David A. Hubbard and Glenn W. Barker. vol. 1. (Waco, TX: Word Books, 1987), 13.

[7] Thomas Dubay, *The Evidential Power of Beauty: Science and Theology Meet* (San Francisco: Ignatius Press, 1999), 115.

[8] John Calvin, *Calvin: Institutes of the Christian Religion*, edited by John T. McNeill, transl. Ford Lewis Battles, vol. xx in "The Library of Christian Classics" (Philadelphia: The Westminster Press, 1975), 63.

[9] Bruce K. Waltke and Cathi J. Fredricks, *Genesis: A Commentary* (Grand Rapids: Zondervan, 2001), 57.

[10] Thomas Dubay, *The Evidential Power of Beauty: Science and Theology Meet* (San Francisco: Ignatius Press, 1999), 134.

[11] Frank E. Gaebelein, *The Christian, The Arts, and Truth: Regaining the Vision of Greatness*, edited by D. Bruce Lockerbie (Portland: Multnomah Press, 1985), 73.

[12] Andy Crouch, "How Is Art a Gift, a Calling, and an Obedience?" in *For the Beauty of the Church: Casting a Vision for the Arts* (Grand Rapids: Baker Books, 2010), 33.

[13] Derek Kidner, *Genesis: An Introduction & Commentary*, Tyndale Old Testament Commentaries, D. J. Wiseman (gen. ed.) (Downers Grove: Inter-Varsity Press, 1967), 60. This imagery of God acting as a potter is re-emphasized in Job 33:6.

[14] Ronald B. Allen, *The Majesty of Man*. Second ed. (Grand Rapids: Kregel Publications, 2000), 84.

[15] Victor P. Hamilton, *The Book of Genesis: Chapters 1-17, The New Testament Commentary on the Old Testament* (Grand Rapids: William B. Eerdmans Publishing Company, 1990), 187.

[16] Wayne Grudem, *Systematic Theology* (Leicester: InterVarsity Press, 1994), 443.

[17] Dorothy L. Sayers, *The Mind of the Maker* (London: Continuum, 1994), 17.

[18] Allen P. Ross, *Creation & Blessing: A Guide to the Study and Exposition of Genesis* (Grand Rapids: Baker Books, 1998), 112.

[19] Franky Schaeffer, *Addicted to Mediocrity: Contemporary Christians and the Arts* (Wheaton: Crossway Books, 1981), 17-18.

[20] Ronald B. Allen, *The Majesty of Man: The Dignity of Being Human* (Grand Rapids: Kregel Publications, 2000), 78-79.

[21] Steve Turner, *Imagine: A Vision for Christians in the Arts* (Downers Grove: InterVarsity Press, 2001), 66.

[22] Waltke, *Genesis*, 66.

Pull Out Quotes:

[i] David Thistlethwaite, *The Art of God and the Religions of Art* (U.K.: Solway, 1998), 11.

[ii] John Calvin, *Calvin Institute of the Christian Religions*, edited by John T. McNeill, transl. by Ford Lewis Battles, "The Library of Christian Classics," vol. 20 (Philadelphia: Westminster Press, 1975), 52.

[iii] *Ibid.*

[iv] Madeleine L'Engle, *Walking on Water: Reflections on Faith and Art* (Colorado Springs: Waterbrook Press, 2001), 7.

[v] Dorothy L. Sayers, *The Mind of the Maker*, edited by Susan Howatch (London: Continuum, 2004), 21-22.

[vi] Francis A. Schaeffer, *Art and the Bible* (Downers Grove: InterVarsity Press, 1973), 52.

Chapter Two

DEFINITION

It's uncomfortable when people stare at a part of your body. I least expected it to happen during a conversation about religion with a gentleman on the street. The conversation was sparked by a street survey I conducted. I listened intently as he shared openly about his experiences with churches and his own perceptions of spirituality, until I noticed he no longer was making eye contact with me but was staring at my left arm. The short-sleeve shirt I wore exposed the deep red birthmark that ran from my fingertips along my arm and disappeared underneath my sleeve.

He finally asked me, "Did you get burned?" I'm okay with people's curiosities about my birthmark, and I'm used to the did-you-get-burned question. But when I told him that it's a birthmark, his response perplexed me. He said, "There are laser treatments nowadays for that. You could get that corrected." Corrected? I never thought my arm needed correcting. I politely responded, "Actually, I don't want my birthmark removed. It's always been a part of me. Anyway, it doesn't hurt or cause discomfort." Still, he had to rebut, "Yeah, but don't you want to make it normal?"

His message to me was that there was an ugliness on my arm, and though it posed no risk, it was still an ugliness that should be corrected to conform to a perception of beauty defined by his concept of normality. He held an assumption he believed to be universal: *the birthmark is ugly and why wouldn't you want it removed?* As much as his perspective of my arm needing fixing perplexed me, my response in not seeing the ugliness on my arm perplexed him. At the end of our ten-minute interaction, we didn't find ourselves at the same definition of what was ugly and what was beautiful…at least when it came to my birthmark.

Though we make evaluations every day about what is beautiful or ugly, we rarely know exactly what we mean. We say phrases like, "That's beautiful" or "She's a beautiful person", but if we had to define what beauty is, we'd likely find ourselves puzzled to articulate what we meant. Defining beauty in our contemporary age can be like trying to handle a wet water balloon—it feels like a slippery task with no concrete end. Our quest toward a definition involves an overall glimpse of society's views on what beauty is through history, and ultimately an exploration of beauty from a biblical view and how that affects our spiritual lives and engagement with contemporary culture.

A Definition That Affects Us

An exercise I enjoy doing with the students of my class at Biola University is presenting to them a series of images and asking them, "Is this beautiful?" Hearing their differing responses illustrates the heavy influence of subjectivity. Some determine it is beautiful because of the colors and content while others see the skillful technique of the artist and still others investigate the message behind the piece.

Marcia Muelder Eaton in *Basic Issues in Aesthetics* identified different perspectives that influence the way we evaluate and experience the aesthetic quality of something. [1] The factor that bears the greater emphasis will more greatly influence

> "Every normal person knows what beauty is, even though few can define its meaning." [i]
>
> —Thomas Dubay

how we discover and interpret beauty. After Eaton's evaluation of the differing perspectives, she proposed that beauty could be defined as something with the "capacity to evoke pleasure that is recognized as arising from features in the object traditionally considered worthy of attention and reflection".[2] The most common understanding about beauty nowadays is that it's something that pleases us or is desirable.

> "If we say that the aim of any activity is merely for our pleaseure, and define it solely by that pleasure, our definition will evidently be a false one."[ii]
>
> —Leo Tolstoy

However, each person's sense of pleasure is a subjective matter that differs from one person to another. The popular phrase, "beauty is in the eye of the beholder", captures the relative perception, which assumes an objective definition is unavailable. But can there be an objective definition of beauty that is a universal, absolute standard that exists independently of our personal opinions and pleasures?

After Leo Tolstoy surveyed extensive theories of beauty in *What Is Art?*, he concluded these theories boiled down to two main views. The first states that beauty is something that has an "independent existence (existing in itself), that it is one of the manifestations of the absolutely Perfect" and the second states that beauty is "a kind of pleasure received by us".[3] He identified a major distinction between the views of objectivity versus subjectivity. Objectivity delineates beauty according to a universal, even cosmic, principle that surmises an authoritative, absolute rule. Subjectivity renders a definition of beauty that is relative to individuals in their contexts, where the only rule is the one you make. Tolstoy had a problem with deriving a definition that primarily centered purely on our biased tastes.

It is fascinating to see how the definition of beauty in society changed from a sense of objectivity to relativity over the last two thousand plus years, an aesthetic evolution that Umberto Eco detailed in his monumental work *History of Beauty*. The ancient Greeks and medieval philosophers predominantly subscribed to a canon or standard of beauty, which held to the qualities of harmony, proportion, goodness and truth. This standard, however, in no way diminished the pleasurable effects beauty has on the one who experiences it. But there is a difference between the definition and the effects.

As Eco tracked beauty's definition over the centuries, he discovered the canon gradually became less popular. Society wanted to push beyond the canon. People wanted to define beauty according to originality, the surprise factor, the genius factor and the passion element. When Eco's research finally landed in our contemporary day of mass media and plurality, he concluded that a single idea of beauty no longer exists. Beauty could be whatever is pleasing, provocative, marketable or consumable. Beauty was defined by "whatever sells", fueling an overall superficial sense of beauty. He reasoned that if a time traveler from the future visited our present-day, he would "have to surrender before the orgy of tolerance, the total syncretism and the absolute and unstoppable polytheism of Beauty".[4] According to Eco, beauty in contemporary time no longer had a unified definition. It's not surprising that the plurality of beauty reflects the plurality of spirituality as well. Tolerance that allows for multiple views versus an objective view of truth became the greatest virtue and definition of ideologies in our time.

To a pluralistic culture the idea of an absolute definition of beauty appears outdated and threatening, because notions of objectivity imposes on our subjectivity. If there were no objectivity, subjectivity reigns supreme. But an absolute or objective notion implies that there is a "right" idea. Objective ideas of beauty infringe on our personal freedom because there would be an expectation to subscribe to objectivity. Conforming to a standard of any sort violates the extreme view of individuality and relativity. The idea of an objective beauty can even seem oppressive because we're required to subscribe to an idea that may be against our feelings and opinions.

Subjectivity centers on what makes us feel good where the only principles we subscribe to are derived from our own tastes and opinions. Immanuel Kant denied the validity of any objective rule to defining beauty, stating that, "If we judge objects merely according to concepts, then all presentation of beauty is lost. Thus there can be no rule according to which anyone is to be forced to recognize anything as beautiful."[5] Kant's influential teachings on aesthetics determined that beauty was subjectively defined by an individual's gauge of pleasure or pain, where one's pleasure determined beauty and one's pain determined ugliness. If it feels good, then it must be beautiful, and if it feels bad, then it must be ugly. But when a person has a subjective experience of the beautiful or the ugly, he does not think it is only true for himself. Rather, he unconsciously universalizes his experience to everyone else, believing that others must also experience the same thing. And so to the individual, it makes complete, logical sense that others should feel the same way even though it was purely a subjective perspective. Kant's view perhaps correctly explains my situation with the man who expected me to think as he did that my birthmark was ugly and it explains his surprise when I didn't agree.

Subjective relativity offers a sense of freedom with our ideals and values shaped after our own appetites. For Christians whose fundamental beliefs are rooted in notions of the absolute and the singular, such as there being absolute truth and one God, the ring of relativism and subjectivity of beauty sounds alarming. But there is truth in a subjective and relative view of beauty. In fact, there is biblical truth to be found in Kant's theory, for everything does exist in relativity. The issue that should challenge us is not whether we need to choose between an objective and a subjective view. The real questions are: "Whose subjectivity are we considering?" and "Could one individual's subjectivity be rightly universalized as an objectivity for everyone else?"

Beauty by The Book

Genesis 1:1 reads, "In the beginning God…". The source of everything was not an inanimate force, a metaphysical phenomenon nor a theoretical concept, but a single, personal individual with an intellect and desires. Everything created by God would exist in relationship to Him. Reality was meant to be personal. The universe was always going to be a question of how it and everything in it related to Him.

Throughout the process of creation, God was the first to determine the definition of beauty as he declared six times what He thought was "good." The word "good" is translated from a Hebrew term, tob, which could refer to something that's desirable, pleasant or beautiful.[6] *Tob* speaks of an aesthetic quality that evokes a reaction of pleasure in someone, like the pleasantness experienced from listening to a fine melody as in 1 Samuel 16:16 or from looking at the attractiveness of a woman as in Genesis 24:10. At various stages of the creative process, God made evaluative pronouncements about His creation. With each ring of, "it was good", He declared that the universe conformed to His pleasures and delights. When God, who is the authoritative absolute, declared what He thought was good, He defined beauty according to His pleasure. And because He is God and there is no other like Him, His pleasure became our standard.

Perhaps the first and most provocative lesson we learn from a biblical view of beauty is God's subjectivity becomes our objectivity. God's assessment of the universe being "good" and finally being "very good" at its completion was a subjective declaration that established an objective view for the universe. So, Kant's theory of universalizing the subjective is helpful for us in understanding God universalizing His subjectivity. Genesis 1 and 2 defends God as the sole, original Creator, which gives Him authority not only to rule the universe but to also define it. As Maker and Cosmic King, His personal tastes became rules and concepts. Truth was defined by a being – God. God's subjectivity over the universe reinforces for us that everything revolves around Him and life exists in relativity to Him. So that what we know of creation, life and beauty is always personal and it is always subjective. A biblical understanding of beauty points us back to the person, works, words and desires of God. The important question is whose subjectivity are we considering if not God's? Absolute rules exist not because they are derived from a neutral state through some phenomenon but from a personal God.

But what do we mean by good? "Good" can be one of those overused terms that either have too many meanings or too shallow of a meaning. For God, when He declared His creation to be "good", He defined beauty.

Design

I vividly remember the images of the 9/11 attack. I just came out of a seminary class and was walking to my mailbox in the student center when

I noticed dozens of my fellow colleagues fixed to a nineteen-inch television. I followed their gaze to the screen and saw the Twin Towers in New York wreathed in smoke. As the hours went by, I watched both towers finally dissolve into dust and ashes, saw people scurrying down the streets and ducking into storefronts to avoid being consumed by the rolling storm of debris, and observed crying women and stunned men coated with a gray film emerge out of the

> "All art is cosmos,
> cosmos found within chaos."[iii]
>
> —Madeleine L'Engle

dust clouds. The chaos was silencing. What I witnessed were the effects of reckless acts to destroy two massive structures, breaking down their form and shape that resulted in havoc and losses of life, leaving in its stead an empty space of rubble and misery. Decomposition, lifelessness, and void vies against our human nature; it reeks of horror and is the very opposite of good.

When God looked at what was there before the universe was created, He saw formlessness and emptiness (Gen. 1:2), a state described by a rhyming Hebrew phrase - tohuwebohu. In other locations of the Bible, this phrase referred to barren wastelands and deserts, depicting conditions that were chaotic, disordered and lifeless (Isa 24:10; 34:11, Jer. 4:23). Both aesthetically and practically, a condition of tohuwebohu was not good, like a heap of trash that fumigates with diseases. It pictured a place with no composition, order, life, diversity, or blessings of the imagination. And because it lacked design, it held no meaning or purpose. God, however, did not find pleasure in chaos (Isa. 45:18-19). For God, "good" is the very opposite of chaos. "Good" has form, design, cohesive diversity, and life.

The quest for achieving beauty was a divine and miraculous act of transforming chaos into cosmos. The universe reverberates of God's goodness that did not leave things in a state of tohuwebohu but made it into a state of tob. Even in this creative transformation of a primordial chaos into cosmos, we see a foreshadowing of God's eventual redemptive act in salvation as a divine act of recreating fallen people, wreaked with the chaos of sin, at the costly price of His Son into a people whom He could call "good". Creation and re-creation in salvation are both forms of turning chaos into cosmos, a sort of redeeming from *tohuwebohu* into *tob*. For God, beauty was about having cohesive design out of diverse parts.

Glory

When I frequent galleries and museums, I enjoy observing people interact with the art. I noticed a common ritual people practiced when they saw a piece they were attracted to. After viewing it for a moment, eventually, they stepped closer, leaned forward and looked at the plaque or at the bottom corner of the piece for the name of the artist. An unspoken rule about art is it stands to exemplify the passion, personhood and power of the artist who made it. In a fundamental way, a great story, film, or art declares the glory of the artist. God determined creation was good because it expressed His glory.

Glory is fame. Through the ages, scientists and philosophers have taken notice of the order and unity in the universe, from the orbiting of planets around a sun to the collaborative inner-working of cells in a body. One particular fascination that indicates God's fingerprint of design on creation is the divine proportion, a concept that has been observed by ancient civilizations like the Egyptians, early Greek theorists like Euclid and medieval mathematicians like Fibonacci. The divine proportion, also called the golden ratio or the golden proportion, referred to a mathematical proportion known as Phi, which is 1.61803:1. This ratio could be found throughout nature from the spirals in seashells, the eye of storms and the shape of human embryos to the generations of a male bee, flower petals and the measurement of a human DNA strand.[7] The unity found on the macro and the micro scales convey a sense of harmony in the universe, where proportion, balance and rhythm connect the parts to a greater whole. This evidence of design gives sensibility to our reality suggesting that the existence of our universe had meaning. This cosmic har-

> "The work of God was in fact kosmos, the order of all things, which stands in opposition to primordial chaos."[iv]
>
> —Umberto Eco

mony suggested an intentional and intelligent design for the universe, giving evidence to the presence of a very powerful and imaginative God. He revealed Himself through the beauty He makes.[8]

Creation like an artwork stamped with God's signature sings of His presence, power and His character of goodness and imagination (Psa. 19:1-6). It was intended that the artwork should hint of the artist (Ro. 1:19-20). Beauty, for God, was defined by whether it expressed His glory[9], a very delineating factor in a fallen world that automatically attempts to diffuse it. The world, however, was meant to be a sanctuary full of God's glory (Isa. 6:3). To experience beauty, the "good" beauty, is to relish in His glory, immersing in the fame of His presence, power and character. For God, beauty was defined by whether it revealed His glory.

Truth

Artists create with a variety of media. For some it is paint, while for others musical notes. God's primary media was His word. He created the earth in three different ways. In one, He said for things to come into being and it happened (Gen. 1:3, 9, 11, 12). In another, He said for things to come into being and He proceeded to make them (Gen. 1:6-7, 14-16, 20-21). Lastly, God spoke to Himself to go and make it and He made it Himself (Gen. 1:24-27). The one constant medium was His *word*. No part of creation came into existence without His word having been a part of its formation. What He said was authoritative. His words expressed truth. Under many classical standards of aesthetics, truth is an essential element for beauty. Socrates argued that creative expressions that tell lies about God cannot be worthy of claiming beauty.[10] True beauty rightly represents God. A defining quality of beauty, for God, was the conveyance of truth, particularly truth about Him.

Pontius Pilate's age-old question seems to echo the voices of our contemporary day, "What is truth?" (John 18:38). He asked this of Jesus but didn't wait for the answer. Since God is the source, the absolute authority and the origin of all reality, He defined truth by who He is, what He says and does, and what He desires or plans (Psa. 25:5, 26:3). As Frank E. Gaebelein wrote, "Truth is of God."[11] Truth is a version of reality portrayed through God's eyes. Beauty is not truth but if beauty is defined by truth, then looking at something beautiful can lead us down a path of illumination.

It was a breathtaking moment when I first saw Michelangelo's *David* statue in Florence. I turned the corner to enter a long, wide corridor. On either side of this corridor were a series of unfinished works by the master artist. My eyes were immediately drawn to the far end where the two-story statue stood in a curtain of white light that poured in through the glass-dome ceiling above. Its massive presence dominated the entire building. As I gradually approached it, I noticed David held a stone in his right hand while his sling was comfortably relaxed over his left shoulder. This statue depicted David before his famous battle with Goliath. Yet the fierce expression on David's face conveyed the kind of faith that claimed victory over Goliath before the fight began. This statue affirmed the truth about faith in God that leads to victory and allowed the audience to experience this biblical story in a compelling way. The truth revealed in beauty may not need to explicitly portray a biblical story or verse. Beauty that reflects God's truth may speak of His goodness, holiness or sovereignty. It may even speak of the detriments of sin. All such things would align with biblical truth.

But what about when we find things beautiful that do not contain truth? This is when truth challenges our tastes of beauty. Do our senses hunger for truth in the things that attract us? Or do we easily settle for superficial pleasures and absorb them without scrutiny? The danger of mere attractiveness without truth is it captivates us, raises itself as an ideal in our minds and lures us to follow it. If what attracts us does not contain truth, then where will it lead us? In the end, what we find beautiful becomes a mirror for ourselves, a self-revelation that leads us to scrutinize not only what we find beautiful but also why we find these things beautiful. We may ask ourselves, "What does what I find beautiful say about who I am?"

When beauty is defined by truth, it will illuminate truth to us. Beauty can speak truth to us by providing conviction through our senses in viscerally supple ways. The search for beauty in all of life extends far beyond decoration. A search for absolute beauty becomes a profound search for truth in all of life. The challenge beauty presents to us is an attractive yet compelling conviction to transform every facet of our lives to reflect truth. Becoming more beautiful means becoming more truthful. Since all truth is from God and truth is the one non-substitutionary medium of God's works of beauty, our gradual conformity towards truth eventually leads us to conform to the likeness of God.

God Himself

A name says a lot about a person. God called Himself, "I am", (Exod. 3:14) because He is the self-sufficient source of all things. He is the to-be verb *par excellence*, the origin of all things good (Jas. 1:17). When He de-fined beauty by declaring His creations to be "good", the basis of His measurement was Himself as *Yahweh*. "Good" flowed from His character of goodness and resonated with His personal cosmos as the triune God who is perfectly individual and communal as

> "God has given us some reflection of his own sense of goodness, so that when we evaluate things in the way God created us to evaluate them, we will also approve what God approves and delight in things in which he delights."
>
> —Wayne Grudem

three in one. "Good" reflected the perfect harmony within Himself as the one whose seemingly opposing attributes of holiness-justice and love-mercy are held in sound equilibrium (Jer. 9:24). "Good" demonstrates the integrity of creation, undefiled with deception or lies, and reflects the purity and truthfulness of God (Num. 23:19, Titus 1:2, Heb. 6:18). "Good" reveals the glory of the eternal and all-powerful Creator (Ro. 1:19-20). The inspiring journey of searching out beauty in the universe is finding hints of the epitome of beauty – God Himself, who is absolute beauty. All things we find genuinely beautiful in the world and in our lives are faint reflections of the beauty of the great *I am*. In the next chapter, we'll devote focused effort to exploring the depths of God's beauty.

Beauty versus Pretty

There is a difference between what is beautiful and what is pretty. One conveys truth, where beauty has the power to prompt reflection, change and conviction, while the other affords nice feelings. This is the fine line between true beauty and sentimentality.

Sentimentality offers a feel-good experience without a genuine encounter with substance. This is because sentimentality lacks truth and godly glory. Sentiments are based on what *feels* good while lacking the substantial "good" God declared. There are many things in our culture that could be considered merely sentimental. It is like the criticism about many contemporary pop songs that have a great tune but greatly lack substantial lyrics that enlighten the listeners or press them toward being better human beings.

> *"Yet all these works are 'beautiful'— a beauty however which does not mean sweetness and sentimentality, nor a beauty in form or language alone, quite apart from content."[vi]*
>
> —H.R. Rookmaaker

The practical danger of settling for sentimentality over seeking beauty is we feel we had a real experience but it was in the absence of God's truth, like eating fast foods that pleasantly satisfy our immediate hunger but offer no nutritional value.

Contemporary society has perhaps been adept at equating sentimentality with beauty, echoing the voice of, "If it feels good, it must be right." If beauty poses itself as a natural ideal for people, then the pursuit of sentiments and good feelings in place of true beauty leaves people bound to a superficial nostalgia. Beauty challenges us with what we really want and need, and that perhaps what we really want is not to feel better but to be changed. Sentimentality trivializes the issues of the world, life and spirituality, by leaving things the same and anesthetizing it with pleasantries. Beauty on the other hand leaves us wanting change in ourselves.

But when beauty is about God's pleasure, then there are times that the same beauty is about our pain, because as fallen people who encounter beauty that reflects God's cosmos, glory, truth and person, we may find ourselves utterly convicted and challenged to change. Where sentimentality will soothe us with the words of "everything is just fine", beauty will at times show us how far we are from being perfect and remind us of our need for redemption. Where sentimentality binds us to the shallow, beauty may stir us to discover truth that sets us free (John 8:31-34). Sentimentality for fallen people is easy. Beauty can be difficult.

A challenge of our contemporary time is not to settle for sentimentality. The danger we face is mistaking sentimentality for beauty. It's difficult for most not to settle for the sentimental, because what simply feels good to us is all we want after facing our struggles in life. But sentimentality is too often the cheap substitute Satan offers to keep us quiet. By pacifying our flesh, he may cause us to ignore the cries of our spirit that genuinely yearns for beauty – the kind of beauty defined by God.

It is in the things that contain cosmos not chaos, His glory, His truth and reflections of who He is that God calls beautiful and delights in. So that, we find at the heart of a biblical view of beauty is God's pleasure – His delight in who He is, what He does and says, and His glory. Seeking beauty in life, society and faith becomes an invitation to pursue God's "good", to find at the center of our own lives a desire for what pleases Him.

Walk in Color

- Make a list of the things you find most beautiful in life – what tangible and intangible things attract you and allure you?
- Re-read Genesis 1 and 2 slowly. Visualize the drama of God's creation account.
- Observe a sunset. Jot down words or phrases of what beautiful qualities you see.

Notes: Chapter Two

[1] Marcia Muelder Eaton. *Basic Issues in Aesthetics* (Prospect Heights: Waveland Press, Inc., 1988), 6-7.

[2] Eaton. *Basic Issues in Aesthetics*, 143. For Eaton, what we determine to be beautiful is what we assess "aesthetic value" to (138-9).

[3] Leo Tolstoy. *What Is Art?* translated by Almer Maude (Bridgewater: Replica Books, 2000), 38.

[4] Umberto Eco (edited). *History of Beauty*, translated by Alastair McEwen (New York: Rizzoli, 2004), 428.

[5] Immanuel Kant, Critique of Judgment transl. J. H. Bernard in *Philosophies of Art & Beauty: Selected Readings in Aesthetics from Plato to Heidegger*, ed. Albert Hofstadter and Richard Kuhns (Chicago: University of Chicago Press, 1976), 290.

[6] The term *tob* carries five semantic meanings, one of which refers to the aesthetic quality of desirability, pleasantness and beauty. The other four semantic meanings are: 1) practical, economic, or material good, 2) quality or expense, 3) moral goodness and 4) technical philosophical goodness. R. Laird Harris, Gleason L. Archer, Jr., and Bruce K. Waltke, "Tob," in *Theological Word Book of the Old Testament*, vol. 1 (Chicago: Moody Press, 1980), 793. Also, Philo substitutes the word "beautiful" with *tob*, when interpreting God's declaration of light as being "good." Philo, "On the Creation," in *The Works of Philo: Complete and Unabridged*. Trans. By C. D. Yonge (Peabody: Hendrickson Publishers), 8.30.

[7] Priya Hemenway, *Divine Proportion: Phi in Art, Nature, and Science* (New York: Sterling Publishing Co., 2005), 124-140.

[8] See John G. Stackhouse, Jr., "The True, the Good and the Beautiful Christian," *Christianity Today* (January 7, 2002): 58.

[9] "Barth and Balthasar show that the theologically significant content of the idea of 'beauty' is found in Scriptures, primarily under the category of 'glory'." Richard Viladesau, *Theological Aesthetics: God in imagination, beauty, and art* (New York: Oxford University Press, 1999), 105.

[10] Hofstadter and Kuhns (editors), *Philosophies of Art & Beauty*, 9-12.

[11] Frank E. Gabelein, *The Christian, The Arts, and Truth: Regaining the Vision of Greatness*, edited by D. Bruce Lockerbie (Portland: Multnomah Press, 1985), 87.

Pull Out Quotes:

[i] Thomas Dubay, *The Evidential Power of Beauty: Science and Theology Meet* (San Francisco: Ignatius Press, 1999), 29.

[ii] Tolstoy, *What Is Art?*, 43.

[iii] Madeleine L'Engle, *Walking on Water*, 8.

[iv] Eco. *History of Beauty*, 83.

[v] Wayne Grudem, *Systematic Theology* (Grand Rapids: Zondervan, 1994), 197.

[vi] H. R. Rookmaaker. *Modern Art and the Death of a Culture* (Wheaton: Crossway Books, 1994), 197.

Chapter Three

ABSOLUTE

W hy do we imagine God looking like Santa Claus? We picture God as a large fellow with broad shoulders and a white, fluffy beard sitting on a big red chair. His grandfatherly appearance and large, cushy thighs beg you to sit on his lap and tell him your wishes. Perhaps the warm appearance of God, the Santa Claus type, reflects our personal longings for the traits we want to see in God. The Santa Claus image is comforting. But if God were to visually depict Himself to us, what would His self-portrait look like?

I've been a Christian since I was twelve years old. I remember in times of disappointment or hurt I found tremendous comfort in pouring my heart out to Him in the solitude of my bedroom. I always knew there was a listening ear. But something was missing from my spiritual life that was present in believers like King David, St. Augustine or St. Bonaventure. I could not help but notice the stark difference between the experiences the Old Testament prophets had with God and my own. Their encounters with Him did not depict them sitting on His cushy lap. Rather, they saw visions of radiance, splendor and unearthly glory that overwhelmed their senses and overtook their souls, driving them to fall flat on their faces before a majestic king. God's voice was not always a soothing, grandfatherly tone but was the sound of a raging ocean. I couldn't help but notice their God looked and sounded different from the mental image I grew up with. They perceived a profound beauty filled with awe and intensity, which I longed for.

I wanted to know God as he presented Himself. No. I needed to know, because I was not satisfied with my subjective, preferential treatment of God. I needed to know Him based on something higher than myself. But there was a danger to this pursuit. There was a vast difference between knowing God according to preferences versus revelation. It can be a scary thing to set aside our preferential biases and step into a reality that God presents, a reality that is untainted by our own subjectivity. Personal preference attempts to change our reality, to bend God around our own ego. Revelation attempts to change us, to bend us around Him.

Have you ever had those experiences where you thought you knew something like the back of your hand until you see it for the first time from a different vantage? When I meditate on how the prophets knew God, or rather on how He revealed himself to them, I sometimes felt like I was being reintroduced to Him. I grew up close to the shore in San Francisco and I regularly visited the beach as a kid, spending time staring into the Pacific Ocean. The ocean was usually covered with fog under an overcast sky. The waves swelled to the size of small hills then charged like a herd of buffalos until they rammed into the shore with an explosion of white water. There were warning signs about going into the water because this turbulent ocean had claimed many lives. The water was grey, foamy and freezing. I hadn't visited other beaches and I thought this was how the Pacific appeared everywhere until I went to Maui.

In Maui, the water was remarkably blue, blissfully calm and comfortably warm. Standing waist-deep in the water, I could see the ocean floor. The tropical fish swam around me as if I was part of their ocean. I spent hours snorkeling, immersing myself in the Pacific, and forgot about time. What I saw and experienced was completely different from what I grew up with and thought I knew. It was the same Pacific. There is only one. But Maui reintroduced me to the Pacific in a way I had never seen or known. The prophets reintroduced God to me.

The Beauty of God

The ancient Hebrews described God with visual delight. The Bible used Hebrew terms such as *yafah* to describe the "fair beauty" of the Lord. It was the same term used to describe the beauty of Sarah (Gen. 12:11), Esther (Esth. 2:7), Solomon (Songs 2:10), Job's daughters (Job 42:15) and a Shunnamite woman (1 Kgs. 1:4). Another Hebrew term used to express God's beauty was *tsebi* (Isa. 28:5), where He was likened to a beautiful wreath, which represented honor.[1] The prophets were not shy about seeing God as beautiful.

Visualize with the prophets and apostles for a moment as they described God's aesthetic self-portraits. In Revelation 4:1-5, John saw a vision of God sitting on a throne with the "appearance of jasper and carnelian", brilliant precious stones that refracted light. Out of His throne came flashes of lightning. In a vision found in Daniel 10:6, the Son of Man[2] looked like lightning and His eyes were like flaming torches. The Hebrew term for "lightning" could describe a blinding burst of light, which depicted Christ's face as a bluish white flash with two reddish-orange infernos for eyes. His body was like chrysolite, a bright, shiny precious stone of yellow or gold color. His feet were like bronze, a metal that was recognized for its mirror-like sheen. God's beauty was characterized with all sorts of lights.

Fire was another kind of light that appeared in God's self-portraits. In Ezekiel 1:27, God's body from the waist up was like some kind of "glowing metal, as if full of fire, and that from there down he looked like fire and brilliant light surrounded him". Like a torrent of roaring flames, God emanated wild rays of light that danced around Him. He appeared as a pillar of fire to the Israelites in the night to illuminate their way in the wilderness. In Genesis 15:17, God's presence was represented with a fiery, smoking pot and a flaming torch glowing in the darkness.

The most intense source of light, the sun, was used to describe the light of God. Habakkuk likened God's splendor to the sunrise, where brilliant rays peered over the mountains and streams of light shot out of His hand (Hab. 3:4). Psalm 104:2 depicted God as being cloaked with beams of radiant light. Psalm 50:1-2 poetically declared God to be perfect in beauty (*yafah*) as He shone like the sun.

The prophets and apostles not only saw radiant light and colors coming from God but they also saw elements associated with Him refracted light and colors. In Ezekiel 1:26-27, God sat on a throne of sapphire while "brilliant light surrounded him". He was embellished in a sea of light. Imagine God's own effervescent light piercing through each sapphire of his throne, refracting brilliant blue colors around Him. Ezekiel mentioned something like a "rainbow in the clouds on a rainy day" enveloped God (Ezek. 1:28). I picture the rainbow as a result of mixing the red and yellow colors from the fiery light of His body with the blue illuminations coming from His sapphire throne. The angelic beings surrounding God in Ezekiel's vision had the appearances of "burning coals of fire or torches" with fireballs flashing back and forth around them (Ezek. 1:13). In Daniel 7:10, a river of fire flowed out from beneath the Lord. The portraits of God were set against surroundings of splendor, beauty and light.

> "[God] is beautiful, 'beautiful in a manner proper to him and him alone, beautiful as the unattainable Primal Beauty, but..., precisely for this reason, beautiful not only as a fact, not only as a force, but rather: as fact and as a force in the manner in which he asserts himself as the one who arouses pleasure (Wohlgefallen), creates desire (Begehren) for himself, and rewards with delight (Genuss) ..., the one who as God is both lovely and loveworthy.'"[i]
>
> —Hans Urs Von Balthasar

Light was a common element in God's self-portrait. Whether it was the light refracted in precious stones or the light from lightning, fire or the sun, every known brilliant source of light was used to describe God's beauty. The apostle wrote, "God is light; in him there is no darkness at all" (1 John 1:5). So what is it about light? Why not flowers?

There is something about light that's both secure because it reveals and illuminates and yet also mysteriously unsettling because it pierces and penetrates. Light represents wholeness and purity which we innocently love. And it embodies intangible values that we can't live without, like hope, ideals, knowledge, goodness and truth. Hans Urs Von Balthasar wrote God's light penetrates our world. Through the ages light was associated with something of a divine, pure and heavenly beauty.[3] "God is therefore identified with the splendor of a sort of luminous current that permeates the entire universe."[4] In His display of light and colors, God demonstrates His glory and perfection. His radiance showed He was the very source and substance of knowledge, life and excellence.

The apostle Philip made an earnest request of Jesus that I believe echoes humanity's heart-cry. "Show us the Father," he said to Jesus, "and that will be enough" (John 14:8). The Greek word for "enough" expressed a feeling of satisfaction or completion. I think our tireless pursuits and chases for fulfillment in life on this earth could end with a real, authentic encounter with God, to know and behold this incorruptible light. At the core of our human souls, we long to behold this kind of beauty because it gives us a taste of perfection amidst our insecure and fading realities. Like a beacon shining across a dark ocean, His perfect beauty is a penetrating hope in uncertain times. To be in the presence of God's light is to find a place of certain hope and solidarity in a fragmented world. It is as the psalmist wrote, "in your light we see light" (Psa. 36:9). But I wonder how ready we are to see the beauty of God.

In Los Angeles, if you say "beauty" it likely conjures up thoughts of cosmetics and plastic surgery. While our contemporary culture typically associates beauty with outward appearances, the beauty of God expressed a perfect authenticity. There is truthfulness about His beauty that is both soothing and convicting. This truthful authenticity is that His outward beauty is a pure manifestation of His inward nature. There is a genuine harmony and not a hypocrisy in who God is. So whole is God's beauty in a world striving for genuine definition of self, it is an ideal we all long for, that is to achieve a sense of wholeness and harmony within ourselves as we see it in God. When the outward appearance is not truthfully representing the inward qualities, there is hypocrisy, which is an outer shell without an inner reality. When the outward and inward are consistent, there is authenticity and integrity. Real beauty is the outward appeal truthfully representing the inward substance. The Bible described the wholeness of God's beauty with two key words - *glory* and *splendor.*

Glory

"Glory" is one of those words that evoke sentiments of honor, dignity and pride. It is a visually charged term that is frequently used to describe God (Exod. 16:7, 24:16, 40:34). "Divine beauty is so endless, so unspeakable, that Scripture has a special word for it, *glory* — an effort to express the inexpressible."[5] Wayne Grudem explained that

> God's "glory" means the bright light that surrounds God's presence. Since God is spirit, and not energy or matter, this visible light is not part of God's being but is something that was created. We may define it as follows: *God's glory is the created brightness that surrounds God's revelation of himself.*[6]

Thomas Dubay in *The Evidential Power of Beauty* wrote this comment on the meaning of glory:

> The divine radiance and loveliness are so endlessly beyond anything we can imagine or experience that revelation chooses a special term to speak of it. That term is glory, a word that occurs repeatedly in Scripture.[7]

The Hebrew term for glory, *kabod*, literally meant "weightiness", a metaphorical way of communicating the immensity of God's worth. In Exodus 40:34-35 when God's glory filled the tabernacle, Moses could not enter it. We generally understand the concept of worth in measurable units, like a dollar amount. But there is no quantifiable estimation for God's worth. In the presence of His glory, we are left with the inexplicable compelling weight of His worth and the natural response to worship Him for it.

Although God's worthiness cannot be quantified, it can be qualified by His character.[8] God's glory tells of His goodness. In Exodus 33:18-19, Moses requested God to show His *glory* to Him. God agreed and said He would cause all His "goodness" to pass in front of Moses. Moses asked to see God's glory and got God's goodness. God didn't misunderstand Moses. The glory of God expressed His complete goodness. As Ned Bustard stated, "we find that His glory *is* His goodness."[9]

What is God's goodness? The goodness of God is the standard of what is right or moral and is also the reason for beauty and delight. It is because of His goodness that He did not make the world to be a place of chaos, emptiness and evil but rather of integrity, fullness and beauty (Isa. 45:18). It is because of His goodness that He cares for creation (Psa. 106, 107), like the feed-

> "But if God is himself good and therefore the ultimate standard of good, then we have a definition of the meaning of 'good' that will greatly help us in the study of ethics and aesthetics."[ii]
>
> —Wayne Grudem

ing of the animals in the wild (Psa. 104:14), and blesses man with delightful things (Psa. 104:15). Out of His goodness comes life and being (Acts 17:28). Augustine wrote, "These things of beauty would not exist at all unless they came from you."[10] The psalmist insists our response to God's goodness should be thanksgiving (Psa. 100:4-5, 106:1), especially when God will not withhold good things from those who follow Him (Psa. 84:11)! David invites us to "taste and see that the Lord is good" (Psa. 34:8). Taste and delight in His glory – in His beauty.

I find David's invitation very provocative. It is disturbingly humbling because I read it as a universal invitation to an aesthetically truthful experience of God in all times. I remember the stories of kids who got mad when they thought they had been good all year long but Santa didn't bring them what they wanted. At the heart of our humanity, we'd like to believe we deserve good things, which drives us to live by merits and not by grace. We like to believe that if I do good, good things will come my way. What if I'm good but good things don't come my way? What if I regularly diet and exercise and still find myself stricken with cancer? Then the question is, *can I still taste and see God's goodness?* Or is His beauty outside of my experiences because life stinks? If I lose sight of His goodness, would I also lose sight of His glory, His beauty and His worthiness of my unlimited worship?

A fallen world isn't a fair place but a potentially hurtful one. To know God's beauty means His character refashions my perception of reality. Faith becomes a matter of defining my experiences based on what I know about God and not defining what I know about God based on my experiences. It is easy to talk and sing about God's goodness, like a cliché, and I think that's the problem. We make it too easy, and we lose a sense of the immensity of His goodness that inspires celebration, humility and hope especially in the worst of times so that the reality we live in is in the context of my circumstances but under the definition of God's goodness.

> "If the very form of his glory – which mere thought can never simply banish – consists 'not only in awe, thankfulness, admiration, and submission', but also in joy, pleasure, and delight in God and in his splendour, 'if the form of his glory is determined precisely by his ability to transport us to joy, and further determined by that joyous rapture itself: how could we then possibly dispence with the concept of the beautiful?"[iii]
>
> —Hans Urs Von Balthasar

The invitation to taste and see God's goodness is for the 42-year-old single woman who fears growing old alone. It is for the single mom who lost her job. It is for the alcoholic who is searching for freedom. It is for the victim of sexual assault who wants healing. To taste and see is about knowing the light under a canopy of darkness. Tasting and seeing God's goodness is an ongoing journey in Christ of knowing and experiencing God as we interact with the brokenness of life and of finding ourselves arrested by moments of uncanny peace, delight and inspiration because we were touched by His beauty in the midst of darkness. It's in having this knowledge of goodness that we begin to comprehend beauty.

Splendor

Another Hebrew term that visually expressed God's beauty is "splendor" (Psa. 29:2, Job 40:10). "Splendor" (or *hadar* in the Hebrew) described something that looked perfect, flawless and desirable (cf. Ezek. 16:14, Lev. 23:40). When the Bible described God as splendorous, it portrayed Him with the image of perfection and excellence. Splendor expressed His attribute of majesty (Psa. 45:4, 110:3), like a magnificent king robed in grandeur (1 Chron. 16:27, Psa. 145:12-13). Isaiah 33:17 promised God's people they would see His majestic beauty that assured hope and confidence for the future.[11] But His splendor reveals something about Him that we may not expect - something disturbing for Santa-lovers.

It is His righteous judgment (Deut. 33:17, Psa. 45:4, Isa. 33:21-22). One passage vividly and alarmingly displays the character of His judgment. He wore a white robe of splendor, and while He was in His best, radiant attire, He went forth and trampled on unrepentant sinners, like a giant squashing grapes in a vat, until the splattered blood of His victims turned His gleaming white robe crimson. Believe it or not, the perfection of God's judgment is part of His splendorous beauty. Digest Isaiah 63:1 and 3 for yourself.

> Who is this coming from Edom, from Bozrah, with
> his garments stained crimson?
> Who is this, robed in *splendor*, striding forward in
> the greatness of his strength?
> "I have trodden the winepress alone; from the
> nations no one was with me.
> I trampled them in my anger and trod them down
> in my wrath; their blood spattered my
> garments, and I stained all my clothing."
> [italic emphasis mine]

The crayon-colored images of God we grew up with in Sunday school dissolves under an unfiltered revelation of His splendor. It's hard to digest that this violent depiction of God is part of His beauty.

It's difficult to swallow the judgment that God could bring on people for unrepentant sin, injustice and immorality. The difficulty is it seems to contradict the wonderfully gracious and loving God we desire. But if we consider the perfect character of God, would we expect anything less than the perfection of all His attributes? If we can purport that God's love is superlative beyond fathom, then it's also reasonable to consider God's holiness is immensely flawless beyond wonder. Scripture portrays God as a Father who loves sinners immensely and as a Judge who judges the unrepentant intensely. Splendor is not a nice notion but an expression of the perfection of His holiness that does not allow sin to go unjudged. Jonathan Edwards, in his sermon, "Sinners in the Hands of an Angry God," ardently argued for the extraordinary magnitude of God's wrath, so that His grace could not be taken for granted in light of His holiness. The totality of God's character defines the completeness of God who judges perfectly without fail and loves incredibly with sacrificial mercy. We see then that what we mean by the perfection of God is the flawless symmetry of His characters of goodness and holiness, where neither diminishes the other.

Theories of aesthetics through the ages recognized the defining qualities of beauty are harmony, balance, and proportion.[12] "Harmony is not the absence of but the equilibrium between opposites."[13] God is beautiful not because *we* find certain qualities about Him favorable. He is beautiful because His character is in harmony, where He is perfectly balanced in His merciful love and in His righteous judgment. Though the extremes of these two characteristics seem to be opposites, they are a balanced complement to each other. Neither one diminishes the other, but both are held in harmonious tension. Jeremiah 9:24 reads

> "But let him who boasts boast about this: that he understands and knows me, that I am the LORD, who exercises kindness, justice and righteousness on earth for in these I delight," declares the LORD.

In fact, God's character was consistently expressed in the gospel message of Jesus Christ. According to Romans 3:25, God sent Jesus Christ as a sacrifice to "demonstrate his justice", and according to Romans 5:8, God sent Jesus Christ to "demonstrate his love". The incarnation and mission of Christ perfectly embodied God's beauty!

Three...One

Did you ever think there was beauty in the Trinity? God is not only perfectly harmonious and proportionate in character but also in nature. God exists as three persons in one essence. This means the three persons, Father, Son and Spirit, are completely separate individuals while yet they are unified to exist as one divine God. Logically, it makes no sense to us since nothing in our created order could exist in such a way. But God the Creator is not creaturely and exists transcendently beyond the bounds of our physical laws. While we cannot rationally explain how three distinct persons could exist as one being, we can believe in it because it is revealed to us in Scripture and we can see the perfect beauty of it. God is perfectly proportionate as an individual (one God) and as a community (three persons). He lacks nothing as an individual or as a community. He is all of that within Himself.

God is harmoniously relational since within the three persons of God there is no competition, but there is a balance in equality and in hierarchical submission. The Father, Son and Spirit are equals because they share the same power (1 Cor. 2:10-11, Col. 1:16), eternality (John 1:1, 8:58, 17:24) and glory (Phi. 2:6-11) as God. But there is also a harmonious submission within the three persons, where the Father sends the Son Jesus (John 15:21, 17:23) and Jesus is obedient to the Father (John 17:4). Likewise the Father and Son send the Spirit (John 15:26) and the Spirit is obedient to the Father and the Son (John 16:13). The nature of God that appears contradictory to us in a fallen and creaturely world but exists in perfect proportion and harmony should put us in awe and wonder of Him. Such perfect equilibrium and perfect harmony could be found nowhere else in creation. Within the Trinitarian nature of God we cannot help but to see a beautiful depiction of the true meaning of individuality in harmony with community and of equality in harmony with submission, something that should astound us with fascination. The perfectly proportioned nature of God idealizes the concept of beauty.

The Attractiveness of Santa and the Beauty of God

So when we have such a magnificent God who flawlessly depicts absolute beauty, why does a Santa-image of God still seem attractive to people? Because Santa is exactly what we want him to be. He determines whether we've been good or bad which feeds our fleshly expectations of earning our gifts, so that the gifts are not really gifts but rewards. Santa is based on a merit system of works, which is logical, sensible and prideful. If we were bad, there would be no consequences because Santa is not punitive. If we were good, he would bring us what we want. He wouldn't give us what *he* thinks we need. He would give us exactly what we ask for.

God, on the other hand, is not beautiful because He fits our expectations nor because He fulfills our wish lists. He is beautiful because of the complete harmony of His character of love and justice and the perfection of His nature as three in one. If He didn't do anything for us, He would still be beautiful, which is why He is truly worthy of worship. His worthiness is not dependent upon my satisfaction, but solely upon who He is. And by who He is, God introduces to us the reality of an absolute beauty. An absolute is an authoritative and universal standard that remains true whether we agree with it or not. I often get asked whether beauty is an objective or a subjective matter. "Isn't beauty in the eye of the beholder?" The answer is yes to both. The objectivity of beauty is defined

> "He that is spiritually enlightened truly apprehends and sees it, or has a sense of it. He does not merely rationally believe that God is glorious, but he has a sense of the gloriousness of God in his heart. There is not only a rational belief that God is holy, and that holiness is a good thing, but there is a sense of the loveliness of God's holiness. There is not only a speculatively judging that God is gracious, but a sense how amiable God is on account of the beauty of this divine attribute."[iv]
>
> —Jonathan Edwards

by God's subjectivity. His subjective character, nature, words and will become our objective standard.

In the face of an absolute beauty, we are left with a choice. Unlike Santa who conforms to our expectations, God's absolute, immovable beauty calls us to conform to Him. When we walk with God in the presence of His beauty, we encounter a paradigm shift from the popular consumerist mentality. For many, and I'm no exception, we approach God as a shopper, picking what we like and leaving the rest on the shelf. If we yield God's beauty to our preferences, we distort Him and unconsciously fabricate a god after our imagination. It's easier and more convenient to worship a god of our preferences rather than the God of revelation. We have to be humble and brave enough to yield to His self-revelation according to His word in order to discern a beauty that exists outside of the limits we set. It means we don't have the luxury of reading certain books of the Bible that make us feel good, like Ephesians and John, while avoiding other books we find disturbing, like Lamentations or Nahum. God's beauty beckons us to enter into that divine space of harmony and tension where He can be discovered.

I find knowing God in all of His beauty to be a challenge. It confronts the presuppositions I rely on, the biases I rest in and the assumptions of what I think I know. But in moments of honesty when I face my brokenness, I see the misleading of my preferences. I find myself hungering for a perfection too deep to comprehend but enough to fall madly in love with. Maybe then, I may know an experience of God that is like Augustine's, who wrote:

> I gazed on you with eyes too weak to resist the dazzle of your splendour. Your light shone upon me in its brilliance, and I thrilled with love and dread alike. I realized that I was far away from you. It was as though I were in a land where all is different from your own…[14]

Jonathan Edwards, a milestone preacher of the First Great Awakening, wrote:

> The Author of human nature has not only given affections to men, but has made them very much the spring of men's actions… These affections we see to be the springs that set men a-going, in all affairs of life, and engage them in all their pursuits… Take away all love and hatred, all hope and fear, all anger, zeal, and affectionate desire, and the world would be in a great measure motionless and dead; there would be no such thing as activity amongst mankind, or any earnest pursuit whatsoever.[15]

All people are driven by something. In a how-to society where we frequently begin with the question of pragmatism, we ignore the question of passion that is the undercurrent for all we do. Effective pragmatism follows true passion. For the Christian, true passion is ignited by God's beauty. Passions subside when we settle for less, and passions are born when something larger than life moves us.

When I sit with the prophets and apostles, I see and hear their responses to God's glory. Ezekiel and the apostle John fell facedown before the sight of God (Ezek. 2:1; Rev. 1:17). When God appeared in a bright cloud, Peter, James and John fell facedown to the ground (Matt. 17:6). After seeing God enthroned in His temple, Isaiah cried, "Woe to me! I am ruined! For I am a man of unclean lips, and I live among a people of unclean lips, and my eyes have seen the King, the LORD Almighty" (Isa. 6:5). When Jesus ap-

> "My understanding is not able [to attain] to that [light]. It shines too much and [my understanding] does not grasp it nor does the eye of my soul allow itself to be turned towards it for too long. It is dazzled by its splendour, overcome by its fullness, overwhelmed by its immensity, confused by its extent. O supreme and inaccessible light; O whole and blessed truth, how far You are from me who am so close to You! How distant You are from my sight while I am so present to Your sight! You are wholly present everywhere and I do not see You. In You I move and in You I have my being…"
>
> —Anselm of Canterbury

peared to Paul in a brilliant, heavenly light, Paul fell to the ground (Acts 9:4). In the ancient near east, there was a common fear of judgment as a result of seeing God. But these prophets and apostles experienced feelings of reverence and awe that I think we lack. Growing up, I domesticated God with gentle, pastel colors when He showed himself in a consuming light. I long to encounter God where I could echo Augustine's feelings of "love" and "dread", and somewhere in between an uncanny passion for God would arise. For it is only in the one that I love with all my heart and dread with all my soul that would impassion me to live, sacrifice and worship.

Imagine being in the presence of God's beauty where our preferences subside and our frustrations fall silent. His radiance is difficult to look at, like the sun, but our eyes can't help but to be drawn to it, for that's what our souls starve for — the light. It feels like a weight that overwhelms us. It's a light that both warms and penetrates our hearts. As saved sinners, we both hate it and are madly in love with it, because it convicts and enriches us at the same time. His loveliness soothes our brokenness and breaks it. How could such beauty affect us so? How is it that we can be immersed in such pure goodness and holiness so that we see life, ourselves and the world differently? Everything around us stands still in God's beauty while everything within us stirs. Unforeseen passions develop, because we've wrestled with this indescribable perfection. We want to write and sing about it. We want to dance to it. We want to furiously paint and sculpt for it. We want to worship. We want to live. Now, imagine letting go of Santa Claus and encountering God in all His beauty daily.

So what does it take to have this kind of encounter? How can we enjoy God's beauty? That's where our journey continues to next.

Walk in Color

- Write down in a descriptive paragraph what your image of God has been. How has that image influenced your spiritual life in the past and present? What do you think informed you of that image you've had of Him?
- I invite you to take a journey of engaging God's beauty by keeping a daily journal for five weeks. Each day jot down attributes of God that you notice around you and in your reading of Scripture. Take note of both his love and justice and his Trinitarian presence.
- Do a careful study of Ezekiel 1, outlining and taking notes of all the elements described. Experience what Ezekiel experienced that caused him to fall facedown before the Lord. Using a Bible dictionary to help understand and appreciate the meanings of the various elements and colors mentioned would be helpful.

Notes: Chapter Three

[1] The term "wreath" (*atara* in Hebrew) used metaphorically to describe the Lord generally meant a crown. It could be a crown of gold or silver or a crown of flowers, like a garland. In the context of Isaiah 28 where the beauty of God was contrasted with the fading beauty of Ephraim's drunkards as like a withering flower (Isa. 28:1), the imagery of God likened to a garland is the most appropriate interpretation.

[2] Some scholars believe the man in Daniel 10 is an angel, such as the angel Gabriel, and not the pre-incarnate Christ. I believe the man in Daniel 10 is Christ because of four reasons: (1) The illustrations of the Lord as the "Ancient of Days" in Daniel 7, of the Lord in Ezekiel 1:24-27 and of Christ in Revelation 1:13-17 were virtually identical to the description of the man in Daniel 10:5-6, indicating the royal, priestly and judicial attributes of the Divine God; (2) The man in Daniel 10 is the same man in Daniel 12 who demonstrated foreknowledge of God's sovereign plans which angels did not have; (3) In Daniel 12, the man is specifically standing "above the waters", a polemic consistent with God as being superior over other gods, such as Baal (cf. Psalm 29:3 11). The arguments against the view of the man being Christ are primarily questioning why Christ would struggle to defeat the king of Persia, a demon, and receive help from the angel Michael in the battle, and why Christ would function as a messenger, a role more congruent with an angel.

[3] Umberto Eco (editor), *History of Beauty*, transl. by Alastair McEwen, second ed. (New York: Rizzoli, 2005), 102.

[4] *Ibid.*

[5] Thomas Dubay, *The Evidential Power of Beauty: Science and Theology Meet* (San Francisco: Ignatius Press, 1999), 75.

[6] Wayne Grudem, *Systematic Theology: an Introduction to Biblical Doctrine* (Great Britain: Inter-Varsity Press and Grand Rapids: Zondervan, 1994), 220.

[7] Thomas Dubay, *Power of Beauty*, 296.

[8] His glory depicts the *excellence* of His character. Thomas L. Trevethan, *Beauty of God's Holiness* (Downer's Grove: InterVarsity Press, 1995), 224.

[9] Ned Bustard, "God is Good Like No Other," *It Was Good: Making Art to the Glory of God*, edited by Ned Bustard, revised and expanded, second ed. (Baltimore: Square Halo Books, 2006), 20.

[10] Augustine, *Confessions*, transl. by R. S. Pine-coffin (London: Penguin Books, 1961), 80.

[11] There is debate about whether "king" (in verse 33:17) referred to God or to an anointed agent of God. In the Hebrew text, the term is without an article, which may suggest a proper title. Also, the context is exalting God and His character. Therefore, I am led to interpret this term as referring to God. Furthermore, verses 33:21-22 addresses God as "Mighty One", "judge" and "lawgiver" of Zion. These titles are congruent with the functions of a governing king.

[12] Eco, *History of Beauty*, 82-97.

[13] *Ibid.*, 72.

[14] Augustine, *Confessions*, 147.

[15] Jonathan Edwards, *The Religious Affections* (Edinburgh: Banner of Truth Trust, 1997), 28.

Pull Out Quotes:

[i] Hans Urs Von Balthasar, *The Glory of the Lord: A Theological Aesthetics, Seeing the Form*, vol. 1 (San Francisco: Ignatius Press, 1982), 53-4.

[ii] Wayne Grudem, *Systematic Theology: an Introduction to Biblical Doctrine* (Great Britain: InterVarsity Press and Grand Rapids: Zondervan, 1994), 197.

[iii] Balthasar, *The Glory of the Lord*, 54.

[iv] Jonathan Edwards, "A Divine and Supernatural Light," *Sinners in the Hands of an Angry God and Other Writings*, "Nelson's Royal Classics" (Nashville: Thomas Nelson Publishers, 2000), 27.

[v] Anselm of Canterbury, *Anselm of Canterbury: The Major Works*, ed. Brian Davies and G. R. Evans (Oxford: Oxford University Press, 2008), 96-7.

Chapter Four

PLEASURE

What child doesn't like entering through those gates, getting his hand stamped and finding himself standing in front of a lawn with Mickey's giant face designed in flowers? Interestingly, it's not a place celebrated only by children, but teenagers and adults still enjoy the make-believe potency of the magical kingdom. The uniqueness of Disneyland is it doesn't merely thrill you; it transports you. All the thematic elements, from the staff dressed in costumes to the artistic facades of buildings and realistic deco, are meant to immerse you in a place of fantasy. The aroma of kettlecorn, the cottage-like shops, the towering castle, and the music of the quartet on the street corner constantly convince you that you've entered "the happiest place on earth", which assumes your normal life isn't at its happiest. During your time there, you could pretend to be a different person — a space explorer, an adventurer, a pirate or a princess. By enticing your imagination through aesthetic sights, sounds, smells, tastes and touch, it creates a surrounding that allows you to escape the humdrum of your normalcy and to embrace an identity that exists only in your daydream. The worst part about Disneyland is leaving it to return to your own reality, something less than the happiest place.

Though practically Disneyland is constructed with facades and costumes, namely the experience it offers is fictitious versus a real transformation, its philosophy to make you believe you're somewhere and someone else where your troubles could be left at the gate speaks deeply of the human desire to know joy. It's not rocket science to know that joy exists in the absence of pain, emptiness and chaos. Perhaps Disneyland is an unconscious attempt to create a self-contained world without the Fall, a place where things are perfect and everyone does smile all the time. It's a place that reminds you through immersion that your dreams can come true if you seek them. However if the world was perfect and people were living out the happiest dreams of their lives, there might not be a need for Disneyland. Maybe Disneyland has to exist in order to remind us that we are flawed and fragmented people grasping for joy.

One of the responses the beauty of God evokes in us is enjoyment. Learning to rejoice and celebrate is an art of life. Under the Buddhist philosophy, which I grew up with, one of the mantras was to purge oneself of all desires, because desires bring suffering and disappointment. I discovered that the Christian faith taught the exact opposite. Though there is a strong element of denying oneself, it is done so in order to embrace something greater. Christianity is, in fact, a very indulgent faith. It is about accumulating joy, increasing our appetites and partying because we always have a tomorrow. Celebration is a vital part of life because we value and esteem what we celebrate. Not to mention that life would be utterly dull without the parties. The imaginative God who relishes in excessiveness by creating a universe of extravagant beauty is anything but dull. The great I AM knew what it meant to have pleasure when He created a world that was good. And, He knew how to share that pleasure when He established the Sabbath day.

The Party Life

People love parties, but few understand the meaning of this enjoyment being rooted in beauty. Genesis 2:1-3 reads:

Thus the heavens and the earth were completed in all their vast array. By the seventh day God had finished the work he had been doing; so on the seventh day he rested from all his work. And God blessed the seventh day and made it holy, because on it he rested from all the work of creating that he had done.

The seventh day is "blessed", literally meaning a happy day. It was a day of festivity, rejoicing and partying. The term for "rested" is *shabat*, which literally means to "cease or desist". God stopped all His activities and simply enjoyed the "good" that He made, a beauty that reflected back to Him His truths, glory and nature, so that His resting was in every way an enjoyment of Himself. With each day of creation, He declared it to be "beautiful" or "very beautiful",

> "True happiness is the perfect good; therefore true happiness must dwell in the supreme Deity."[i]
>
> —Boethius

expressing His delights over His accomplishments. The seventh day was a "blessed" day, because it was a day of rejoicing – the celebration of His completed masterpiece. It was not a private day only for God, but He set it as a day of rest for all people. Everyone on earth was invited every week to join God in this rest, in a time of ceasing and enjoying the "good" He has done and the good that He is.

The first day after the human race would've been foreign to us. Man and woman were created on the sixth day and the very next day of their lives after their creation was the Sabbath (Gen 1:27-2:2). The first activity of Adam before Eve was made was to name the animals (Gen. 2:19-20). But when humanity was completed with the creations of both Adam and Eve who were given the task to care for the earth (Gen. 1:26), their first activities were not to go feed the sheep, groom the lion, prune the trees or till the soil. It was to rest. It may seem illogical to the got-to-get-things-done lifestyles that the first activity of completed humanity was to rest.[1]

"So what are we going to *do?*" Adam might've asked if he were the modern man standing in the middle of God's paradise on the first official day of their human existence.

"Nothing," God would say, "Rest. Enjoy with me."

"Rest? But we haven't done anything yet," modern Adam would retort with confusion.

"That's right, you haven't," God would reply with a smile as He looked at His craftsmanship of Adam, Eve and the landscape behind them, "But look at all that *I've done.*"

Their first day on the job was a day-off. Their first lesson in being human was to cease, stop and celebrate all that God had *already* done. Because God finished the work and made the masterpiece, a day of rest exists for everyone. He earned it for everyone so that even rest would be grace to everyone.

The pattern of the world is to work in order to earn rest, such as working hard to earn a retirement or a two-week vacation. But the initial establishment of the work-and-rest pattern in the Bible is contrary to social expectations. When rest and celebration precede our work, then our work is done out of a foundation of faith in the goodness and grace of God. We can work out of a sense of what He has already achieved. This rest then is no longer a mere slump at the end of a hard week, but an empowerment for the beginning of a week. Humanity's first lesson was one of grace and glory, grace in that they did nothing to earn that day of rest but God did and glory in that the Sabbath was about learning to enjoy God's achievements before we set out to do our own work. The Sabbath was a blessed and holy day because it would teach us how to enjoy life by depending on God's grace and relishing in His glory.

> "Primarily the Sabbath reclaims us because it enfolds us in the grace of not doing work, of not needing to accomplish anything, of not having to be in control, of living by God's values instead of society's."[ii]
>
> —Marva J. Dawn

Learning the primacy of rest, celebration and enjoyment of God was not an optional request. It was law. Forced vacation seems unnecessary, but we are a people who need to be told to rest; otherwise we won't. Observing the Sabbath is the fourth commandment among the Ten. There are at least a few premises for God in implementing the "forced" time-offs.

First, God tells us to observe the Sabbath (Exod. 20:8) because God made the world in six days and rested on the seventh, and therefore we should too. He uses the initial pattern He set at the foundation of creation as the basis for our rest, calling us to emulate Him. There is no greater quest for beauty than to emulate God, following a pattern that reflects His character.

But for centuries people have had difficulty with resting. In Exodus 16:23-30, some of the more compulsive and worrisome Israelites did not rest on the Sabbath from going out to collect the manna despite God's prohibition. He earnestly reminded them, "Bear in mind that the Lord has given you the Sabbath; that is why on the sixth day he gives you bread for two days" (Exod. 16:29). "Rest," God said. He won't shortchange anyone because He provided bread for two days on the sixth to cover for the seventh. Our choosing to rest is an act of faith, trusting that God will provide. The Sabbath reminds us that God is the Creator, the source of all things good and the great I AM. The Sabbath is a cyclical release from our compulsivity to worry, so that we would have the freedom to enjoy God. It is a release from the fixation with ourselves and our achievements, so that we could trust in who God is and what He does. When we don't celebrate the Sabbath, it suggests that we don't trust God or that what He does is not enough for us. What if Adam and Eve on that

> "Now then, little man... make a little time for God, and rest for a while in him. Enter into the chamber of your mind, shut out everything but God and whatever helps you to seek him, and, when you have shut the door, seek him. Speak now, O my whole heart, speak not to God: 'I seek thy face; thy face, Lord, do I desire.'"[viii]
>
> —Anslem of Canterbury

seventh day said, "God, we can't rest yet. There's too much to be done"? Their resistance to rest with God would've denied God's finished work and His declaration over His work as being "very beautiful". Rest is faith that honors God's beauty and His works of beauty.

Second, while creation is one reason for the Sabbath at the front end, redemption is the other reason at the back end. Deuteronomy 5:12-15 recaps the fourth commandment and offers a second reason for observing the Sabbath – that God redeemed Israel out of their bondage in Egypt and made them a nation, giving them their own identity and purpose. The Sabbath was a day of remembrance and celebration of God's deliverance of them from slavery. The redemptive idea of the Sabbath is further defined by God's work accomplished through Christ. Hebrews 4:1-11 invites us into this rest found in Christ.[2] This day of redemption, then, served as a prophetic day for the Israelites to look forward to the future redemptive act of Christ's first advent when people would be delivered from sin and death and for Christians to look forward to Christ's second advent when God's work of redemption will be finally completed (Rev. 1:10).[3] Peter C. Craigie explained the significant meaning of the Sabbath eloquently:

> We are creatures of our Creator God, and there-
> fore dependent on him for our life. We are partic-
> ipators in that tradition which goes back in history
> to the Exodus, when God revealed to his people
> his activity in human history by liberating his chosen
> people. We are reborn through our identification
> with the risen Christ, who may work in us a new
> creation, recalling the first creation (Exod. 20:11)
> and the creation of the people of Israel (Deut.
> 5:15).[4]

Through the creation-redemption motifs, the Sabbath celebration encompasses the biblical story of God's quest of redemption and humanity's journey towards freedom. Whether in creation or redemption, we find

God as the constant author and authority. The Sabbath is pregnant with theological significance that we should welcome into our weekly lives.

But there is a negative taste to "law". When something is law, it gives a sense of obligation where we feel we must serve the law out of compulsion. That, however, is not the principle behind this commandment. In Exodus 16:29, God said, "Bear in mind that the Lord has *given you* the Sabbath." Jesus said to the Pharisees, "The Sabbath was *made for man*, not man for the Sabbath" (Mk. 2:27). The Sabbath is not a burden; it is a gift. It is a blessing from God, inviting people to bask in beauty – His beauty – to live in faith and to enjoy His accomplishments in creation and redemption. If life were void of practicing the Sabbath, we would always be carrying a load that's too much for us to bear and striving to become something we were never meant to be – gods. When we lose sight of the Sabbath and its spirit of resting and celebrating, we minimize the truth of creation and redemption and attempt to live as people who need neither. Without the Sabbath we lose sight of His beauty and the beauty He makes. It's on the Sabbath that God invites us to be human by reminding us that He is God. He reminds us of the blessings of being human by welcoming us into the pleasures of His own beauty.

Sabbath and Beauty

Disneyland is not usually associated with the Sabbath. Disneyland is pictured as joyful, festive, musical, colorful and full of laughs. People generally view the Sabbath as being solemn, subdued and depressing, like a church service. But the Sabbath as a "blessed" day (Gen. 2:3) should be joyfully festive. In fact, the Sabbath was meant to set the pattern for the other Jewish feasts and festivals.[5] It was supposed to be a day of delight (Isa. 58:13). The Sabbath is a party; it is a one-day per week of rejoicing (Hos. 2:11) and delighting (Isa. 58:13-14).

> "Fully to enjoy is to glorify. In commanding us to glorify Him, God is inviting us to enjoy Him."[iv]
> —C.S. Lewis

The Purple Curtain

The people of God are meant to rejoice and party on a regular basis with Him as the host. In fact, God expresses His desire to celebrate with us, enjoying Him and the fruit of His hands and the glory that comes from Him. God promises that His people will rejoice and "sing out of the joy of their hearts" (Isa. 65:13-14) and God will "rejoice over Jerusalem and take delight in [His] people" (Isa. 65:19). In the parable of the talents and the servants, one of God's rewards for faithfulness was the invitation, "Come and share in your master's happiness" (Matt. 25:21, 23). In the parable of the prodigal son, the immediate event after the son's return was a big feast and party with the father (Luke 15:23). The father's simple words were, "Let's have a feast and celebrate." In contemporary terms, that would be, "Let's eat and party!" It is an oddity to be a Christian and not know how to party when God loves to. The Sabbath is a deliberate space for celebrating God with God.

> "...his happiness flows from his perfections, including the perfection of his infinite power. It is this immeasurable power that guarantees the freedom of God's delight in all that he does. His delight is the joy that he has in the reflection of his own glory in the person of his Son. But part of that glory is infinite power. And the unique function of his power is to make way for the overflow of his joy in the work of creation and redemption. It is his power that removes (in God's time and God's way) any obstacles to the accomplishment of his good pleasure. Thus the declaration that God does all that he pleases is a declaration of his power."
>
> —John Piper

The Sabbath is essential for experiencing beauty because it is a day to enjoy God, who is the absolute beauty. God declared in each day of creation that His works were "beautiful" and the final completion of creation was "very beautiful". The following Sabbath day was not called beautiful but "blessed", because it was a day to enjoy the beautiful. The Sabbath was the wrap-party at the end of a masterful project. This blessed day was the celebration of God's glory and the power of His divine nature shown in His beautiful works (Ro. 1:19-20). The Sabbath celebrates who He is, what He does and what He delights in (the definition of absolute beauty), and so to deny the Sabbath is to diminish His beauty. The invitation to enter into His rest is one that calls us to remember and enjoy the beauties that resound of His glory. The person who celebrates is someone who experiences beauty.

It's ironically self-inflicting when we don't celebrate the Sabbath, because God bars people from the Sabbath experience as a way of judgment! Psalm 95:11 reads, "So I declared on oath in my anger, 'They shall never enter my rest'" (see also Heb. 4:3-5). Could it be that we unknowingly place ourselves in the conditions of judgment when we forsake the Sabbath? Judgment can simply be the removal of a blessing, where outside of God's goodness only misery awaits us. The barring from sharing in the blessed day and knowing God's beauty through the Sabbath removes not only the savory of life but more importantly a witness of the goodness and glory of God that defines our sense of what's true, worthy and everlasting. Apart from God's beauty, then, we are left to our own vices, however limited and unsatisfying they may be.

The Sabbath invites us to enjoy God with God. This is *God's* rest that He calls us into (Heb. 4:10). It is not *a* generic rest but a rest that belongs to Him. He invites us to share in *His* happiness (Matt. 25:21, 23). As we saw in the previous verses in Isaiah, He calls for people to rejoice and He would rejoice, too. The Sabbath is about knowing God's rest, happiness and joy, to understand what God means by "good" as it reflects backwards on His creative acts and also forwards on His redemptive vision. The Sabbath is not simply about knowing *a* rejoicing but *God's*

> "If, therefore, pleasure is the union of the harmonious with the harmonious, and if the Likeness of God alone contains in the highest degree the notion of beauty, delight and wholesomeness and if it is united in truth and intimacy and in a fullness that fulfills every capacity, it is obvious that in God alone there is primordial and true delight and that in all our delights we are led to seek this delight."[vi]
>
> —Bonaventure

rejoicing. It is about embracing what God calls good and beautiful. To share in His happiness is to enjoy what He enjoys, and in doing so, we expand our appetites, because the things that God enjoys are far greater than the petty joys of the world. For God promised us that

> "If you keep your feet from breaking the Sabbath
> and from doing as you please on my holy day,
> if you call the Sabbath a delight
> and the LORD's holy day honorable,
> and if you honor it by not going your own way
> and not doing as you please or speaking idle
>   words,
> then you will find your joy in the LORD,
> and I will cause you to ride on the heights of the
>   land
> and to feast on the inheritance of your father
>   Jacob."
> The mouth of the LORD has spoken.
> (Isa. 58:13-14)

An Appetite for Beauty

The Christian faith should increase our appetites. Christianity teaches us how to be better indulgers. We are called to a life of sacrifice, but our sacrifices do not leave us empty. We're called to let go of the minute things in order to embrace the greater beauties, like truth, goodness, life and freedom. I like C.S. Lewis' claim that, "We are far too easily pleased." Our problem with not wanting to let go of the superficial things of the world is not that we lack restraint; it is that we do not know how to indulge. There are attractive things of the world that fade and do not possess God's eternal goodness (Jas. 1:10-11). The Christian truth teaches us to discern between the lesser and greater beauties, since we will pursue and hold on to what we believe to be most beautiful. His word reveals to us the greater beauty that reflects His character, so that we may let go of the fading things and embrace the things He would call "good". It is as if God says to us, "You're hands are so full of the trivial stuff that I can't give you the treasured stuff."

Most would not think that learning Biblical Greek would be too exciting, but I'll never forget this one lecture as our class read through Ephesians 1 in the original Greek. Dr. Jay Smith from Dallas Theological Seminary picked apart the lavish promises and blessings of God piece-by-piece in this chapter, elaborating on Paul's description of God's grace, love, eternal rewards, calling, purposes and power that are

> "...if we considered the unblushing promises of reward and the staggering nature of the rewards promised in the Gospels, it would seem that Our Lord finds our desires not too strong, but too weak. We are half-hearted creatures, fooling about with drink and sex and ambition when infinite joy is offered us, like an arrogant child who wants to go on making mud pies in a slum because he cannot imagine what is meant by the offer of a holiday at the sea. We are far too easily pleased."[vii]
>
> —C.S. Lewis

generously bestowed on Christ-believers. One would've never thought this chapter was written by a man who had been through tremendous suffering, embarrassment and persecution and whose very life was threatened. Then Dr. Jay Smith said to us in the most animated way I had ever seen of him that we too easily lose sight of the incredible lavishes of God by worrying over the petty and trifling things of the world.

What we do and create in the other six days of the week is defined by what we remember on the seventh. The working person will find no greater motivation to work than the compelling of God's glory. The drug addict has no greater hope than the redeeming beauty promised by God. The musician cannot hear a melody greater than the harmony of God's goodness in the universe. The artist can have no greater vision than the one inspired by the vision of God's beauty. How easily we tend to forget. The Sabbath is a day to remind us.

A New Reality

Like Disneyland, the Sabbath offers an alternate reality. Unlike Disneyland, the Sabbath doesn't offer a façade but an actual image of the reality to come. The festivity of the Sabbath is colored with aesthetic delight, casting an aura on the day of rest as one that should be savored and filled with praise. The Sabbath festivities offer a glimpse and a taste of the reality God promises in eternity with Him. Disneyland portrays an imaginary fantasy. The Sabbath reveals a promised paradise. The world of Disneyland only feels real until you leave the park. The Sabbath reminds us we have yet to enter the actual reality in heaven but we can now taste and see it on earth by our observances of the Sabbath (Heb. 11:1). Celebrating the Sabbath is celebrating the beauty of God's creation and the beauty He will create in the end.

> *"God and true happiness are one and the same."*[viii]
>
> —Boethius

What Do You Do When You Do Nothing?

Sabbath does not mean, "do nothing". *Shabat* means to cease and desist from work, but it means to do something else. So what do we do that defines ceasing on the Sabbath? First off, Hebrews 4:1 tells us that the invitation to enter into "his rest" remains open for all people who believe in the gospel. The writer of Hebrews encourages us to "make every effort to enter that rest", which is accessed by faith (Heb. 4:11). The first and foremost activity of the Sabbath is a celebration of Christ in our lives, praising our Savior who has championed the conquest over sin and death. There is no legalistic way for how the Sabbath must be observed, but one activity that should be essential on the Sabbath is worship and praise, a way of celebrating God for being God. If we are truly enjoying God, experiencing the "blessed" day of the Sabbath according to His Word, then as C.S. Lewis wrote, "…all enjoyment spontaneously overflows into praise…".[6]

Second, the Sabbath as a day of resting *with* God calls for communing with Him, intentionally setting aside time to talk with him in prayer. God would want nothing less than an honest conversation that entails praise, thanksgiving, confession and requests (Phi. 4:6, 1 Jn. 1:9). Sometimes our talks mean venting to God as the psalmists did. But at the end of our rants and vents we should find our hope and trust in Him also as the psalmists did.

However, at times our prayers mean ceasing with silence where we are in a state of listening to God's Spirit. Our prayers can be most fervent when we have specific requests of God. But try praying and meditating without an agenda. Come to God simply to know Him and to contemplate on His beauty. Learn to practice the spiritual act of silence before God. The author of Ecclesiastes wrote:

> "Guard your steps when you go to the house of
>   God. Go near to listen rather than to offer the
>   sacrifices of fools, who do not know that they
>   do wrong.
> "Do not be quick with your mouth,
>   do not be hasty in your heart to utter anything
>   before God.
> God is in heaven and you are on earth,
>   so let your words be few"
> (Eccl. 5:1-2).

Oftentimes the best things we could offer to God are our ears. *Shabat* means to pause from the humdrum of daily responsibilities and to silence the noise of a busy world in order to curb the worries of life. Our pause creates space to ponder. "The Sabbath offers the magnificent gift of an entire day to ponder God's truth instead of our work, to

> "God does not only 'demand' praise as the supremely beautiful and all-satisfying Object. He does apparently command it as lawgiver."[ix]
>
> —C.S. Lewis

notice God's creations of beauty, and to relish goodness in our closest relationships," wrote Marva Dawn.[7]

A way of hearing from God is to be in the Scriptures. It was by His word that the universe was made in six days and that He declared the seventh day to be blessed and holy. If the Sabbath is a day to know God and His rest, then dwelling in His word is essential. Jesus taught God's words in the synagogue on the Sabbath (Luke 13:10). Since God could only be found in truth (Psa. 145:18) and because in Him there is no lie (Titus 1:2, 1 Jn. 2:21), we can encounter God's presence by dwelling in His truth. Jesus who said He is "the truth, the way and the life" leads us to the Father when we engage the truth in faith (Jn 14:6).

Expectations are a filter for everything, even when we approach the Bible. For many, we come to the Bible looking for answers, which is a good thing since we believe that the Bible has the answers we need. But there are times when the practice of ceasing before God should also suspend our expectations and questions, where we don't come looking for something but we come to listen. What would God say to us if we simply let Him speak through His word? If we allowed the voices in our minds that echo our frustrations, worries and desires to subside, what would we hear from God? When truth is revealed, we have one of two responses: to suppress it (Ro. 1:18) or believe it and let it have its way in us (Heb. 4:12).

Third, the Sabbath is a day to do "good", doing acts that bring about some level of beauty and healing in a needy and broken world. Even Jesus showed mercy on the Sabbath by healing others. The Pharisees wanted to trap Jesus for breaking the law because He healed a crippled man on the Sabbath (Mk. 3:1-6). They misunderstood the meaning of the Sabbath, where they saw it only as a day for refraining rather than as a day for redeeming. Jesus asked them, "Which is lawful on the Sabbath: to do good or to do evil, to save life or to kill?" In a similar way, Jesus healed a crippled woman on the Sabbath and defended his actions by saying, "…should not this woman, a daughter of Abraham, whom Satan has kept bound for eighteen long years, be set free on the Sabbath day from what bound her?" (Luke 13:16).

The Sabbath is a day for people to find deliverance and freedom as Jesus pointed out. The seventh day celebrated all the good God did in creating the cosmos out of chaos. In a similar way, every act of mercy, kindness, charity and service to others in need brings a level of cosmos out of chaos in our society (which we'll discuss in a later chapter). We could unfold a glimpse of the beauty God delights in by our acts of healing, grace and goodness, which fundamentally represents the Sabbath. Whether we're helping at a soup kitchen, listening to a friend's troubles or aiding an old lady with her groceries, the Sabbath can be a day to know beauty by participating in the beauty that God makes in the world.

And finally, the Sabbath is a day to gather together. The Christian faith should not produce loners, especially not when we were adopted into a family (Ro. 8:15-16). Our faith is one to be shared with one another who know Jesus and to others who don't. Hebrews 10:25 reads, "Let us not give up meeting together, as some are in the habit of doing, but let us encourage one another – and all the more as you see the Day approaching." Our reservations to cease from working will impede our relationships. The Sabbath day is a Family Day for the family of God. Let the Sabbath ring with laughter, prayers, encouragements, service, singing and dancing! Let it be a time of partying with God as the host and the guest of honor.

A Week's End and Beginning

"Six days you shall labor and do all your work, but the seventh day is a Sabbath to the Lord your God" (Deut. 5:13-14). The seventh day comes at the end of each week. The magic of the Sabbath being on the seventh day is we live the other six days in looking forward to the seventh. Knowing what is impending casts a shadow over everything that comes before it. Since we anticipate the coming of the seventh day, it affects how we prepare and labor on the other six days. We find ourselves making sure we plan our six days well in order to keep the Sabbath. So the seventh day causes us to live out the other six days faithfully in view of His rest.

But the seventh day is also the forerunner for the first day of the week, establishing God's grace, goodness and glory as the introduction for each workweek. The Sabbaths are an enclosure for the entire week, so that even the work done in-between the Sabbaths are done out of a sense of holiness and faithfulness unto God because we work with the Sabbath in mind. The work that we produce in the six days should reflect God's notion of goodness and beauty to be enjoyed on the seventh day. At the same time, His beauty that prefaces each week drives us toward creating beauty through creative and redemptive acts. Beginning the week with grace on a Sunday, it should not be unusual to find ourselves Monday through Friday helping old ladies carry their groceries, offering courtesy to those who offend us, painting and writing with inspiration and being charitable to strangers.

When we take time to pause and honor God's holiness by celebrating Him, we grasp a sense and definition of His beauty, not only on the seventh day but throughout the week. When we rest with God, the Sabbath becomes a space to know, encounter and enjoy beauty – the beauty of who He is, the beauty He makes and the beauty we partake in. Under this pattern of live-work-play, we weave throughout the rhythm of our weekly lives the relationship between worship and beauty, something that's vital to our lives and that we explore in the next chapter.

Walk in Color

- Take a Sabbath day of enjoying God who enjoys being God. Go on a personal retreat. Leave your cell phone and laptop. Have an ipod, a good book, a journal or sketch pad and your Bible. Take pleasure in God. Read Psalm 104 aloud.
- Gather together with other lovers of God and celebrate the beauty of God and the beauty He creates in life.
- Do good on the Sabbath. Bring a measure of joy and pleasure into someone's life by doing one specific task that reflects the beauty of God to them.

Notes: Chapter Four

[1] Marva J. Dawn, *The Sense of the Call: A Sabbath Way of Life for Those Who Serve God, the Church, and the World* (Grand Rapids: William B. Eerdmans Publishing Co., 2006), 36.

[2] Paul Ellingworth, *The Epistle to the Hebrews: a Commentary on the Greek Text* from *The New International Greek Testament Commentary* edited by I. Howard Marshall and W. Ward Gasque (Grand Rapids: William B. Eerdmans, 1993), 255-6.

[3] Peter C. Craigie, *The Book of Deuteronomy* from *The New International Commentary on the Old Testament* edited by R.K. Harrison and Robert L. Hubbard, Jr. (Grand Rapids: William B. Eerdmans Publishing Co., 1976), 158.

[4] *Ibid.*

[5] J.G. McConville, *Deuteronomy* from *Apollo Old Testament Commentary* edited by David W. Baker and Gordon J. Wenham, vol. 5 (Downers Grove: InterVarsity Press, 2002), 128.

[6] C.S. Lewis, *Reflections on the Psalms* in *The Inspirational Writings of C.S. Lewis: Surprised by Joy, Reflections on the Psalms, The Four Loves, The Business of Heaven* (New York: Inspiration Press, 1984), 179.

[7] Marva J. Dawn, *The Sense of the Call: A Sabbath Way of Life for Those Who Serve God, the Church, and the World* (Grand Rapids: William B. Eerdmans Publishing Co., 2006), 42.

Pull Out Quotes:

[i] Anicius Manlius Severinus Boethius, *The Consolation of Philosophy*, transl. H. R. James, intro by Michael V. Dougherty (New York: Barnes & Noble, 2005), 63.

[ii] Marva J. Dawn, *The Sense of the Call*, 35-36.

[iii] Anslem, "An Address (Proslogion)" from *A Scholastic Miscellany: Anselm to Ockham*, ed. Eugene R. Fairweather, Ichthus ed. (Philadelphia: The Westminster Press, 1982), 70.

[iv] C.S. Lewis, *Reflections on the Psalms*, 180.

[v] John Piper, *The Pleasures of God: Meditations on God's Delight in Being God* (Portland: Multnomah Publishers, 1991), 52.

[vi] Bonaventure, "The Soul's Journey into God" from *Bonaventure: The Soul's Journey into God, The Tree of Life and The Life of St. Francis*, transl. Ewert Cousins (Mahwah: Paulist Press, 1978), 73.

[vii] C.S. Lewis, *The Weight of Glory and Other Addresses* (New York: HarperCollins Publishers, 2001), 26.

[viii] Boethius, *The Consolation of Philosophy*, 66.

[ix] C.S. Lewis, *Reflections on the Psalms*, 178.

Chapter Five

WORSHIP

W hen I read the headlines on the Internet that Michael Jackson died, I was at a pastor's conference in Minneapolis. Growing up, I was among the many young admirers of the King of Pop who listened to his songs and learned his dance moves. I watched "Thriller" dozens of times. I was too young to appreciate how much the world loved MJ, but I do remember seeing the effects he had on people. I was puzzled by the images of girls crying uncontrollably with contorted faces at his concerts. They looked like they were in agony. I realized later they were expressions of overwhelming passions. People raised their hands towards him, sang along with him and mouthed the words, "I love you". Young people imitated him in dress and demeanor from the white glove and black hat to the moonwalk and voice pitches. MJ had a hold on the world that inspired people not only to fall in love with him but to praise him.

What was it about MJ that captured people's love and praise and motivated a following to look and act like him? Society perceived a beauty about him, whether it was his music, talent, dance-style, stage-presence, or originality. People he never met developed a kind of relationship with him that could be likened to a kind of worship.

Worship may seem like a heavy word, but its fundamental meaning is to honor someone we exceptionally esteem by offering praise, exaltation and devotion in individual and corporate settings. According to the *Evangelical Dictionary of Theology*, the word worship "means 'worthship', denoting worthiness of an individual to receive special honor in accordance with that worth". [1] The act of worship and attributing worth are inseparable. We worship whom we give worth to. We give worth to what we find most beautiful since beauty conveys to us the ideal and perfect. Beauty inspires worship.

> "...if they do not enjoy worshipping the great God Almighty that made them, they find something else to worship.
>
> "If a person does not have God, he has to have something else. Maybe it is boats, or maybe it is money, amounting to idolatry, or going to parties or just simply raising the devil." [i]
>
> —A. W. Tozer

Human beings were built to look to someone greater than ourselves. Our finiteness and fallibility inform us of how small and limited we are in the universe, and, therefore, we naturally look to someone greater that gives inspiration, hope and purpose to our imperfect world. We are ready-made worshipers only needing an object for our worship.

Our definition of beauty is crucial. Beauty captures our attention, takes the spotlight in our eyes and humbles us in its presence. It will lead us to fall to our knees in reverence. A misconception of beauty then leads us to adore, devote to and even sacrifice for something that may not be worthy of our worship. Idolatry is a natural danger for a misunderstanding of beauty. In a world of many things where God is not always the central attraction for people, anything can be an idol.

Enticed to Worship

I am intrigued at seeing how society treats esteemed celebrities. They get the "red carpet" treatment. All eyes, lights and cameras are on them as they're thought to be the most beautiful people in the world. We get the sense that these individuals are treated with a higher sense of worth. That treatment is what God deserves from us.

King David wrote: "Splendor and majesty are before him." David was moved by God's beauty, like the splendors of diamonds and gems and the majestic awe of pearly white towers that inspire reverence and adoration. Because of God's beauty, the natural response is to, "Ascribe to the Lord the glory due his name" and to "worship the Lord in the splendor of his holiness" (1 Chron. 16:27, 29). The language that describes God's beauty expresses His limitless worth. When we encounter the beauty of God, we embark on an endless journey of worshiping Him for His infinite worth.

God shows off His beauty to draw and inspire us to worship Him. Worship is recognizing that God is worthy of praise, admiration and devotion. His beauty demands the spotlight, and He doesn't share that praise for His beauty with any other because no one compares to Him (Ps. 89:6, Isa. 40:18). Our worship of God alone expresses that we see Him as the most beautiful being in the world and nothing in it could compete with Him. In fact, He is jealous of His beauty and disgusted by misdirected worship given to someone else unworthy of it (Exod. 34:14). The most essential function of God's beauty is to prompt worship by drawing attention to Himself and wowing us with His eternal worthiness. The immensity of His beauty causes us to realize that no breadth of worship could equate to the depth of His worthiness. It's this inexhaustible depiction of His worthiness that fuels a passion for eternal worship.

I want to invite you to think about the things you do on a regular basis. Wash up. Go to work. Clean your house. Take the kids to soccer. Clean your car. Get gas. Buy groceries. Wash the dishes. Get dinner. How often does worship register as an activity in our daily schedules? Worship is a necessary activity in daily life if we recognize God for His beauty. The absence of worship indicates our lack of noticing God's beauty. God's spotlight attempts to shine in the midst of our cluttered lives because His beauty attempts to convey to us His worth—a worth deserving of worship.

Worship Reveals More Beauty

While on the one hand God's beauty is a cause for worship, worshiping Him further reveals His beauty to us. When God brought the Israelites out of Egypt, having seen much of His glory in the pillar of cloud and fire and the mighty acts of the plagues and the parting of the Sea of Reeds, He gave them plenty of reasons to worship Him. But we see a difference in the revelation of God's glory when worship was added. In

> *"...it is in the process of being worshipped that God communicates His presence to men. It is not of course the only way. But for many people at many times the "fair beauty of the Lord" is revealed chiefly or only while they worship Him together."[ii]*
>
> —C.S. Lewis

one instance, they saw Moses enter the Tent of Meeting with God's glory guarding the entrance while God spoke with Moses inside the tent (Exod. 33:8-11). Then God instructed them to worship Him by giving of their talents, time and gold to the building of the Tabernacle that would be a place for worship and for His presence to dwell (Exod. 25:1-9). After the Tabernacle was built and worship was offered there, a new experience of God's beauty unfolded as His glory filled the Tent of Meeting which Moses this time could not enter (Exod. 40:34-35). Moses and the people saw another aspect of God's glory they had not witnessed before.

My high school choir director said something to me that seemed nonsensical at the time. She said when life is rough and you can't find the reasons to praise God, praise Him anyway. Worship begins with God's worthiness not with conditions of life. As worship occurs it uncovers for us more of the unchanging beauty of who He is in spite of our circumstances. While at times encountering God's beauty in nature or miracles is enough to stimulate worship, at other times it's our worship of Him that allows us to see more of His beauty. When we give God what He deserves, we are blessed for it.

True worship exists as a central facet of our lives that should weave throughout the fabric of our identity and daily duties, rather than as an extra-curricular activity. The presence of authentic worship indicates that we have discovered true beauty worthy of our devotion. "Worship is therefore a *direct* expression of our ultimate purpose for living…"[2] wrote Wayne Grudem. We are identified by whom we worship, and meaning in life is determined by our worship.

If we have not discovered the compelling and truthful conviction of worshiping God as central to our lives, we have discovered neither true beauty nor the ultimate purpose of our existence. The absence of worship in our daily lives is likely an indicator of our lack of recognizing God's beauty daily.

What We Give God

Worship is an art of giving. We can't give to God what He already has, but we can give what is due to Him. He doesn't need worship but He deserves it. Psalm 96:8-9 reads, "Ascribe to the Lord the glory due his name… Worship the Lord in the splendor of his holiness…". To "ascribe" literally means "to give".[3] Between verses 7-9, the call to ascribe to the Lord was repeated three times before telling us to worship the Lord.

> "That biblically defined purpose is that we might worship God and enjoy Him forever. Apart form that, man has no other purpose; and short of that, man wanders in a spiritual disorientation taking him further from finding his created purpose."[iii]
>
> —A. W. Tozer

The act of "giving" and "worshiping" are synonymous. The beauty of His splendor, majesty and glory described in Psalm 96:6 warrants us to give Him the honor that fits His beauty.

A wonderful thing happens in worship when we create beauty for someone who is already beautiful. When you send fan mail to a celebrity, telling him or her how much you admire his or her skills, talents and achievements, your praise of the person doesn't add anything to your icon's qualities. You don't increase his abilities or achievements. But your praise is honoring and, therefore, in a way fulfilling to the one who receives it and to the one who gives it. "In praise we bring new beauty to Him who is altogether beautiful!"[4] In worship, beauty is created for one who is ultimately beautiful.

Worship becomes a matter of creating beauty because we've been inspired by beauty. We create beauty in music, poetry, art, drama or dance. We create beauty in praise, preaching, doing the work of God and loving another in honor of God. Things we do in honor of God out of reverence for Him and because of His worthiness become a matter of making beauty to one who is beautiful. In light of making beauty for beauty, we find that worship is not only inspired but also fitting. Worship as beauty-making for one who is beautiful is natural.

Beauty inspires beauty. Dr. Ronald B. Allen commented that the Hebrew verb for "to praise" (*nawa*) in Exodus 15:2 means "to beautify, to make beautiful".[5] Since worship is giving beauty to God, we make expressions of beauty through the songs we sing, the dances we do, the prayers we say, and the poetry we write to Him. The more we worship, the more beauty we make and the more our lives become focused on absolute beauty. Worshiping God becomes a redemptive activity that fosters beauty in our lives and brings a measure of wholeness out of our brokenness, as worshiping Him centers us on what's truly beautiful — His character, words and deeds and desires.

The vastness of God's beauty moves His worshipers on a quest towards building an array of worshipful expressions with ever increasing creativity. Listen to the psalmist's enthusiasm for varied praises:

> Praise him with the sounding of the trumpet,
> praise him with the harp and lyre,
> praise him with tambourine and dancing,
> praise him with the strings and flute,
> praise him with the clash of cymbals,
> praise him with resounding cymbals.
> Let everything that has breath praise the Lord (Ps. 150:3-6).

The worship described in this psalm was a big party with dancing at the center of the list. There is no limit to how creative and far we could strive to worship God, where in the wake of honoring God's worthiness, worship becomes a passionate pursuit of making beauty.

Beauty by Immersion

What better way to change a worshiper than by immersing him or her in an experience? The idea of immersion in order to create a make-believe experience by Disneyland is genius. You may recall the sound of "It's a Small World," the touch of the furry, life-size Mickey, the sights of the Haunted Mansion, the cool, dark cavern of the Pirates of the Caribbean, and the ruins of the Indiana Jones Adventure ride. The idea of make-believe is to *make you believe.* Through immersing your aesthetic senses and captivating you with the decorative beauties of the park, Disneyland is a faith-instilling place if it can steal you away even for a moment from the reality of your normal identity and world, and make you believe you're someone and somewhere else. The Tabernacle was an immersion experience to make you believe.

God liberated the Israelites from their bondage in Egypt to create a nation of worshipers (Exod. 7:16). The Tabernacle provided one of the most significant experiences that shaped the Israelites' understanding of worship. According to the rule of proportion, the amount of written space devoted to a subject in the Bible suggested its importance. About one-third of the book of Exodus describes the Tabernacle, between chapters 25 and 40! Perhaps in our past lessons in the book of Exodus, we focused on the ten plagues and the parting of the Sea of Reeds, but we paid little attention to the art at the end of the story. Yet, the art takes up a significant space in the story.

Experience Worship: Tabernacle Tour

God did not spare any elaboration in describing the artistry of the Tabernacle, and so we will immerse ourselves into the experience of the Tabernacle through a tour of it and discover the meaning of worship through this immersion experience.

Let's make believe you're a Hebrew high priest entering the Tabernacle, like Aaron (Exod. 28). You put on a decorated ephod "of gold, and of blue, purple and scarlet yarn", a blue robe, a gold breastpiece, a sash and a turban. You feel the weight of the gold chains and rings hanging from your ephod and the twelve stones fastened across your attire that represent the twelve tribes of Israel and the promises of God. The four rows of precious stones, including rubies, topaz, amethyst and chrysolite, mounted across your robe shine and sparkle. As you feel this beautiful garment envelop you, you feel the weight of approaching God's presence (Exod. 29:29). You put on clothing of beautiful dignity to approach the God of infinite worth. In a similar way, the believers of Jesus are clothed with Jesus Christ (Gal. 3:27) and are called a nation of priests (1 Pet. 2:9).

Walking into the first of the three sections of the Tabernacle, you enter the "courtyard", a spacious area with only the open sky and a canopy of evening stars as the ceiling (Exod. 27:9-19). The walls are made of linen, held together by posts mounted on shiny bronze bases. As you stand at one end of this perfectly rectangular court, measuring seventy-five feet by a hundred and fifty feet, your gaze is naturally drawn forward.[6] This rectangular shape created a tunnel effect where your inclination is to move towards the building in the center. But your path is lined with stages.

You first approach a brilliant bronze basin of water that sits in front of the Tent of Meeting (Exod. 30:18).[7] As you wash your hands and feet, the cool water runs over the dirtiest part of your body and heightens your sensitivity to God's holiness. You know that unless you washed up, you would die before Him (Exod. 30:17-21). Because, before a holy God there was a strict need for purity.[8] There could be no blemishes, stains or adulterations in us. In other words, only beauty could stand before beauty. The refreshing, cool water running over your hands reflects on the cool water running over the disciples' feet when Jesus washed them and told them unless they were washed, they could have no fellowship with him. Purity was necessary to be in God's presence and Christ's service to us offered the ultimate purity for our bodies and souls.

You, then, take two steps back to where you had passed the bronze altar, the station of sacrifice (Exod. 27:1-7). You lay your hands on an innocent, perfect sheep to transfer the guilt of your sins and your people's sins onto it before you kill it. The fading guttural sound of the sheep when you disembowel it sends a jarring shrill up your spine that stuns you with the paradox of the unjustifiable act of killing an innocent creature to justify a guilty people. But without this paradox there is no redemption. The aesthetic vision of this scene is a trailer for Jesus' embodiment of this paradox for our justification.

The reek of raw blood reminds you that you are approaching a most holy God as an imperfect person among imperfect people in need of His mercy.[9] As you burn the animal on the altar, the scent of grilled meat rises with the smoke and dissipates into the sky. An imagery of God's delight over your faith comes to mind, for this is a "pleasing aroma" to Him (Exod. 29:18). And still yet, this scene of delight foreshadowed a more beautiful imagery to come in Jesus as the perfect Lamb who was a pleasing aroma to God on the cross (Isa. 53:10, Eph. 5:2, 1 Pet. 1:19). You wash your hands and feet once more at the basin, to clean off the blood, before finally entering the Tent of Meeting.[10]

Your worship journey continues as you pass the water basin and stand at the entrance to the Tent of Meeting, which is the building in the middle. The door is a curtain of blue, red, and purple with masterfully embroidered cherubim which was crafted by an artisan (Exod. 27:16). The curtains match the breastpiece and ephod you're wearing, except your robe is missing the cherubim. You pause to ponder on these mythical creatures because they do not resemble any beasts on earth with their human faces, lion-like bodies and eagle's wings. These celestial creatures evoke a sense of awe within you over the transcendence of God and His other-worldliness.

As you part the curtains to enter in, the sound of bells announce your entry (Exod. 28:35). You stand in a mysteriously dim room, lighted by a seven-candle lampstand. The light gently refracts off the gold overlay on the furnishings and tent frame, but is accentuated by the dark background of the black goat hair on the walls.[11] On the opposite side of the lampstand is the table of shewbread. The ever-burning candles on one side and the ever-present shewbread on the other communicates that God's constant presence surrounds you. The altar of incense is in front of you (Exod. 25:30, 27:21). This rectangular room is called the Most Holy Place.

You notice the tactile juxtaposition between the curtains of goat hair, ram skins and sea cow hides[12] covering the Tent on the outside and the precious acacia wood and gold on the inside (Exod. 26:7-29). You see the harmony in the contrast of materials. The ram skins and goat fur express God's atonement and mercy, while the gold and bronze express God's divinity and authority. Within the equilibrium of these juxtapositions you behold the harmony of God's attributes, which is quintessential to His beauty.

> "The priest, enveloped by the sweet fragrance of the cloudy incense, must have been lifted to inexpressible heights of blessing as he communed with God in this sanctified place."[iv]
>
> —David M. Levy

You also observe the progression of value in the materials from the outer to the inner—from the sea cow hides, rams skin, black goat hair, acacia wood to the gold overlay. As you see this increase of worth in materials, you get the dramatic sense of God's worthiness.

And then, there's the fragrance! Like being in a busy Italian restaurant at dinnertime, the smell is all around you, a mixture of cinnamon, myrrh, olive oil, and dried flowers. Everything – the walls and furnishings – was anointed with a blend of these fine spices, the combination of which was eloquent and exhilarating.[13] You couldn't find this scent anywhere else because its formula was applied only here (Exod. 30:32-33). But there was one more fragrance to ignite. The special incense you sprinkle over the hot coals on the altar of incense kindles an aromatic smoke, intoxicating you with a sense of God's fair beauty. It is refreshingly novel,[14] because it is a recipe that is exclusive to the Lord, reminding you of His uniqueness and sacredness (Exod. 30:34-38). The blend of all the fragrances forms a new kind of invigoration, one that extols God's complex creativity and immeasurable goodness.

Finally, behind the altar of incense you see through the hazy smoke a "shielding curtain" (Exod. 40:21), made by a craftsman "given special divine wisdom in the making of this beautiful veil, which has never been duplicated."[15] Behind it is not another rectangular room but a square one, for this is the final destination of your journey. It is the Holy of Holies, the throne room of God. If there were a time to feel a quiver in your knees, it would be now. The Ark of the Covenant, a highly ornate box covered in gold and remarkable engravings with two cherubim atop its lid, sits in the middle of the room. If this were the Day of Atonement, you would enter the Holy of Holies to sprinkle an animal's blood on the cover of the ark for the atonement of your and your people's sins.

You notice the mixture of the red and gold now on the ark being faintly illuminated by the hot coals from the altar of incense. The colors on the ark cast yet another paradoxical truth about glory and sacrifice. It reminded you that for broken, sinful people to behold beauty, there must be a sacrifice. This sacred box is a mystery, communicating the majesty of God as His throne and yet the mercy of God as it represents His covenant with us. It is a box that tells us God reigns supreme and loves us. He is the ultimate judge but He forgives us by grace. He is transcendent and yet He desires for His presence to be with us. Somehow worship is not only an activity but an understanding of our existence within the paradox of brokenness and beauty.

Why the Box?

The "why?" sneaks into the equation of worship. We know we need God, but God doesn't need us. So then, why the box? Especially when you had to go through so much trouble outside the Tent of Meeting just to be able to approach the box. But perhaps it is the unanswerable question about the mystery of the box that drives the definition of worship further in that worship exists because God initiated with us – worship exists because He gave us the box. We didn't do something to earn it. Part of the profundity of worship is that God doesn't need people, but He still gave His people the box as a lasting covenant and promise of His presence. For these Israelites who were taken out of Egypt, it was God's redemption of them that initiated their worship.

Redemption remains the precedence for worship. It would always be about what God first does for us that makes worship possible. But even the covenanted presence of God found in the beautiful ark foreshadowed a greater covenantal beauty of His presence found in His Son on the bloody cross. Worship will always be about the fact that God started it, by showing us His beauty and drawing us to Him by redemption.

Somehow in this space between the majesty and the mercy of God, you find yourself at peace with the harmonious tension of revering God's holiness and relishing in His goodness. Every aesthetic aspect, the sight, sound, tactile feel, smell and kinesthetic movement, was part of the worshipful experience. But it was an experience of substance, because every element expressed a theological truth about who God is and who we are in relation to Him, from His goodness and holiness to our sinfulness and need for atonement. We realize the Tabernacle experience did not immerse us in the beauties of gold, furs and fragrances, but in the beauty of God. For, all the earthly, material beauties resound of God's character and worthiness of worship. Authentic worship must happen in the presence of God's beauty. The absence of worship in daily experiences means an absence of His beauty in life.

But beauty also fosters something else that is akin to worship; something we and our society find necessary and puzzling – love. Without love the enjoyment and worship of God could not be fulfilled. Love is next.

Walk in Color

- Read Exodus 25-40 carefully and take note of the various artistic elements of the Tabernacle. Take note of where the emphases are placed through repetitions, reiterations or detailed explanations.
- How can the Tabernacle experience model a life of worship for you?
- What tangible and creative things could you do to immerse yourself in God's beauty and express your worship to Him?
- Take a sketch pad (no lines). For a month, take a journey of worshiping God and journal in this pad daily. Write, sketch, doodle, draw. Record what you notice about God's beauty and worth and your expressions to God in worship.

Notes: Chapter Five

[1] *Evangelical Dictionary of Theology* (1997), s.v. "Worship," by E. F. Harrison.

[2] Wayne Grudem, *Systematic Theology*, An Introduction to Biblical Doctrine (Leicester: InterVarsity Press & Grand Rapids: Zondervan, 1994), 1004.

[3] Francis Brown, S. R. Driver, and Charles A. Briggs, *New Brown, Driver, Briggs: Hebrew and English Lexicon*, 1095.1.

[4] Ronald B. Allen, *The Wonder of Worship: A New Understanding of the Worship Experience* (Nashville: Word Publishing, 2001), 73.

[5] Ronald B. Allen, *The Wonder of Worship*, 78.

[6] John D. Hannah, "Exodus," edited by John F. Walvoord and Roy B. Zuck, *The Bible Knowledge Commentary: An Exposition of the Scriptures by Dallas Seminary Faculty, Old Testament* (Colorado Springs: Chariot Victor Publishing, 1985), 147.

[7] The bronze wash basin is the last piece of furnishing described but the first in practice to encounter. Its order of mention emphasizes its practical purpose and highlights the importance of God's holiness in a memorable way as an item that averts death. (Also see comment in Hannah, "Exodus," 154).

[8] John I. Durham, *Exodus*, edited by David A. Hubbard and Glenn W. Barker, Word Biblical Commentary (Waco: Word Book Publishers).

[9] David M. Levy, *The Tabernacle: Shadows of the Messiah* (Bellmawr: The Friends of Israel Gospel Ministry, 1993), 30.

[10] *Ibid.*, 33.

[11] Ted W. Bronleeve, "The Significance of Colors in the Tabernacle Worship of Israel," Th.M. thesis, Dallas Theological Seminary, 1977, 51.

[12] It is uncertain what the "sea cow hides" (an NIV translation) are. Sarna translates it as "dolphin skins." (Nahum M. Sarna, *Exodus*, edited by Nahum M. Sarna, The JPS Torah Commentary (Philadelphia: The Jewish Publication Society, 1991), 157.

[13] Spices were priceless commodities in the ancient world and highly prized. Sarna, *Exodus*, 197. The sheer amount of them (e.g. 500 shekels of myrrh was equivalent to 12.5 lbs) was invaluable.

[14] Novelty, originality and uniqueness were recognized as defining characteristics of beauty particularly beginning with the movement of mannerism and extending into our contemporary time. Umberto Eco, *History of Beauty*, transl. by Alastair McEwen (New York: Rizzoli, 2005), 220-221. But novelty was not new to the definition of beauty. We saw it manifested in God's original creation – originality was akin to the word *bara* ("to create").

[15] David M. Levy, *The Tabernacle: Shadows of the Messiah*, 70.

The Purple Curtain

Pullout Quotes:

[i] A. W. Tozer, *The Purpose of Man: Designed to Worship*, ed. James L. Snyder (Ventura: Regal, 2009), 44.

[ii] C.S. Lewis, *Reflections on the Psalms*, The Inspirational Writings of C.S. Lewis: Surprised by Joy, Reflections on the Psalms, The Four Loves, The Business of Heaven (New York: Inspirational Press, 1994), 178.

[iii] Tozer, *The Purpose of Man: Designed to Worship*, 28.

[iv] David M. Levy, *The Tabernacle: Shadows of the Messiah*, 59.

Chapter Six

LOVE

iving is assumed but having a purpose for living is discovered. How many people in the world run through life without having realized what they lived for? Young adults are ardent about pursuing success until they re-evaluate the worthiness of that pursuit. Women in their late thirties grow tired of their careers and not knowing what they really want to do with their lives. Men in their sixties carry regrets over not having lived out a more significant life. Purpose for many is elusive and some never discover it. There is one central factor that defines our purpose – it's our love. Jesus said where your treasures are is where your heart is. The question of what is our purpose is answered by what we love most, for that love will drive us towards pursuit and sacrifice. What we love is what we will give ourselves over to. In the end how we have lived will be defined by what we have loved. That love will become for us our true north.

For survival in the wilderness, a compass is necessary, especially in the backcountries where there are no tourist stations or kiosks with maps. When a group of us backpacked in the Tuolumne Meadows, the hovering trees and mountains scrambled our bearings as we journeyed deep into the wilderness. But if we got lost, we at least knew to head west to find civilization. All we needed was a compass. A compass' job is simply to point you north — it always points north. Once it tells you where north is, you then know where every other direction is in reference to it. The simple question is: have we found our true north that makes sense of everything else in our lives?

Of all the things God wants from us, it's not pilgrimages, constructions of church buildings, or giving of our assets. His greatest commandment to us is to love Him (Mk. 12:30, Matt. 22:37-38). From a practical standpoint, that seems like a small request from the Almighty God. You mean He doesn't want us to build a massive pyramid or walk to Jerusalem at least once? God knows our love means we give of ourselves, not just our things. Jesus explained that the greatest commandment is like a coat rack for all the other commandments to hang on; loving God made sense of all other endeavors and religious acts (Matt. 22:40). Without a love for God at the center of our lives, everything we do or pursue is meaningless. Life would be busy but lacking purposeful cohesion. Loving God is both a goal and a reference point for life, the true north for every human being.

However, the beauty of loving God is it doesn't begin with us. It begins with Him. 1 John 4:19 reads: "We love because he first loved us."

The Beauty of Being Loved by God

I saw a picture of love in my neighbor and his handicapped father. I first met Dan in the parking lot while I was moving into our new apartment. Dan, who looked like a man in his mid-forties, lived in the same unit for thirteen years with his parents whom he took care of. His father was eighty-some years old with balding white hair. His eyes didn't focus on anything. His "O"-shaped lips didn't speak, and his curved back led me to think that at one time he was taller.

Dan parked in the same spot in front of their apartment and helped his father out of the SUV onto the sidewalk. He held his father's hand and led him slowly to their home as Dan took one slow step and waited for his father to make five small-shuffling steps. "Come on, Dad," Dan would say encouragingly. Then came the two flights of stairs to get to the front door. The father had trouble with that and not just physically. He seemed afraid of the step. Dan grabbed both his father's hands and pulled him up the step. Eventually they made it up the first flight, but as they turned the corner to the second, the father resisted. The old man pulled on Dan's hands, leaning away from the step with all his weight. Now they were stuck halfway up the stairs. Then, Dan wrapped his arms around his father's back and hoisted him up each step to help him get home.

Many pay for the services of a convalescent home to care for their elderly parents but not Dan. Dan did this dance regularly with his father. Never did I notice Dan lose his patience or raise his voice. I've never heard Dan say he loved his father or any other types of endearing words, but their dance was a perfect performance of love.

Umberto Eco in *History of Beauty* wrote that at one period in history, a kind of love described as a *je ne sais quoi*, or a "I don't know what", expressed a beauty that extended beyond verbal description.[1] It was the sort of incredible love, which befuddles our minds and forms a stirring picture of beauty that inspires mystery and escapes sensibility. Dan's dance with his dad displayed such beauty.

The psalmist sang of this incredible love.

> *Praise the Lord.*
> *Give thanks to the Lord, for he is Good;*
> *his love endures forever*
> (Ps. 106:1).

One of the beauties of God is His incredible love for us, artistically depicted in the Old Testament with open flowers.[2] In the Tabernacle, the lampstand was crafted out of gold with almond-shaped flowers in bloom (Exod. 25:31-34). Why almond flowers? In Numbers 17:10, Aaron's staff budded with almond blossoms as a warning of judgment from God for his sins. The intention of the warning,[3] however, was to give Aaron and his tribe a chance to repent so that God wouldn't punish them but show them mercy instead. The almond flowers, though pointing out their guilt, refreshingly reminded them that God does not desire to punish people for their wrongs (Ezek. 18:23) but to forgive them out of His love by patiently (Ro. 2:4) giving them chances to repent. If God wanted to judge us, He would not give warnings of judgment. The warnings are opportunities for grace.

As the lit lampstand reminded the people of God's presence, the shimmering almond flowers affirmed God's gracious love that generously flowed from His presence. In the Temple, the generic open flowers engraved on the walls symbolized the same goodness and grace of God. These floral symbols reminded people of God's *hesed*, a mysterious Hebrew term that has no equivalent translation in our English language but is best described as God's covenantal love that is unending in faithfulness and loyalty.

The *je ne sais quoi* quality of God's love is it defies sensibility because He chooses to forgive out of love those who offend Him when He has every logical right to punish them. It is an impossible kind of love because it was fully expressed through the sacrifice of His Son (1 Jn. 3:16). And it is a fully selfless love because though people need God, God does not need people. God's sacrificial love evokes a *je ne sais quoi* beauty. John the apostle wrote: "This is love: not that we loved God, but that he loved us and sent his Son as an atoning sacrifice for our sins" (1 Jn. 4:10). The fundamental premise to loving God and discovering our true north is to understand what it means to be loved by Him according to the gospel. The moment we take the gospel for granted, minimizing it as something elementary and familiar, we dismiss the mysterious depth and *je ne sais quoi* beauty of imperfect sinners being loved by the perfect Father.

His love draws us into a beautiful dance with Him that arouses, even demands, a love from us in return. But we might learn that loving God may involve a greater level of complexity than we thought.

Genuine Love Purified by Beauty

Jonathan Edwards, the preacher of the Great Awakening in America in the 1800s, wrote an insightful and provocative book called *The Religious Affections* that challenged everyday Christians to honestly discern their motives for loving God. He addressed a people who were so marinated in the customs of consumerism that they might not have been aware of their own hypocrisy. He made this soul-searching statement:

> "This infinite excellency of the divine nature, as it is in itself, is the true ground of all that is good in God in any respect; but how can a man truly and rightly love God without loving Him for the excellency in Him which is the foundation of all that is in any manner of respect good or desirable in Him? If men's affection to God is founded first on His profitableness to them, their affection begins at the wrong end; they regard God only for the utmost limit of the stream of divine good, where it touches them and reaches their interest, and have no respect to that infinite glory of God's nature which is the original good, and the true fountain of all good, the first fountain of all loveliness of every kind, and so the first foundation of all true love."[4]

Edwards points out that many deceive themselves by thinking their love is genuine when it is merely self-serving. As Edwards wrote, sometimes people love God for their own "profitableness". The payoffs are their primary reasons for believing God. Faith in this sense is a reasonable transaction rather than an enthrallment with God whose beauty warrants their devotion and love. Edwards calls the beauty of God, "his excellency". A love for God that is not motivated by His beauty is a self-love.

We're all driven by something, Edwards wrote, some by ambition, hate, anger or jealousy. If you take away these motivations, our lives would cease to move.[5] But there are drives in life that are "holy affections", which belong to true religion.[6] He beckons us to become aware of what drives us to do, pursue and believe. We pursue only what we love and we love only what is

> "A natural principle of self-love may be the foundation of great affections towards God and Christ, without seeing anything of the beauty and glory of the divine nature."
>
> —Jonathan Edwards

beautiful to us. If God's beauty is not at the core of our gaze in life and faith, then what is?

There are two crimes for a religion driven by self-love. First, it is exploitative. Self-love exploits God, reducing Him to a means for gaining things, whether salvation, blessings or comfort, without realizing a greater worth for loving God. He becomes a means rather than an end. It is not to say that God does not graciously give good gifts, but if the gifts are the highest ends of our desires and not God himself, then God is simply reduced to a dispenser. This kind of faith is like a good business deal, where we offer our faith and professed love for God in exchange for good things from Him. On the other hand, self-love is Pharisaic because it is a love for one's own standing and gain versus a love for God's beauty. The only encounter self-love grants us is an encounter with ourselves since we think that our own rewards are the highest ends.

At our most basic, human instinct we all ask the question, "What's the payoff for me?" I've often heard it asked by Christians struggling with why they would follow God and not the things of the world, attempting to rationalize the motive for being a Christian by weighing out the tangible rewards. This is a sensible question that is concerned with the natural desire for self-preservation. But so long as the greatest question that drives our faith is what we can get out of God, we would never develop eyes to see God's beauty that charges us with a greater sense of purpose for living that exists beyond ourselves. "What's the payoff?" is an age-old question that even Satan asked.

Satan asked, "Does Job fear God for nothing?" (Job 1:9-11). *The only reason Job follows you, God, is because he gets something out of it. He's in it for himself and not because he finds you worthy,* Satan claimed. This wasn't so much a challenge to Job as it was to God. This was a challenge of God's worthiness of being loved merely for who He was and not for what people got from Him. If He didn't do anything for a guy like Job, no protection and no blessings, would God's glory, splendor and beauty be enough to deserve Job's love? Or is God only loved because of what Job gets out of Him? So, God did something none of us would ever want happen to us – He stepped up to Satan and gave him the permission to remove all of

Job's blessings, sparing only his life and a faithless wife. When a person is stripped bare of his possessions, you see nothing but his heart. Job questioned God about the reasons for his sufferings as any normal person would, though he never rejected God. By the end, God revealed His splendor to Job. In the midst of Job's emptiness, God showed him the beauty of His attributes, and it was enough to warrant Job's devotion (Job 42:1-6). If we

> "There is a difference between having an opinion, that God is holy and gracious and having a sense of the loveliness and beauty of that holiness and grace... The former may be obtained by hearsay, but the latter only by seeing the countenance. When the heart is sensible of the beauty and amiableness of a thing, it necessarily feels pleasure in the apprehension. It is implied in a person's being heartily sensible of the loveliness of a thing, that the idea of it is pleasant to his soul, which is a far different thing from having a rational opinion that it is excellent."[ii]
>
> —Jonathan Edwards

were Job, how would we fair? Would we love God for who He is or would we validate Satan's suspicions that we don't love God for nothing? Why else do we love God if it's not for His beauty?

Gaze

I find Augustine's notion to be both accurate and profound, that we fall in love with what we find most beautiful.[7] In our contemporary society where the concept of beauty is diluted by mass media, we forget that beauty captures our hearts and intends to allure us. There is nothing simple about beauty because it evokes a love in us.

If our love for God is really a self-love, then we have yet to encounter God's beauty. But, a sincere love for God is *je ne sais quoi* because it is prompted by a beauty, or excellency, of God that extends beyond human comprehension. David, known as a man after God's own heart (Acts 13:22), wrote in Psalm 27:4,

> *One thing I ask of the LORD,*
> *this is what I seek:*

that I may dwell in the house of the LORD
all the days of my life,
to gaze upon the beauty of the LORD
and seek him in his temple.

The context of this psalm, according to verses 1-3, was wartime as armies besieged David and the city. The typical practice of an ancient Mesopotamian king about to go to war was to enter the temple of his god and plead for a victory so that the name of that god may be honored. David wrote about having strength in war in the first three verses.

Then in verse 4 he made an unparalleled expression, describing a single-focused desire, "One thing I ask of the LORD...".[8] There's one thing arresting David's heart. *What is it? As war is about to break out, what do you want? Power? Victory?* Instead of immediately requesting the obvious in light of his circumstances, he expressed his utmost desire to dwell in God's house where he found refuge. He wanted to stay in the tabernacle for the rest of his life so that he could "gaze upon the beauty of the LORD". The term "to gaze" meant to stare in wonder. It was the same term used in the Song of Songs to refer to a person staring at the beauty of another in admiration (Songs 6:13).[9]

> "There is no condition God must meet before we are under obligation to love Him with all our heart, soul, strength and mind. He is altogether worthy of that love, and every creature who owes his very existence to his Creator and who lives and moves and has his being in that Creator owes the honor and esteem that is inherent in His eternal perfection to the Creator."[iii]
>
> —R. C. Sproul

In the tabernacle, David would've gazed at the Ark of the Covenant,[10] which he knew well, celebrated and loved even as he danced with it back to Jerusalem during its retrieval (2 Sam. 6:12-16). Perhaps his cry expressed his longing for the glory of God to fill the tabernacle while he dwelled in it and to allow the weight of God's worthiness to surround him as he basked in its brilliant light and relished in God's glory. The Ark, a highly ornamented chest, symbolized God's beauty and echoed His promises and presence.[11] And where God's beauty was, David wanted to be even as he cried:

> How lovely is your dwelling place,
> O LORD Almighty!
> My soul yearns, even faints,
> for the courts of the LORD;
> my heart and my flesh cry out
> for the living God
>
> (Ps. 84:1-2).

What we genuinely love most becomes our true north. But if what we love most is a misplaced love on an unworthy object, then nothing else we have will bear proper meaning. For those of us who are lost in the woods and don't have a clear sense of true north, a raw encounter with God's splendor may definitively move us to cry, *I love you, O Lord, my strength* (Ps. 18:1).

Perhaps for some of us, true north feels like a moving target because we've been so consumed by the worries of our needs that we haven't sought an honest encounter with God's *je ne sais quoi* beauty expressed in His sacrificial and covenantal love. Perhaps for some of us, religion has been more about our needs than God's beauty. We've been distracted by a love for our own gain and we've missed a pure love for God that stems from knowing Him. Perhaps we're missing true north because we haven't been asking ourselves what is the one thing we desire most that captures our gaze.

Desire and Drive

Augustine, though a revered theologian and bishop in our church's history, wrestled with desires of the flesh over his love for God. Through his internal quarrels, he came to this principle: "If the things of this world delight you, praise God for them, but turn your love away from them and give it to their Maker, so that in the things that please you you may not displease him."[12]

There is a difference between loving things from a worldly attitude (1 Jn. 2:16-17) and receiving blessings from God that are meant to be enjoyed (Eccl. 2:24-25, 3:22, 5:19). These blessings include tangible gifts, even the rewards earned from your labors. It would be unfaithful to decline those blessings and equally unfaithful to feel that you could not ask God for blessings. In fact, the psalmists were realistic about their plights, and they had no qualms about asking God for concrete results and tangible deliverances.

> *"For wherever the soul of man may turn, unless it turns to you, it clasps sorrow to itself. Even though it clings to things of beauty, if their beauty is outside God and outside the soul, it only clings to sorrow."*[iv]
>
> —Augustine

But our problem is not our inability to curb or restrain our desires. It's that our desires are too small. We're too ready to settle for the smaller things of the world, and God wants to increase our appetites. I find myself agreeing with C.S. Lewis' statement,

> If we consider the unblushing promises of reward and the staggering nature of the rewards promised in the Gospels, it would seem that Our Lord finds our desires not too strong, but too weak. We are half-hearted creatures, fooling about with drink and sex and ambition when infinite joy is offered to us, like an ignorant child who wants to go on making mud pies in a slum because he cannot imagine what is meant by the offer of a holiday at the sea. We are far too easily pleased.[13]

Even though God would still be worthy of our love if He didn't give us anything, out of His goodness and through Christ He pours out spiritual blessings on those who love Him (Eph. 1:1-14). So God does not want us to be anorexic about our desires and the receiving of good things from Him. In fact, He said to test Him and see how He would pour out so many blessings that we couldn't contain it (Mal. 3:10). But even in Malachi, the drive was not a love for the blessings; it was a love for God and His kingdom.

It's a paradox to hear people's perceptions of Christianity as a religion of reservation, that is of wanting less. "Why would I want to be a Christian," I've heard many ask, "when all that means is I have to give up everything?" The Christian faith, however, is not about lessening our appetites; it is about increasing them by turning our cravings on the truly valuable things. In the middle of Jesus' famous Sermon on the Mount, He delivered a message about treasures and worries (Matt. 6:19-34). He didn't tell us to stop storing up altogether. It wasn't the act that was in question, but the object. He said stop amassing worldly treasures that corrode and deteriorate, but instead amass eternal treasures. The keen insight He provided was *where our treasures are is also where our hearts are*. Another way to express it is: what we treasure is what we love.

Jesus further drove home the point with his analogy of the eye being a lamp for the body and qualifying the eye with the terms "good" or "bad", where "good" had a double meaning (Matt. 6:22-23). In R.T. France's analysis of this term, it could mean "sound" but also "single-mindedness".[14] The eye that was fixed on the right things cast a light upon the soul, enriching the heart and spirit of the person. But our fixations on corruptible things only bring deterioration upon ourselves. The worth of a person's life may be reinforced or debased by the things he loves.

Jesus explained that a person could only truly love one or the other: either God or the material treasures of the world (Matt. 6:24). Jesus knew this axiom well even while He was tempted by Satan, who showed Him all the beauties of the worldly kingdoms and offered it to Him if only He bowed down to Satan (Matt. 4:8-9). It's intriguing that Satan never asked Jesus to deny God but simply to worship Satan; it was a request to *add* another master. But Satan knew that in the event Jesus accepted that offer of idolatry Jesus could not love God anymore, because one cannot love two masters. The nature of love is there is only one great beauty that arrests our hearts. Only one. We would be fooled to think that we could have it all.

Jesus had still yet to pose the more profound consideration as He connected our treasures to our worries (Matt. 6:25-34). That consideration is the question: *don't you realize you're more important than the corruptible worldly things you worry about?* He made it clear that we only worry about what we treasure. If our greatest concerns in life are over the corruptible things of the world, then perhaps we don't have a sense of our own self-value, at least not a value for our humanity as defined in the eyes of the heavenly Father. Perhaps we don't really see the beauty of our humanity made in the image of God. The common struggle for people with materialism versus godly pursuits is not merely a matter of virtue. It's about one's self-evaluation, for our greatest treasures and worries are indicators of how we think of ourselves. For many of us, we have yet to come to a realization that we are worth more than the fleeting things of the world. For the person who has entered into the *je ne sais quoi* beauty of God's love, we have the opportunity to recognize our self-worth beyond the valuations of worldly things.

In the end, Jesus again tried to increase our appetites by calling us to fix our hearts and eyes on God's kingdom and all the heavenly things associated with it, such as God's fellowship, goodness, righteousness, joy and reign. Love the greater things of God that can't spoil, Jesus said, and even the lesser things which God is aware that you need and desire will be provided for you (Matt. 6:33).

So how do we know if we love God and His kingdom above everything else? Simple. Do we worry about it above all other things?

How Do We Love God?

In my upbringing, the words, "I love you", never came from the lips of my family. It was understood that our actions concretely exposed our hearts. For my parents it was their provisions for our needs that expressed those three, unspoken words, and for the children it was our obedience. Of course growing up, I didn't appreciate the power of actions to incarnate authentic love. In contemporary perceptions, obedience tends to have a ring of oppression and control, bearing a negative connotation of suppressing one's freedom and individuality. But there is a theologically rich meaning to obedience because it embodies love. Obedience encompasses faithfulness, discipleship and trust, all of which in their absences would only afford an empty love based on words alone. Obedience is how God defines a genuine love for Him.

Soon after Philip asked Jesus for a theophany in John 14:8, "Show us the father and that would be enough," a request to see God in all His beauty and glory which would gratify the desires of life, Jesus explained to His disciples in his last hours before the crucifixion the meaning of love.

> "The whole Christian life is compared to a warfare, and fitly so... True Christian fortitude consists in strength of mind, through grace, exerted in two things; in ruling and suppressing the evil and unruly passions and affections of the mind; and in steadfastly and freely exerting and following good affections..."
>
> —Jonathan Edwards

"If you love me, you will obey what I command," Jesus said (Jn. 14:15, also see Jn. 14:21). In a reciprocal way, to follow Jesus' commands allows us to be recipients of His love (Jn. 15:10). Jesus blurred the seam between love and obedience, where obedience is the fulfillment and expression of love. Jesus himself modeled a *je ne sais quoi* kind of love in His obedience to the Father (Jn. 14:31).

On that dark, cold night, at the quietly awry place of Gethsemane, Jesus would've rather walked away from the road to the cross than to suffer the agony set before Him. During my own trials, I've often reached to comprehend the volume of Jesus' agonizing words on that nightly hill, "My soul is overwhelmed with sorrow to the point of death" (Matt. 26:38). And I've sought further to understand and even embrace the kind of love Jesus had for the Father when His obedience to follow God's will decided the matter as "he fell with his face to the ground and prayed, 'My Father, if it is possible, may this cup be taken from me. Yet not as I will, but as you will'" (Matt. 26:39). His love for the Father overrode his love for self. It was *je ne sais quoi*. His love for God expressed with total obedience was a model for us on how to love God.

Obedience to Jesus redefines our understanding of morality in light of love. In this light, sin and morality is a relational matter. Right-and-wrong is not just about an impersonal code of ethics but it has to do with how we relate to God. Preserving purity and integrity becomes a form of behavioral management of do's and don'ts when obedience is a mindless act apart from love. But obedience is empowering when it is a matter of nurturing one's relationship with Jesus and a way of loving Him. Obedience in love conveys faithfulness. In a surprising paradox, obedience is not more confining but liberating because we discover a more genuine and beautiful humanity, which is free from sin and corruption. It's by our obedience to Jesus that we fulfill the call to deny ourselves (Lk. 9:23), freeing us to embrace a beauty that is outside of us and greater than us; obedience is the key to discipleship as we follow the one we love.

> "I began to search for a means of gaining the strength I needed to enjoy you, but I could not find this means until I embraced the mediator between God and men, Jesus Christ, who is a man, like them, and also rules as God over all things, blessed for ever."[vi]
>
> —Augustine

But why love Jesus when the commandment is clearly to love God (Deut. 6:5, 1 Jn. 5:3)? Because to love Jesus, who is the second person of the Trinity, the mediator between humans and God, and the manifested beauty of God in human form (2 Cor. 4:4-6, Heb. 1:3), is to love God. Even God directed us to obey Jesus when He said out of a supernatural cloud, "This is my Son, whom I have chosen; listen to him" (Lk. 9:35). Jesus' response to Philip's request to see the Father was if you've seen Jesus then you've seen the Father (Jn. 14:9). We cannot know or love God without knowing and loving His Son, so that the kind of loving relationship we enter into with God is a Trinitarian one. Obeying Jesus as His disciples is essential to loving God.

In the end, how we have lived is defined by how we have loved because it is our greatest love that marks the greatest beauty that has captured and defined us as our true north. Followers of Jesus being madly in love with God likely look strange to the world. But then again, the picture of my neighbor Dan with his dad, I think, looks pretty strange to most. That's the beauty of the *je ne sais quoi*. The surprising amazement of such love, particularly the godly love, is otherworldly, even heavenly. And while it might be strange, it offers a view of beauty that a broken world needs to see.

Walk in Color

- Describe your greatest experience of love.
- How well do you believe you honestly know God's love for you? How would you honestly evaluate your love for God? If you could paint a verbal picture of what your love for God would ideally look like, how would you describe it?
- Read and meditate on Romans 8:36-39. Then read Matthew 22:37-40.
- How could knowing God's beauty infuse a greater love in you for Him?

The Purple Curtain

Notes: Chapter Six

[1] Umberto Eco, *History of Beauty*, translated by Alastair McEwen (New York: Rizzoli International Publications, 2004), 310.

[2] Leland Ryken, Jim C. Wilhoit, and Tremper Longman III, "Flowers," in *Dictionary of Biblical Imagery* (Downers Grove: InterVarsity Press, 1998), 294.

[3] The *"waw"* in Num. 17:10 is a *voluntative waw* which denotes intentionality or purpose, i.e. "so that," whereby the intention behind the warning of the almond flowers was not judgment but to provide a chance for the receiving of grace out of love. (The "voluntative waw" category is described in Brown, Driver, and Briggs, "waw," *Hebrew Lexicon*, 254.1)

[4] Jonathan Edwards, *The Religious Affections* (Carlisle: Banner of Truth Trust, 1997), 168-9.

[5] *Ibid.*, 29.

[6] *Ibid.*

[7] Augustine, *Confessions*, translated by R.S. Pine-Coffin (London: Penguin Group, 1961), 83.

[8] Peter C. Craigie, *Word Biblical Commentary: Psalms 1-50*. Edited by Bruce Metzger, vol. 19 (Waco: Word Books, 1983), 232.

[9] David's choice to use the Hebrew term *hatah*, versus *ra'ah*, communicates his desire not to see a prophetic vision but to be enraptured by God's beauty. The term complements the object of his gaze which was God's *na'em* (beauty, delightfulness and pleasantness).

[10] Craigie, *Word Biblical Commentary: Psalms 1-50*, 232.

[11] *Ibid.*

[12] Augustine, *Confessions*, 82.

[13] C.S. Lewis, *The Weight of Glory and the Other Addresses* (San Francisco: HarperCollins Publishers, 2001), 26.

[14] R.T. France, *The Gospel of Matthew* in The New International Commentary on the New Testament (Grand Rapids: Wm. B. Eerdmans Publishing Company, 2007), 261.

Pull Out Quotes:

[i] Jonathan Edwards, *The Religious Affections* (Carlisle: Banner of Truth Trust, 1997), 169.

[ii] Jonathan Edwards, *A Divine and Supernatural Light* in *Sinners in the Hands of an Angry God and Other Writings* (Nashville: Thomas Nelson, 2000), 27-28.

[iii] R. C. Sproul, *Loved by God* (Nashville: Word Publishing, 2001), 148-9.

[iv] Augustine, *Confessions*, translated by R.S. Pine-Coffin (London: Penguin Group, 1961), 80.

[v] Jonathan Edwards, *The Religious Affections*, 277.

[vi] Augustine, *Confessions*, 152.

98

Chapter Seven

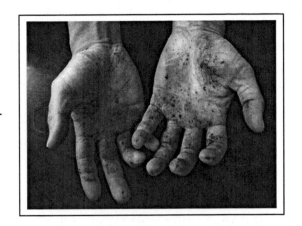

UGLINESS

Ug ● ly: unpleasant or repulsive, esp. in appearance; involving or likely involving violence or other unpleasantness; suggestively unpleasant; morally repugnant (*The New American Oxford Dictionary*).

You probably won't like this chapter, but I challenge you to read it.

Soiled underwear in a pile of trash infested with flies, a decapitated road-kill rotting on the hot asphalt, the moaning sounds of zombies from George A. Romero's "Night of the Living Dead", or the screeching of nails scraping a blackboard are examples of what repulse us. They make us grimace and shirk away, causing us to feel sick in our own skin. "Something is wrong with this," we think to ourselves. We'd describe these things as nothing less than disgusting. They are what we'd call "ugly".

Ugliness is not a foreign idea to our pop culture. Our culture unabashedly finds amusement in gruesome horror films based on sadism, like "Saw", "The Texas Chainsaw Massacre" or "Friday the 13th". Though they evoke feelings of repulsion, fear and disgust, the ugliness portrayed on screen is popularly consumed as entertainment.

Why do so many enjoy blockbuster horror films that depict grotesque, gruesome and gory scenes? Films like "The Grudge", "The Ring" and "Paranormal Activity" show frightening images of people distorted by demonic forces. Horror films and stories have remained a favored pastime, with classics like "The Exorcist", "Jaws" and "Poltergeist". Even the television screen has been haunted by shows like "Tales from the Crypt", "True Blood" and "Supernatural". I personally could never stomach horror movies too well though I shared a twisted fascination for them while growing up. I used to watch Chinese vampire movies as well as American films of the undead. I was guaranteed to have nightmares after each movie. Horror films were also popular in the Hong Kong cinema. Why are horror films popular across western and eastern cultures? They make us squirm, give us nightmares and ruin our appetites. We wouldn't eat a juicy cheeseburger while watching a zombie movie. And yet, many of us keep coming back to these films.

I've heard some say they watch horror films for the adrenaline rush. They like to feel their blood surge, their hearts race and the hair on their arms stand. I've also heard some say that horror films connect with something we all understand but fear – it's death and destruction. These are realities we comprehend and yet are perplexed by because we don't know what to make of them. We can't really explain death and destruction or make sense of it but we know it's real. Horror entertainment both reminds us of our broken reality and gives us a sense of connectedness to this dreaded and perplexing reality. Fictional horror reminds us that real ugliness exists in life and the world.

But when we talk about ugliness, what is it?

Throughout history, the perception of ugliness has varied in different periods and cultural settings whether in art, music, literature, fashion, life experiences or world events. Umberto Eco observed that historically few theories on ugliness were created.[1] Ugliness was generally understood as a matter of relative taste – what is ugly to one person may be attractive to another. For example, "to a westerner an African ritual mask might seem hair-raising — while for a native it might represent a benevolent divinity".[2] Our relative sense of ugliness is determined by what makes us feel repulsed or disgusted. For different people the threshold of disgust also differs.

But amidst the diverse opinions, there is a general commonality to what people find disgusting or repulsive.[3] Eco asserted that there is a universal agreement on what is ugly, such as the images of starving children reduced to skeletal forms and stories of people being tortured and raped by invaders from other countries. The difference between these and slasher-horror films is the reality versus fiction. Horror could be entertainment as long as it remains fictional. Real inhumane acts and conditions are universally agreed to be ugly. Eco wrote in *On Ugliness*,

> We all know perfectly well that such things are *ugly*, not only in the moral but in the physical sense, and we know this because they arouse our disgust, fear, and repulsion… No knowledge of the relativity of aesthetic values can eliminate the fact that in such cases we unhesitatingly recognize ugliness and we cannot transform it into an object of pleasure. So we can understand why art in various centuries insistently portrayed ugliness. Marginal as the voice of art may be, it attempted to remind us that, despite the optimism of certain metaphysicians, there is something implacably and sadly malign about this world.[4]

If atrocities are universally perceived to be ugly, would then even the perpetrators agree that their own acts were ugly? Did they simply have a twisted proclivity for doing what's ugly? Or maybe they didn't recognize their atrocious acts as being ugly at all.

So how do we define ugliness? Immanuel Kant explained that, "all judgments of taste are *singular* judgments. For because I must refer the object immediately to my feeling of pleasure or pain, and that not by means of concepts, they cannot have the quantity of objective generally valid judgments."[5] He echoes the popular sentiment that ugliness is defined by personal feelings towards something, that is if it causes you "pain" (or disgust) to experience it, then it is ugly *to you*. But our subjective opinions are not the only ones we should consider. If we take again into account the subjective tastes of God, then the possibility of an objective definition of ugliness could be found in the one Creator who has the authority to establish His subjectivity as an absolute for everyone else. The concepts of beauty and ugliness are based on His delights and disgusts. His subjectivity becomes our objectivity. So, the question is *what does God find ugly?*

God and Ugliness

If we are to form a definition of ugliness based on God's disgust, let's first look in the Bible at a few emotionally charged Hebrew terms that honestly express His disgust: *tow 'ebah, shiqquwts, ga'al* and *naqa*. *Tow 'ebah* in particular could be translated as, "disgusting, disgraceful, detestable, horrible, abominable, abhorrent, reprehensible or loathsome". Things that cause *tow 'ebah* are likened to the churning feeling in the bowels from food poisoning, spoiled milk or the putrid smell of feces. They are things so gravely offensive that they immediately instigate violent reactions, and relief is not found until you turn away from them or they are expunged from your system. Though God is not a physical being, the Bible's descriptions of His disgust conjure memories of reprehensible tastes, smells, sights and touches, so that we could grasp a sense of His repulsion towards certain things.

The things God finds repulsive, even hateful, include sexual sins (Jer. 13:27, Lev. 18:6-23), dishonesty (Deut. 25:16), hypocritical worship and injustice (Amos 5:21-24), perverse desires (Prov. 11:20), empty prayers of the unfaithful (Prov. 28:9) and, above all, idolatry (Deut. 7:25, Deut. 27:15, 2 Kgs. 17:12). God said, "*Do not do this detestable thing that I hate! But they did not listen or pay attention; they did not turn from their wickedness or stop burning incense to other gods*" (Jer. 44:4-5). Idols looked and smelled ugly to God; idols to Him are like soiled menstrual pads (Isa. 30:22). The lukewarm faiths of half-hearted Christians were like a bitter taste in Jesus' mouth that

He wanted to spit, or more graphically vomit, out (Rev. 3:15-16).[6] These moral and spiritual depravities are ugly to God because at a fundamental level they violate His truths. Romans 1:18 reads, *The wrath of God is being revealed from heaven against all the godlessness and wickedness of men who suppress the truth by their wickedness.*

Nobody likes being told a lie. Idolatry, sexual immorality and other sins are based on lies. They are actions that are manifested from a false premise, a denial and violation of God's truth. In order to sin, we have to form a lie, in particular, about God. In the moment we sin, we have to assume the belief that God is not worthy of being honored with righteousness or that He's not really holy. He's not omniscient so He doesn't see what we're doing. He's not omnipresent so He's not there while we're sinning. Or, He's not really God so we could do whatever we feel like. These are all lies we tell ourselves about God in order to justify our sin, if even for a moment.

Lies about God were thought to be most ugly and repulsive in ancient philosophy. Socrates said that lies about spiritual matters were despicable: "deception, or being deceived or uninformed about the highest realities in the highest part of themselves, which is the soul, and in that part of them to have to hold the lie, is what mankind least like; – that, I say, is what they utterly detest."[7] The late H.R. Rookmaaker, a respected theologian of the arts, commented that certain modern artworks are ugly not because of style or form, but because of their denial of truth. "What is the difference between the beauty of these 'horrible' works and the horrible we find in modern art?" He wrote, "Again, it is a matter of truth. Modern art often speaks of (or rather swears at) the ugliness of God's creation, or of despair without hope or of the meaninglessness of the meaningful: insofar as these things are lies they are never beautiful."[8] Regardless of our personal tastes for particular styles of art, Rookmaaker's point is that expressions denouncing God's biblical truth, including His existence, character, creation, gospel or judgment of sin, are ugly. The apostle Paul explained that when people suppressed God's truth, they surrendered true beauty (i.e. God's glory) and embraced acts of ugliness, like idolatry and sexual sins. The birth of ugliness begins by renouncing truth (Ro. 1:18).

In a fallen world we should expect ugliness to be prevalent, whether in stories that advocate we live in a godless world or pornographic films that defy biblical truths about sexuality. Ugliness is the contradiction of *tob* (good). The good expresses God's delight, and the ugly offends it. The ugly is absent of grace, holiness, righteousness, love and truth. And, if *tob* describes the perfect and whole, the ugly is the broken and depraved.

How we deal with the reality of ugliness in our world and in ourselves is often the path to how we discover beauty. The things that cause us feelings of disgust, even shame, remind us of the unsanitary brokenness we live in and alert us to the need for redemption. God's expressions of disgust towards facets of our world and humanity are often divine cries to penetrate our cover of busyness, wishful thinking and temporal satisfactions. Until we are able to honestly sense God's *tow 'ebah*, we remain aloof to the decay of our brokenness and detoured from His *tob*.

Meet the Monster

Monsters have been a universal symbolism for ugliness in many cultures. Every horror film or adventure tale had to have a monster or two. There had to be cyclops in Homer's *Iliad* and the *Odyssey*, Grendel in *Beowulf*, the giant shark in "Jaws", the zombies in zombie-films, the demonized girl in "The Exorcist", Sauron in *The Lord of the Rings*, the wicked witch in *The Chronicles of Narnia* or Voldemort in *Harry Potter*. Monsters in stories have symbolized evil, tragedy and hurt that must be conquered in order to preserve peace and harmony in life. They are the embodiment of ugliness and they seek to cause more ugliness. Stories demonstrate that the more we know about the reality and nature of monsters the more we realize our own weaknesses and real life problems and what it takes to triumph over them.[9]

Sin and Satan are the monsters of the human story. Sin brings death (Ro. 6:23) and Satan lures people towards sin. The Bible portrays sin as the monster that waits outside our door ready to devour us if we give it the chance. God said to Cain, *"Why are you angry? Why is your face downcast? If you do what is right, will you not be accepted? But if you do not do what is right, sin is crouching at your door; it desires to have you, but you must master it*" (Gen. 4:6-7). Sin is the ugly beast or the creature of the story, and our task is to master the monster. Our quest is to overcome the ugliness that violates God's beauty.

But what is the real monstrosity? Monsters have typically been portrayed as grotesque, hideous and deformed. But stories have revealed that monsters were not always defined by ugly appearances but by character and nature. Stories like *Twilight* challenged the conventional understanding of vampires by redefining the "monsters" as those who did harm to others while those who knew how to love were beautiful.

Quentin Tarantino films are either loved or hated. I found his film "Inglorious Basterds" brilliant and disgusting at the same time. In a WWII context, one would readily assume who was good and who was evil since it seems clear that the Nazis were the monsters that ruthlessly conquered others and attempted genocide. But "Inglorious Basterds" re-evaluated the arrogant assumption that *we* are good. In the film, there were no characters with redeeming qualities, but all were overtaken either by bigotry, hate, selfishness, cowardice or vengeance. Amidst the depictions of ruthless violence and bloody scalping, you want to cringe and ask yourself, "Why am I watching this?" But, the film leaves you with the unsettling suggestion that *we're all* inglorious bastards, a title not reserved for an especially evil group of people but a label suited for the common debasement of our humanity. This film and others, like "Seven", do not offer feel-good moments, but express honestly about humanity's ugliness and how sometimes we resemble the monsters we fear in the stories.

In the world of three-dimensional art, Alberto Giacometti (1901-1966) was known for his famous bronze sculptures of elongated, thin, anorexic and distorted human figures. Instead of creating typically full-formed figures, this late post world war artist depicted human beings in a state of alienation, isolation and loss in the world.[10] The figures look as if the space around them pressed the life out of them. The rough, agitated surface of the figures with limbs that could be likened to chopsticks portrayed a frail, deformed and depressed humanity. Having lived through the history of the most violent and bloodiest of wars, his works spoke of "the despair in the aftermath of world war".[11] His figures show the monstrosities of war, but even more so, the monstrosities of despair wrought on those who survived the violence.

From the music front, the late rapper Tupac Shakur (1971-1996) sang a song, called "Changes", that depicted the monstrosities of racism in societies, where "there's war on the streets and in the Middle East". Having come from the slums, his firsthand experiences fueled his music. He sang about the social depravities, like the unjust ways of making money, the racism of police authorities and the mindsets of living in such environments. But the real problem is whether society will ever change. One of the lines in his song reads, "Take the evil out the people, they'll be acting right." The monstrosities Tupac rapped about resided in our sin nature.

I consider these artistic expressions to be like the harassing nag of the prophets in the Bible, who tried to enlighten people about their sinfulness and broken societies. Eco wrote art that portrays ugliness is a voice that tries to shake us from our generic, numbed optimism. Ugliness reminds us that we're not in heaven. Without a sensitivity toward ugliness, we may actually recline to an unsubstantiated optimism over a desperate humanity. Jesus said, "When [the Holy Spirit] comes, he will convict the world of guilt in regard to sin..." (Jn. 16:8). Experiencing the ugly moments are sometimes God-moments where He gives us the grace to intuit on some level His revulsions and call for repentance. Without a sense for the ugly, we would not know the need for redemption and remain ignorantly in debasement. And there is no ugliness of humanity that cries out louder for redemption than what we will consider next.

Ugliness in Death

I remember my first funeral. I was about six years old when my great-grandfather died. To be honest, he was sort of a scary, old man to me. Don't get me wrong. He wasn't mean. He was just wrinkly and hunched with darkened skin and blackened fingernails, and he had this moaning-voice. But he always loved me more than anybody else, which was scarier for me because his loving expressions appeared to me as an old man who was "after" me. His eyes got big and watery whenever he saw me walk into his room at the convalescent home. He'd pick up a piece of fried drumstick off his plate, the best piece according to Chinese customs, and extend it to me with his quivering fingers. I didn't realize the sadness of his death until many years later.

But I vividly recall his funeral. I didn't understand what was happening as my family members and I sat in front of an open casket with my great-grandfather lying peacefully in it. Why wasn't he moving? Where were his big watery eyes? Why wasn't he offering me a fried drumstick? What's wrong? "He's sleeping," my mother told me. But I knew he wasn't sleeping. No one sleeps like that. Something was wrong, but I didn't comprehend it.

When a college assignment had me research my family history, I learned my great-grandfather was the first emigrant from our family to the U.S. and his 30 years of sacrifices paved the way for our family to establish our lives in the States. When I integrated what I learned in my adulthood with my memories of him from my childhood, I re-experienced that funeral day and realized the meaning of it, that a wonderful man was lost to this world and to me. I comprehended then the sadness of death in a new way. The unsettling mystery of death haunted me because I believed death should have no place in life. Death was wrong.

Death is wrong because it has no part in God's original design for humanity. Human beings possessed a measure of glory when God artistically sculpted them out of clay (Gen. 2:7) with His own image as the blueprint (Gen. 1:27) and when He called us "good". Humans had honor as rulers and stewards of God's creation (Gen. 1:28). Relationally, they were in harmony with God and one another. Psalm 8 praised humanity's place in the universe as being slightly lower than the angels.

> "O pitiful lot of man... he has lost the blessedness for which he was made, and has found the misery for which he was not made. That without which nothing is happy has deserted him, and that which by itself is nothing but misery has remained. Then, 'man ate the bread of angels,' for which he hungers now; now, he eats the 'bread of sorrow,' of which he knew nothing then."
>
> —Anselm of Canterbury

Paradise for man was not merely a place, but a state of being – a state of beauty.

But sin forced us into a world of *"thorns and thistles"* where our existences would end in *"dust"*. Genesis 3:17-19 reads:

> *"Cursed is the ground because of you;*
> *through painful toil you will eat of it*
> *all the days of your life.*
> *It will produce thorns and thistles for you…*
> *By the sweat of your brow*
> *you will eat your food*
> *until you return to the ground*
> *since from it you were taken;*
> *for dust you are*
> *and to dust you will return."*

I know this sounds morbid, but the curse from the original sin changed humanity's reality drastically. Instead of a world of pure beauty, dignity, honor and meaningfulness, the plight of human life is about painful work in order to survive and all our hard work may not amount to anything except for thorns and thistles. A reality of thorns and thistles means a world where two plus two does not always equal four. It may equal zero.[12] It is a reality where we could work hard and save responsibly for years but still lose our

> *"To this day I do not know what they mean when they call dead bodies beautiful. The ugliest man alive is an angel of beauty compared with the loveliest of the dead."*[ii]
>
> —C.S. Lewis

retirement because of someone else's wrongful actions. It is a reality where we could eat right, never smoke and exercise daily and still wind up with a rare cancer. And when we have toiled long enough, striving for fruit and hoping we don't get thorns and thistles, we die. We decompose back into the raw material from which we were made. No matter what people lost or gained in life, the end result is dust. It's no wonder everyone craves a sense of significance in what appears to be a meaningless existence. We work, strive and grasp for something meaningful – maybe we'll find meaning in the success of our careers or in our families. But the meaningfulness we desire is elusive because we face the ugliness of thorns, thistles and dust.

I liken death to an account of Michelangelo's famous *Pieta*, a life-size sculpture depicting Mary cradling the body of Jesus after He was taken down from the cross. One day while it was on display, a deranged man charged the statue with a hammer, shattering the arm of the masterpiece. For many devout viewers, this representation of Mary and Jesus was more than artistic – it was sacred. While some responded with shock and agony at the destruction of a revered sculpture, others clambered at the fallen pieces in a frenzy. Specialists were able to recover some of the pieces and reassemble the broken parts but much of the original pieces were lost. Similarly, human life is God's masterpiece and the destruction of it is an unspeakable tragedy, a desecration of something sacred. Death sends us back to the dust from which we were made (Gen. 3:19), a disassembling of masterpieces, an undoing of the "good" God

> "It's like a dream I once had, though I didn't know then how true it was. I dreamed I was lying dead – you know, nicely laid out in the ward in a nursing home with my face settled by the undertaker and big lilies in the room. And then a sort of a person who was all falling to bits – like a tramp, you know, only it was himself not his clothes that was coming to pieces – came and stood at the foot of the bed, just hating me. 'All right,' he said, 'all right. You think you're mighty fine with your clean sheet and your shiny coffin being got ready. I began like that. We all did. Just wait and see what you come down to in the end.'"[viii]
>
> —C.S. Lewis

made. Death is destruction. It is chaos on order. It is deforming the harmonious. It is no wonder the images of death and decay in horror films and stories harrow our minds with a mixture of grief, fear and disgust.

Popular films portraying the afterlife, such as "The Sixth Sense", "The Crow" and "Ghost", and films depicting characters wrestling with death, like "The Bucket List", demonstrate our compulsion to address the issue of death. Is there an afterlife? Can we find peace in death? Will doing everything we desire in life before we die give us that sense of significance?

> "I will ransom them from the power of the grave; I will redeem them from death."
>
> "Where, O death, is your victory? Where, O death, is your sting?"[iv]

Death is something we all must deal with, as The Teacher wrote, *"for death is the destiny of every man; the living should take this to heart"* (Eccl. 7:2). We live life based on how we have addressed death. The reality is we all live in the present under the overcast of our destinies. If we can triumph over death, we no longer live in the shadow of an impending doom yet to be resolved. There can be no real peace in Middle Earth as long as Mordor still remains. We begin living when we've overcome dying (1 Cor. 15:26). Then, we can live from a place of fullness out of the life we have and not from a place of trying to compensate for our future destruction.

It may be presumptuous for me to comment on how people should or should not meet their ends when death knocks, since I haven't had such an experience and there are no other experiences that I could compare to the feeling of impending death. However, I frequently recall an inspiring colleague who had big dreams but died too young. While on his deathbed at home after battling a rare form of cancer for over a year, his friends and family surrounded him and his newly wedded wife. In his last moments, he asked for his Bible and expressed his nervousness and excitement over meeting Jesus. I recall his good-bye to me a month before his passing. I was in denial at that time, but he knew his end was coming. He had a lot he could've been angry and remorseful about, but he met his end with grace, gratefulness and courage because he had something not everyone finds — redemption. How my friend met death revealed what he found in life — Jesus. If death is an ugly distortion of life yet to be reconciled through redemption, then no beauties in this temporal world will satiate our souls in the end. Apart from the redemptive sacrifice of Christ Jesus, people remain under the monsters of thorns, thistles and dust. Death serves as a nagging reminder of our quest to recover the lost beauty of our humanity.

Death in Hell

I hate writing this part. But death can't be fully explained apart from mentioning hell, which for an unredeemed humanity is a reality according to the Bible. We don't know the details of hell's circumstances, but the Bible tells us it is a real place of pain. If there were an icon for ugliness, it might be hell. The Greek term for hell is gehenna, derived from the imagery of a physical place in the Ancient Near East called the Valley of Hinnom. It was a dreadful place that always smelled like burnt carcasses, because pagans burned human sacrifices there. The Valley of Hinnom provided a depiction of a dark place in the afterlife.

> *"We have been sent from our fatherland into exile, from the vision of God into our own blindness, from the delight of immortality into the bitterness and terror of death."*
>
> —Anselm of Canterbury

Hell, according to the Bible, is a place of eternal judgment (Matt. 25:46), where there will be *"weeping and gnashing of teeth"* (Matt. 25:30), *"eternal fire"* (Matt. 25:41), *"darkness"* (Matt. 25:30) and *"worms"* that don't die (Mark 9:48). It is like the most nightmarish horror film come to life. In Dante's *Divine Comedy*, he contrasted the unimaginable effervescent beauty of the heavenly paradise (*Paradiso*) with the malicious ugliness of hell (*Inferno*). All the feelings of bliss and awe evoked by eternal beauty were juxtaposed with the horrors of hell's torment. Hell as the fulfillment of death is the ideal ugliness, where its chaos and destruction of life is ultimate. But even a bit of hell's ugliness can be experienced in the present.

The Walking Dead

Moon-size comets smashing into the earth, hundred-feet tidal waves rushing a coastline, earthquakes that swallow up towns and fireballs raining down from a black sky are popular images of God's wrath. His wrath is typically thought of as an impending apocalypse. But what if we realized that His wrath already arrived in more subtle yet no less potent ways? The elusive tragedy of humanity is that the destructive force of death is present in our waking days. The apostle Paul told us that apart from redemption in Christ, we're all <u>dead</u> *in our transgressions and sins* (Eph. 2:1). Sin that destroys life with physical death also enslaves daily life with spiritual death.

I can't stand zombie movies. The emasculated corpses haunting people with their moans and awkward movements repulse me. I think to myself there's nothing worse than being a zombie! Paul's jarring statement that we are dead in our sin implies that death has already happened to us spiritually, mentally and morally. We move through this earth and go about our days, but without Christ we are animated corpses – the walking dead outside of grace.

Many assume we begin life in the neutral with the chance to prove our innocence with good deeds. But Jesus said that those who do not believe in Him are condemned *"already"* (Jn. 3:18) because sin is in our nature not simply in our actions. We are sinners not because we sin; we sin because we are sinners. And death is sin's closest companion. No matter what amount of good things we do, we do them as already condemned people ruled by death (Rom. 3:9, 5:12).

> "The Scripture sets before us a man who is not only bound, wretched, captive, sick and dead, but who, through the operation of Satan believes himself to be free, happy, possessed of liberty and ability, whole and alive. Satan knows that if men knew their own misery he could keep no man in his kingdom; God could not fail at once to pity and succour wretchedness that knew itself and cried to Him, for God is proclaimed with mighty praise throughout the Scripture as being near to the brokenhearted."[vi]
>
> —Martin Luther

What is this present death? It is an existence of guilt without grace, remorse without resolve, faults without forgiveness and the waking attempt to be human without knowing the Creator. It is a life of the "already condemned" that leaves a trail of insecurity, dissatisfaction and regret because condemnation presents no hope. Like a prisoner who may do good deeds in prison but has yet to change the fact that he is still a convicted prisoner in prison, he is enslaved to sin without life in the Spirit. The already condemned could be businessmen who create portfolios and artists who make art, and by God's common grace[13] they can make good things but they still function from a place of death apart from Christ. When redemption from death is not yet discovered, people wrestle with the emptiness of life, the frustrations of limited time and the fear of insignificance in a vast eternity.

Reinventing Ugliness

"Seeing is believing" is a popular phrase and one that holds much biblical truth. Faith is based on perception (Matt. 13:14-15). We make choices based on what we see and we cannot choose genuine beauty if we cannot perceive it.

Romans 1:18-32 offers us a view of the cycle of ugliness. The apostle Paul explained that when people were presented with absolute beauty through God's creation and scriptural truths, they didn't appreciate His beauty. Instead, they traded the knowledge of His beauty for corruptible things and succumbed to idolatry (Ro. 1:20-21). *They became fools and exchanged the glory of the immortal God for images made to look like mortal man and birds and animals and reptiles* (Ro. 1:22b-23). The Greek term for "to exchange" described a business transaction, where the principle was to trade something of lesser value to gain something of greater value. Because the people could not perceive true beauty (God's glory), they traded it for artworks of wood and stone to be their gods. Trading God's glory for corruptible idols does not go unjudged (Jer. 2:11).

Their beliefs followed their misperceptions of beauty. People choose what they perceive is beautiful even if they are ugly to God. Their idolatries were detestable to God and their beliefs were based on lies, which led them to greater depths of ugliness even as Jeremiah wrote, "*They followed worthless idols and became worthless themselves*" (Jer. 2:5, also 2 Kgs. 17:15). In other words, their choosing to value ugliness (defined in God's perspective) brought greater ugliness upon themselves. There is no separation between what we choose and what we become. Embracing ugliness makes us ugly.

An important principle about worship is *we become like who/what we worship*. If we worship the God of absolute beauty, our lives become more beautiful, but if we worship corruptible things, we become depraved. Ugliness is formed from spiritual blindness that drives us to choose ugliness. Paul explained that because people didn't choose absolute beauty, they became unwise and God surrendered them (*gave them over*) to further depravity in three ways: physical degradation in terms of what was done with their bodies (Ro. 1:24-25), relational degradation from lust, abuse and perversion (Ro. 1:26-27) and intellectual depravity (Ro. 1:28-31). The idea of "surrendering" people was to dismiss them from God's truth, grace and goodness and release them to the demise of their own misperceptions, giving them over to ugliness in *all* spheres of life. The shocking news is this rendering of ugliness *is* God's wrath (Ro. 1:18). What began with spiritual blindness towards truth resulted in ugliness as human beings. Ugliness became their punishment.

Ugliness as a punishment may seem superficial on the surface. Yet, if beauty communicates worth and honor, ugliness is the opposite and the punishment of being made ugly is the reduction of one's humanity. It is a removal of dignity and honor. Ugliness as an expression of judgment is a solid biblical depiction. Ezekiel 16 metaphorically depicts Israel as an infant that grew up in the Lord's care. The descriptions of God beautifying this child conveyed the goodness and blessings He lavishes on His people. They were a people with esteem and loveliness. But their betrayal of God by turning towards idols resulted in God stripping them of their beauty, leaving them in shame and degradation. For people who are living under thorns, thistles and dust and who are grasping for significance and meaningfulness, the removal of dignity and honor as humans is poetically and excruciatingly a tragic punishment.

> "O Lord, from my soul, in thy light and blessedness, and so it still dwells in darkness and in its own wretchedness. For it looks all around, and does not see thy beauty. It listens, and does not hear thy harmony. It smells, and does not sense thy fragrance. It tastes, and does not recognize thy sweet savor. It touches, and does not feel thy softness... the senses of my soul have been frozen and stupefied and blocked up by the ancient enfeeblement of sin."[vii]
>
> —Anselm of Canterbury

Romans 1 echoes the rendering of ugliness as judgment on people whose misperception of beauty and truth led to reinventing more ugliness in themselves and in others (Ro. 1:32). Romans 1 speaks not only to "them" but to us — to those of us who have subscribed to thinking we're getting away with continual sins because we don't see any consequences. It speaks to the porn addicts, the greedy, the liars and the abusers. What we're not realizing is our sins *are* the consequences because we've been surrendered over to a state of dehumanized disgust. Just because God lets us have what we want doesn't mean we're not being judged. God doesn't need to send a hailstorm on our heads to punish us; He simply releases us from His goodness. If we find ourselves outside of His goodness, we find ourselves in judgment. By forsaking God's beauty and choosing the things that are ugly to God, we choose a condition of judgment.

Engaging and Entertaining Ugliness

If ugliness exists in us, it also exists in our society. A pressing question that naturally arises is how and when should we interact with ugliness in our society. My approach is that ugliness needs to be engaged honestly, critically and biblically. Beneath all ugliness is likely a pain that has not found healing from a Savior. If we become cold towards the cries in our society — the cries of inhumanity, injustice, immorality and spiritual depravity — we will also become cold towards God's quest for redeeming broken people and restoring broken societies.

However, we should not so easily fling open the doors of our souls to all kinds of ugliness without careful thought. After all, we are moldable and impressionable people. Steve Turner wisely wrote in *Imagine: A Vision for Christians in the Arts,*

> We should respect the power of art. We can't let our spirits take any amount of punishment and expect to emerge unscathed. Sometimes we give ourselves permission to watch, listen or read such material because we say it's 'just for a laugh' or 'a bit of fun.' But that usually means our critical faculties are relaxed, and it is precisely at these times

that our thinking can be shaped by ideas that are antago-
nistic towards faithful living.[14]

Pride and a lack of respect for the ugly will cause us to let our guards down and forget that our souls can be affected. Some things need to be avoided for moral reasons while others need to be engaged in critical dialogue. It is the fine treading between being in the world but not of it (Jn. 17:15-16). We're called neither to escape nor embrace the world but to engage it with truth and compassion. Engaging culture, for its beauty and ugliness, is faithful and responsible on our parts. Despite how ugly the world may appear to God, He still loves it. That's why He's called us to still be a part of it. It's easy to try and escape it by avoiding the world altogether; then, we don't have to deal with it. And it's easy to let ourselves go and embrace the world. But God has called us to do neither. Only by engaging the world are we able to interact sensitively and faithfully with the world without becoming a part of the world.

Perhaps some of the artists of culture are companions to the prophets and apostles of Scripture, by illustratively affirming the truth of sin and death. Having an honest awareness of the ugliness in life, humanity and society awakens us to our deepest needs.

But having an awareness of ugliness is not the penultimate goal. The journey from ugliness to beauty achieved through redemption is. Redemption is our next chapter.

Walk in Color

- In the next three films you watch, note the antagonists (either tangible or intangible) in the films. Describe what about the antagonists and the effects they bring make them ugly. What is the ugliness the film is portraying about society or humanity? How does this portrayal of ugliness compare with a biblical perspective of ugliness?
- Read Exodus 32:1-33:6. If this were a screenplay for a film, describe the ugliness portrayed as if you were Moses seeing and hearing God and the people. Be detailed in your description and discussion.
- What is the ugliness, or monster, you are wrestling within yourself?[15]

Notes: Chapter Seven

[1] Eco, *History of Beauty*, 8.

[2] Eco, *Ibid.*, 10.

[3] Umberto Eco, *On Ugliness*, transl. by Alastair McEwen (New York: Rizzoli International Publications, 2008), 421.

[4] Eco, *Ibid.*, 436.

[5] Immanuel Kant, "Critique of Judgment: Critique of the Aesthetical Judgment, First Division, Analytic of the Aesthetical Judgment," *Philosophies of Art and Beauty: Selected Readings in Aesthetics from Plato to Heidegger*, ed. by Albert Hofstadter and Richard Kuhns (Chicago: University of Chicago Press, 1976), 289.

[6] The reference to the lukewarm taste alluded to the water that flowed from the hot springs of Hierapolis into Laodicea through a system of aqueducts, since Laodicea lacked its own natural water supply. The water was hot when it first came out of the hot springs, had a medicinal function and was soothing to drink, as was the cold water in Colossae (sister city to Laodicea). But as the water from Hierapolis flowed through the aqueducts, it cooled in temperature and picked up sediments, making the water bitter and nauseating to drink. (see G.K. Beale, *The Book of Revelation*, "The New International Greek Testament Commentary" (Grand Rapids: William B. Eerdmans Publishing, 1999), 303; Craig S. Keener, *The IVP Bible Background Commentary: New Testament* (Downers Grove: InterVarsity Press, 1993), 774).

[7] Plato, "The Arts and Measure," *Philosophies of Art and Beauty*, 13.

[8] H. R. Roomaaker, *Modern Art and the Death of a Culture* (Wheaton: Crossway Books, 1994), 234.

[9] While monsters have been a prevalent symbolism of evil and ugliness, cultures have also developed various appreciations for the monstrous and in some ways analyzing the beauty of their curious features, like dragons and other mythical beasts. But a general perception of the immoral significance of monsters has traversed across cultures. Eco, *History of Beauty*, 147-152.

[10] Fred S. Kleiner & Christin J. Mamiya, *Gardner's Art Through the Ages*, 12th ed. (Belmont: Wadsworth, 2005), 1036.

[11] *Ibid.*, 1037.

[12] I am not making a propositional claim about the basic laws of logic and arithmetic but rather an expression about the uncertain and unfair results of hard work and the sense of futility that comes with it.

[13] God's common grace is His measure of grace bestowed on all people, saved and unsaved, that enables them to produce good and worthy things. Gaebelein writes that, according to the doctrine of common grace, "God enables fallen men and women, whether saved or unsaved, to make positive contributions to the fulfillment of the cultural mandate through art. And he does all this through his Spirit working in the world and through human life." Frank E. Gaebelein, *The Christian, The Arts, and Truth: Regaining*

the Vision of Greatness, ed. by D. Bruce Lockerbie (Portland: Multnomah Press, 1985), 76.

[14] Steve Turner, *Imagine: A Vision for Christians in the Arts* (Downers Grove: InterVarsity Press, 2001), 42.

Pull Out Quotes:

[i] Anselm, "An Address (Proslogion)" from *A Scholastic Miscellany: Anselm to Ockham*, ed. Eugene R. Fairweather, Ichthus ed. (Philadelphia: The Westminster Press, 1982), 71.

[ii] C.S. Lewis, "Surprised by Joy," *The Inspirational Writings of C.S. Lewis: Surprised by Joy, Reflections on the Psalms, The Four Loves, The Business of Heaven* (New York: Inspirational Press, 1994), 12.

[iii] C. S. Lewis, *Perelandra* (New York: Scribner, 2003), 144-5.

[iv] Hosea 13:14 & 1 Corinthians 15:55

[v] Anselm, "An Address (Proslogion)," 71.

[vi] Martin Luther, *The Bondage of the Will*, transl. J. I. Packer & O. R. Johnson (Grand Rapids: Fleming H. Revell, 2003), 162.

[iii] Anselm, "An Address (Prosloglon)," 84-85.

Chapter Eight

REDEMPTION

People like to put things together. We like to see how things fit, whether this tendency first showed itself when we played with Legos, made our first drawings or began planning out our careers. I believe we all have an appetite for *cosmos*, that is a desire for wholeness and purpose since we bear the image of God who created the cosmos and called it beautiful. We see our attempts at composing cosmos in our cities when we construct new freeways to bring greater organization or in our daily lives when we plan our weeks. We enjoy seeing order in the universe from knowing that the planets still orbit the sun to knowing that traffic is still regulated by red and green lights. Cosmos gives us a sense of meaningfulness, harmony and design. Things make sense in cosmos.

The interesting contrast is we are chaotic people because of our fallen nature. We are by nature separated from the Creator of the cosmos by our sin. We experience chaos when we're conflicted over the dilemmas of our habits, addictions, regrets and guilt. But, I believe the *imago Dei* within us reminds us that we were meant for cosmos. Hence, when we see our brokenness and ugliness, whether personally, relationally, spiritually or culturally, we yearn for cosmos. We yearn for wholeness. We long for things to make sense. Our present conditions of chaos and aspirations for cosmos mark the beginning and end points of our quest in life. Who we become and what we do or create is a journey from brokenness to beauty. The question remains: *how do we accomplish this journey of chaos to cosmos?* Or, how do we conquer the ugly monsters of sin and death and achieve God's intended beauty for our humanity?

Growing up as a Buddhist and animist and becoming the first Christian in my family, I can say that "not all roads lead to Rome". All religions do seem to have the commonality of addressing the question of salvation, but the path in Christianity is not like all religions. Some religions are about amassing good deeds to increase one's likelihood of entering heaven and others teach about a spiritual or mental enlightenment as the means to salvation. But the path presented in the Bible is one of *redemption*.

Trash

We can appreciate redemption when we begin with the nature of trash. Trash is a nuisance. It's what we discard because it is the refuse of human life and society. Once things are used up, they lose their value or worth and are simply meant to be thrown away—unless an artist comes along to do something about it.

Contemporary artists like Robert Rauschenberg, who "much like a composer making music out of the noises of everyday life, constructed works of art from the trash of urban civilization."[1] Visionary artists like Jean Shin took $24,496 worth of non-winning lottery tickets that were thrown away and constructed an amazing cityscape with them.[2] Or, the late John Chamberlain, who is well-known for his "junk sculptures", looked at a heap of scrap metal from automobiles and called it "marvelous"[3] because they were converted into incredible sculptures at his hands and were "composed in such a way that they form a new entity...rather than the crumpled automobiles to which they once belonged".[4] The average person sees trash as annoying, worthless and rejected. However, a masterful artist sees a vision in trash and the possibility of refashioning it into a work of beauty. The formation of a "new entity" as in Chamberlain's works is key to this redeeming form of artistry, where the trash that's refashioned no longer resembles the refuse it once was. Creation and redemption run in the same vein, where creation is bringing cosmos from chaos and redemption is refashioning beauty out of brokenness.

Need, Free & Cost

Redemption is an act that re-creates someone who was rejected, discarded and depraved into a person of dignity, worth and beauty. It is a process of taking something lost or bound to corruption and refashioning it anew, granting it the freedom to become a being of beauty. Many popular films consist of characters having redeeming moments, where a lesson is learned or an effort is made that saves the character and/or others from error or harm. These redeeming moments are inspiring because the characters exhibit honorable virtues, like love, courage and honesty, that overcome corruptible traits, like selfishness, materialism or hate. The recurring themes of redemption in stories echo people's prevalent desire to find redemption in themselves and in their societies. These themes show we have a deep longing for beauty to arise out of our brokenness.

While redemption is a frequent theme in films, redemption according to God requires one distinct element – a price must be paid by someone. This biblical concept of redemption that's conditioned upon a sacrifice is portrayed in films like "Braveheart", "Saving Private Ryan", "The Green Mile", "The Lord of the Rings", "The Gran Torino", "District 9" and "The Matrix." Redemption is free for the one who receives it, but there is always a high cost for the one who gives it. In "Saving Private Ryan", there was a theme of redeeming one individual in the middle of a chaotic war. When Private Ryan discovered the sacrifices that were made to bring him home alive, his response was, "It doesn't make any sense, sir. Why? Why do I deserve to go home?" An incomprehensible and seemingly illogical price was paid to save Private Ryan. The incredible price for redemption leaves the undeserving recipient confounded. Redemption in itself is a beauty without words. Redemption brings cosmos at a price that always seems insensible.

How often do we celebrate the free gift of redemption through Christ to an error? We call this grace and none of us could be saved without it. Yes, it is a free gift. But that doesn't mean it was without a cost. We just didn't have to pay it. Redemption according to God always comes at a high cost. The cost was the Son of God who stepped down from heaven to embrace sinful humanity and die a criminal's death that meant a physical destruction of his body and a spiritual separation from God (Phi. 2:6-11, Mk. 15:34). Salvation, redemption and grace are anything but cheap. The price is more than we could possibly imagine. Our propensity to overemphasize the free aspect of grace and redemption creates a spoiled Christianity that takes for granted the true wonder of grace. The paradox between the free and cost aspects are both equally at work in redemption. It is in this harmonious paradox that we find a unique beauty. A redemptive beauty.

A biblical imagery for redemption comes from the slave market. The one needing redemption is in a state of ugliness because he or she is a disposable commodity. A slave is in bondage and has had his dignity and worth reduced to a mechanism that serves another's selfish purposes. As portrayed in the classic television series "Roots", slaves were showcased in the nude, women were assessed for their childbearing potential to produce future slaves and men were examined like cattle. The person who is bound in slavery lacks the beauty of honor and dignity a soulish person should possess. The act of redemption is a benevolent person buying the slave's freedom at his own expense. The Scrip-

> "Still thou dost conceal thyself, O Lord, from my soul, in thy light and blessedness, and so it still dwells in darkness and in its own wretchedness. For it looks all around, and does not see thy beauty. It listens, and does not hear thy harmony. It smells, and does not sense thy fragrance. It tastes, and does not recognize thy sweet savor. It touches, and does not feel thy softness...the senses of my soul have been frozen and stupefied and blocked up by the ancient enfeeblement of sin...Lift me up from myself to thee. Cleanse, heal, sharpen, 'enlighten' the eye of my mind, that it may behold thee."[i]
>
> —Anselm

tures tell us that apart from Christ we are slaves to sin and death (Ro. 6:6), slaves to the fear of death (Heb. 2:15), captives in the dominion of darkness (Col. 1:13) and followers of Satan (Eph. 2:2). Outside of the redeeming work of Christ we are captives of the monster and ridden with the ugliness it brings. The first step in redemption is an honest admission that we are broken, bound and in need of the Master's redemption at the cost of Christ.

God's act of redemption restores a person to his or her intended beauty. We behold and become beautiful when we embrace redemption, or rather when redemption seizes us. This redemption is not found in a principle, rule or mystical spirituality. Surprisingly to the world, it is found in a person.

See Jesus

Jesus. Prophet. Teacher. Leader. Politician. Cynic. Extremist. Moralist. Fanatic. For over 2,000 years, people held differing views of Jesus. Who is He? He is perhaps the most debated figure in our last two millennia. He stirred a controversy because unlike other religious men who claimed to be a prophet, spiritual teacher or moral activist, He claimed to be the Son of God and, under a trinitarian understanding, He claimed to be God Himself. Others claimed they received messages from a divine source, like Muhammad, or discovered enlightenment, like Siddhartha Gautama (Buddha). Jesus, however, claimed to be the second person of the Triune God (Father, Son and Spirit). Being simultaneously human and divine, He taught and performed miracles not merely as a messenger or a vessel but as God. The question for the world is how accurate were the reports about Jesus: did God Himself actually penetrate our broken reality as one of us? If He didn't, the world goes on as it has and our natures and destinies are unchanged. But *if He did*, that is if He personally touched our humanity by being born a human and if He died by crucifixion but resurrected on the third day, then everything changes.

The Son of God stepping into our world means He presented us an image the world had never seen before – the image of the Divine in a perceivable, tangible human being. Jesus was a form of an icon.

Icons popularly found in medieval cathedrals were more than pictorial messages; they were visible representations of spiritual truths or realities. The icons were created with masterful skillfulness and theological acuity to accurately portray a biblical reality.[5] Icons, as sacred art, were windows to invisible truths. In our contemporary culture, we are somewhat removed from the iconographic style of art but the desire of artists to represent supernatural and invisible realities has not disappeared. Makoto Fujimura, a contemporary artist in New York who was appointed to the National Council on the Arts by George W. Bush in 2003, aims to convey a biblical reality through his art. He wrote,

> Many, seeing my paintings today, would call my works abstract, or semi-abstract... I see abstraction as a potential language to speak to today's world about the hope of things to come...I believe that in many ways, spiritual qualities and ideas can be more readily accessible in abstraction than they would be in representational art.[6]

Regardless of our preference for style, various artists and audiences through the centuries have viewed art as serving a sacred purpose of revealing spiritual realities and truths. These artists devoted themselves to this sacred task with seriousness, for they knew that on some level art could lead one to truth or mislead them to sin.[7] Unexpectedly, there was no greater icon that perfectly revealed to the world the reality of the invisible God than the one born of God.

Jesus is called the "image" of the invisible God according to Colossians 1:15. The term "image" in this verse is translated from the Greek term *eikon*, where we derive our English word, "icon". While in some occasions, the image referred to artworks that were idols (Ro. 1:23), an *eikon* could also be understood to be an accurate visual representation, portrait or artistic expression of something or someone. In the context of Jesus being referred to as the image of God, it meant that Jesus was the perfect self-portrait of God. He revealed the radiance of God (Heb. 1:3), a visual quality of God described in the Old Testament. The face of Christ was the very glory of God (2 Cor. 4:6). The resurrected and ascended Jesus appeared in a celestial vision likened to the visual theophanies of God in the Old Testament (Rev. 1:13-16). In essence, God's incarnation made Him visible and tangible (Ro. 8:3), being an icon to the world.[8] Even as John the apostle wrote, "*We have seen his glory, the glory of the One and Only who came from the Father, full of grace and truth*" (Jn. 1:14). Jesus was the image of absolute beauty, not only reflecting but also sharing all of God's splendor and glory.

The Picture and 1000 Words

The idea of an image was not taken lightly by the early Christians. The image or artistic representation of someone was understood to carry that person's *numen*, or "guiding spirit".[9] To worship the image of the person was understood to be the same as worshiping the person himself.[10] According to Deuteronomy 4:15-18, people were not allowed to create images of God since He was invisible to them and no one knew what He looked like.[11] He deliberately did not show people any physical images of Himself. So, they should not make any artistic representations of Him. This command protected them from fabricating a God out of their own imaginations, which would demean the person of God, and from idolatrous worship.

The portrait of God was sacred and it was His right to reveal it to us; His absolute beauty could not be assumed or conjectured. It could only be received. God's beauty that is sacred should be revered and received through revelation. It is a beauty that is uncreated and exists outside of our craft or control. In Deuteronomy 4:16, the first and most important warning was that people didn't make an image of God to look like a man.[12] This prohibition prophetically reserved the sacred privilege of God to reveal Himself in the image of the man, Jesus Christ.

Bonaventure called Christ the Eternal Art that reveals the ultimate beauty of God to us.[13] Jesus is the *uncreated* Eternal Art, unlike any other icon. His existence did not begin with his birth on earth, but He co-existed with the Father God before time (Jn. 1:1). In fact, Jesus' involvement in creation was essential, whereby without Him nothing would've been fashioned into existence (Jn. 1:3; Col. 1:16). As the Eternal Art, he has no beginning or end. It is because Jesus shares God's eternality, divine nature, power and glory that he can be His perfect icon. As the icon of God, it means He perfectly expresses the beauty of God in a language that we could comprehend.[14] He was fully God so that He perfectly represented God and He was fully human so that we could grasp Him. God who was Spirit and imperceivable by our aesthetic senses became tangible, reachable and perceivable to us in Christ, not only as the image but also as the Word.

Hear Jesus

Where the image is seen, the word is heard. While Paul referred to Jesus as the icon, John the apostle referred to Jesus as the word (Jn. 1:1, 14; 1 Jn. 1:1), translated from the Greek term *logos*. The logos was a matter of speaking one's mind, for it was understood that one's words clearly expressed one's thoughts and intentions.[15] Even before the birth of Christ, "Greek philosophers began to adopt the word and use it to signify that which gives shape, form or life to the material world".[16] The creative and revelatory power of the word was known to the Judaic faith for millennia, where God's word was respected throughout the Old Testament as the vehicle to carry out His will, whether in creation, judgment or deliverance. D.A. Carson noted that the word of God enacts creation, revelation and salvation.[17] It is also by God's

> "Everything human in Christ is a word, an image, a representation, and an expression of the Father."[ii]
>
> —Hans Urs Von Balthasar

word that He establishes unbreakable covenants and promises with His people. Jesus as the incarnated Word of God means He enfleshed the intangible will and thoughts of God and the creative and salvific plans of God. He is the final fulfillment and revelation of God's promises (Heb. 1:1-2).

Conversation

Since the word is a matter of speech, it invites dialogue unless the word falls on deaf ears.[18] Speech both reveals one's thoughts and invites a wrestling of ideas. Jesus as the incarnated speech of God is expected to evoke a conversation with God. Good art can never be ignored; it provokes conversation and thought. Jesus, therefore, as the image and word of God is meant to provoke conversation between the God of absolute beauty and sinners of utter ugliness. The gospel message invites a dialogue, where the broken may find faith in the Beautiful.

When we take something for granted or perceive it to be elementary, we stop talking about it. The cross is simple, but there's nothing simple about it. By introducing Jesus as the Icon and Logos to the world, God communicated the incommunicable, invisible qualities of His absolute beauty. God "has spoken to us by his Son" (Heb. 1:2). When God introduced Jesus to the world as the image and word, He spoke to us about receiving His beauty in the midst of our brokenness. He began a complex conversation about brokenness and beauty that candidly exposes our ugliness in order to show us our need for beauty. It is a conversation confounded by the immensity of grace and yet simplified by faith. It is a conversation that invites us to enter into a journey of redemption by accepting this confounding grace through simple faith.

> "Since orthodox Christianity has always held firm to the basic belief that it is by looking at Jesus himself that we discover who God is, it seems to me indisputable that we should expect always to be continuing in the quest for Jesus precisely as part of, indeed perhaps as the sharp edge of, our exploration into God himself."[iii]
>
> —N. T. Wright

Nowadays, it seems there are more conversations about the attendance and activities at churches or the latest issues and scandals about churches than about the person of Jesus Christ. Jesus as the absolute beauty who embraced broken humanity is the most reawaking point of conversation between God and sinners from which redeeming faith can be birthed. I believe it is the church's role to make Jesus the topic of conversation, never allowing the gospel to fall silent in a world that is silent towards God. When we stop conversing about Jesus, we settle into the familiarity of our brokenness and lose a sense of what is truly beautiful.

Absolute Beauty in Jesus

What does it mean for Jesus to be the perfect representation of God's absolute beauty? It means that Jesus bore certain qualities distinctive to God and God alone. First, as the Son of God, He is equal to God (Jn. 5:18) because He is of the same divine nature as God (Phi. 2:6). Nothing created is of divine nature, whether the earth, humans or angels. In sharing the divine nature, Jesus is the second person of the triune God who exists as three persons in one essence.

Second, Jesus is eternal as God is eternal. People saved from death through Christ will have no end to their lives, and hence they achieve a state of eternity in salvation. God being eternal means He also has no beginning (Col. 1:17), which cannot be true for anyone that was created since everything created had a beginning. Jesus being co-eternal with God means He was not created and He existed before birth (Jn. 8:58).

Third, Jesus participates in the divine works of God in creating, sustaining and redeeming the universe (Col. 1:16-17, Heb. 1:2) and in saving it (Col. 1:20). The works or actions of Jesus are divine in nature.

Fourth, Jesus shares the same glory that is due only to God. God is a jealous God (Exo. 34:14) and so He doesn't share His glory with anyone because there is no one like Him deserving such glory (Deut. 4:39). God declared that He is one of a kind (Deut. 6:4). But when God declares Jesus' supreme glory, one that warrants worship (Matt. 28:17), He acknowledges Jesus' divine status (Phi. 2:9-11, Rev. 5:13).

Finally, Jesus bears the same sacred name as God, the great "I am" (Exo. 3:14, Jn. 8:58). By this name, he claims to be the same self-sufficient, life-giving and all-powerful being as God. Also, Jesus declared in a divine vision that he is, "The Alpha and Omega... the Almighty" (Rev. 1:8). "His *person* is the manifestation of the glory of God. To see him as he really is means seeing the infinitely valuable beauty of God."[19]

> "Whoever sees him [Christ] sees the Father – provided that one sees him as he must be seen and as he intends to be seen: as the Word of the Father."[iv]
>
> —Hans Urs Von Balthasar

Jesus offers a broken world an unprecedented encounter with awesome beauty, for to know Jesus is to look into God's face (Jn. 14:9).

By these attributes, Jesus exhibits the very beauty of God (2 Cor. 4:4, 6) because he bears the same perfect character, glorious status and divine nature as God. Jesus told the Apostle Philip that the miracles He did were evidences of His divine nature because they were miracles that only God could do. His teachings were also evidences of His divinity because they

> "The Word is in a way the art of the Almighty God."
>
> —Augustine

revealed knowledge from God (Jn. 14:10-11). These evidences of Jesus' identity were recorded in the Bible so that by faith we may encounter this absolute beauty that entered our world 2,000 years ago (Jn. 21:24, 1 Jn. 1:3).

One of the profundities of Jesus' incarnation is the reality that absolute beauty stepped into our brokenness, giving our imperfect existences the graspable opportunity to encounter perfection. Though Jesus was untainted by sin and existed as the only sinless human being, He embraced the nature of a frail humanity susceptible to temptation, pain and death, making Him the perfect atoning sacrifice for our sins (Heb. 4:15). The atoning ministry of Jesus' death and resurrection welcomes us to behold God's beauty by grace through faith and redemption from the chaos of our fallen nature (Heb. 4:16).

If David's "one thing" prayer of gazing into absolute beauty echoes the universal cry of the human heart (Psa. 27:4), then knowing Jesus is the fulfillment of humanity's cry, because to know Jesus is to see God's glory. But, *how do we "see" Jesus?*

Seeing & Believing

The apostle Philip echoed the cry of our human spirits when he said to Jesus, *"Lord, show us the Father and that will be enough for us"* (Jn. 14:8). He asked Jesus for a theophany, an unfiltered vision of God in all His glory and beauty. And for the disciples, the result of seeing God would be "enough", a word translated from the original Greek term *arkeo*, which on the surface expresses simple "contentment". The term also expresses complete sufficiency, lacking nothing and leaving nothing else in want (e.g. 2 Cor. 12:9).[20] Philip expressed that an experience of God's glory would make life complete. This satisfaction wouldn't just be for Philip, as he said it would be "enough for *us*", where "us" referred to the desire of all the disciples and symbolically referred to the universal desire of the human heart. Even D.A. Carson explained that Philip wanted to join the list of humans throughout history who

> "Christ, through the work of the Holy Spirit, awakened us to our true purpose in life. Now our days are filled with praise. And we praise Thee with our whole being, honoring Thee, adoring Thee in the beauty of Thy Holiness. Amen."[vi]
>
> —A. W. Tozer

"rightly understood that there can be no higher experience, no greater good, than seeing God as he is, in unimaginable splendour and transcendent glory."[21] However much we have defaced the image of God within us and perhaps because our image of God has been defaced, we especially "still yearn for the *visio Dei*, the vision of God" to make life complete.[22]

But how do we who live 2,000 years after Jesus' incarnation on earth see this beauty that was revealed to the world? We live in an especially visually oriented culture, where people are convinced if something can be seen on YouTube.com, then it must be believable. So how do we grasp the divine Icon when He appeared in a time before cameras, camcorders and webcams? How do we who live under the notion that seeing-is-believing see God as the absolute beauty?

I believe for broken people like us who are naturally captivated by the things of the world, acknowledging a "Philip's desire" within us is the first step. Our hunger for divine beauty can be too easily pacified by the cheaper and temporary fixes the world offers. We satiate our senses with the pretty things, that is the sentimental things which give feelings of contentment but lack the luster of beauty defined by God's character. Increasing our desire to exceed beyond sentimentality is required to find a life that is enough. Honestly and dependently allowing our appetite for God's beauty to burgeon in us is the beginning of seeing. Without acknowledging this hunger, we would not humbly nor sincerely seek it. Allowing our hearts to echo Philip's cry is saying, "That's all we want."²³ We only search for what we desire and beauty is meant to evoke desire. Our desire for God's beauty needs to be permitted to awaken. The psalmist wrote, *My soul thirsts for God, for the living God. When can I go and meet with God?* (Ps. 42:2).

Seeing through the Word

I think one of the most important sources of revelation of beauty we take for granted is the Word. Jesus' answer to Philip's request was that they had already seen the Father when they saw Jesus (Jn. 14:9). I'm sure they were puzzled. Jesus revealed the Father to them through His words, works and miracles (Jn 14:10-11). The truths Jesus taught and the power He displayed showed the glory of God in Him. The intent of the gospel writers was this: *these were written that you may believe that Jesus is the Christ, the Son of God, and that by believing you may have life in his name* (Jn. 20:31). Those who wrote the Scriptures had us in mind. They were voices moved by God to tell the account of what they saw and heard in order that through their words we may see and hear it, too (1 Pet. 1:21, 1 Jn. 1:3). The Bible tells the timeless story of the Logos and paints a portrait of the Icon for every future generation.

Our generation focuses on two things: what works and how it makes me feel. How many of us honestly come to the Bible with these goals? We read it to find out practical to-do steps or to make us feel better. We search for pragmatism and sentimentalism in the Bible. It's no wonder absolute beauty eludes us. Richard Foster wrote, "In our desire for a packaged, user-friendly, 'just tell me what to do' life of faith, we distort the Bible into an owner's manual for successful living."²⁴ We unknowingly water God's Word down to a fix-it or self-help book. The Bible is revelation to form a relationship with God. Its truths are the companion tools of the Holy Spirit for the completion of God's sanctifying work in us (2 Thess. 2:13). Every time we open our Bibles during services, quiet times or small groups, we are opening an opportunity to perceive divine beauty. The Holy Scriptures cannot ever be taken for granted as merely a book. A mere book is written from the will of men. The Bible is written by the will of God (2 Pet. 1:20-

21). But then, why is it so often the content of Scripture seems irrational or plain boring? Why don't we always see beauty in the Bible?

Brokenness means our senses are impaired. It is the combination of our fallen human nature and Satan's work in blinding the minds of people that keeps people from seeing the glory of God in Christ (2 Cor. 4:4). We're like nearsighted people trying to make out the letters of a street sign two blocks away. The more appropriate question is not why doesn't God show His beauty to me, but why can't I see it? What specific burdens of our brokenness hinder us? What sins, bitterness, regrets or guilt?

St. Bonaventure wrote that our mind's eye, the faculty within us that allows us to perceive God, truth and beauty, was "deformed by sin" and needs to be "reformed by grace".[25] We are dependent upon God's grace and the work of His Spirit to revive our senses, for we need the touch of the Master Craftsman to reform our ability to perceive. Without this touch of grace, Jesus would merely appear as the ordinary man described in Isaiah 53 as the one who lacked any kind of attractiveness according to the world's standards (Isa. 53:2). In fact, all we may notice about Jesus is the brokenness He bore without the beauty He brought (Isa. 53:3).

We need a measure of faith to heal our sight in order for us to see and believe. Sometimes biblical truth doesn't make sense because we lack the belief that allows us to perceive it. Faith is not always the product of evidence seen but the precursor to seeing truth, where understanding is not the prerequisite for believing but believing is the access to understanding. Anselm of Canterbury wrote, "I desire to believe that I may understand." This is not to say faith is blind. God expects us to think rationally, which is why Jesus provided evidences of who He was through His miracles and teachings and God appealed to Israel through reason. The Bible intends to offer us enough information that allows us to develop faith. Faith that precedes understanding is not about blind belief but about having the

> "Only Jesus can make him known in truth and fullness (Matt. 11:27). Therefore, look steadily at Jesus and pray that he would reveal God as compellingly beautiful."[vii]
>
> —John Piper

right conditions of our hearts that are open, humble and ready to receive. Too often we come to the Bible with skepticism and demands for proofs when the core of the issue is the disposition of our hearts. God responds to faith. Faith calls for God to reveal His truths to us. When we have faith in Christ, Christ then redeems and recovers our senses for the beautiful, allowing us to see the glory of God in Him.[26]

Beauty through Brokenness

It is ironic that the path of bringing us beauty is through a gruesome and ugly form of execution, the crucifixion. The cross was not made of gold or marble. It was crude, rough and smeared with blood from a broken man nailed to it. The cross was a simple mechanism invented by a cruel mentality intended to terminate life through a tormenting experience. The crucifixion was meant to be grotesque to demonstrate the horrific consequences for breaking the Roman law. The cross is a killing machine designed to slowly and gradually drain the life of its victim. On this cross we see the Icon beaten, broken and battered and hear the Logos cry out in agony, "*My God, my God, why have you forsaken me?*" (Mk. 15:34). And yet, it was God's desire to "crush" His own Son whom He was pleased with and loved (Isa. 53:10, Matt. 17:5). The Hebrew term for "to crush" (*daka*) can be translated as "to destroy" or "break into pieces". In the moment of Christ's death on the cross, black clouds covered the sky and blocked out all sunlight (Lk. 23:44). There are a few symbolic meanings for darkness or blackness. It can represent death and evil forces.[27] It also symbolized God's judgment and wrath (Ex. 10:22).[28] On that cross, God subjected Jesus to death, the forces of evil and His wrath.

God brought chaos on the One who helped to create the cosmos. He brought the One who revealed absolute beauty to a state of ugliness in order that we who are ugly might know beauty. God brought beauty into our fallen world through the brokenness of the only perfectly beautiful human being.

It was the brokenness of Jesus that fully satisfied the apparent juxtaposition of God's justice and love (Rom. 3:25, 5:8), His justice in that Jesus' death paid the penalty for our sins and His love in that Jesus' death offers us mercy and grace for salvation. It is the juxtaposed qualities of God that makes Him perfectly beautiful, and we find it is the complete brokenness of Jesus that fulfills the perfect beauty of God.

The True Beauty of the Cross

Many of us have come to love the image of the cross, despite its representation of horror, its intent to break people and its often bloody and dehumanizing associations. Many would even call the cross beautiful, because it symbolizes the greatest sacrificial love ever known. It is because of the extent of ugliness that was brought upon Jesus for our sakes that we see the cross as beautiful. We reap the benefits of life, love and mercy from the cross, and therefore see it as attractive. But I believe the cross beckons us to go a step further by seeing the beauty of the cross for God's sake.

For God's sake means that the cross is utterly beautiful because it satisfies the perfect character of God. The cross demonstrates to us that God is serious about who He is and nothing of His balanced perfection can be diminished, whether His attributes of justice or mercy. For it was because of God's justice and mercy that Jesus died for sinners (Ro. 3:25-26). Somebody had to assume the consequences of sin and Jesus, an innocent man, took it on our behalf. That's justice and mercy. Therefore the cross does not emphasize one attribute over the other. The cross holds God's character in perfect harmony. The wonders of the cross have to do with the benefits of salvation it offers us, but even more so, it expresses the complete beauty of God's character, which makes it a perfect bridge for broken people to discover and embrace true beauty.

In a very unexpected way for our culture, the cross shows us that brokenness can be a path to beauty. Some who have a handle on this idea express it in their art. Makoto Fujimura sees the metaphor of beauty brought about through sacrificial destruction from the style of nihonga painting where the materials have to be "pulverized" in order to draw out their true beauty.[29] Through his style of painting he sees a symbol for the gospel.

Jesus' slain body absorbed our anger and defiance, but more important, it absorbed God's just anger toward us. In that moment, all of what was most fair and beautiful in Christ became the hideous stench of a dying beast. Beauty was literally pulverized, destroyed, and the Eternal experienced the decay of death.[30]

This path of brokenness to achieve beauty was not a new concept. In the Old Testament, God invited people to offer to Him their brokenness.

The sacrifices of God are a broken spirit;
a broken and contrite heart,
O God, you will not despise
(Ps. 51:17).

It is no wonder that Jesus invites us to follow Him on the path of the cross: "*If anyone would come after me, he must deny himself and take up his cross daily and follow me*" (Lk. 9:23). What God made apparent to us through Christ and the cross is beauty is not seized through optimism or sentimentality. Beauty will be seized through brokenness, first through the brokenness of Christ on the cross and then through a confession of our own brokenness before God.

For a fallen race in need of redemption, beauty will be discovered by way of surrender, sacrifice, and self-denial. Those who come to God with their brokenness are not the proud, the powerful or the self-sufficient. They are the needy, the weak and the dependent. It is like Jesus' parable about the Pharisee, who boasted about his righteous standing in contrast to those obvious sinners, and the tax collector, who simply cried out for mercy (Luke 18:9-14). In a comedic way, it will be the unexpected people who recognize their brokenness that discover true beauty which doesn't come from themselves but from the brokenness and beauty of the cross. Even as Jesus said from the Sermon on the Mount that it will be the meek, poor and lowly that will inherit the blessings of God (Matt. 5:1-12). Jesus was not merely addressing the social conditions of people but also their spiritual dispositions. The emphasis was the "poor in spirit", a quality of which even the socially powerful and rich could have. His socially radical message expressed a spiritually redeeming means for attaining beauty.

Redemptive Beauty

Brokenness is the path to beauty because the beauty we discover in the end is a *redemptive* beauty, where we find God taking our fragmented nature, spiritually dead selves and hearts tainted by burdens, baggage and demons and refashioning us into a work of art. The language of renewal, new creation, new birth, and the new person versus old person is replete throughout Scripture. In the Old Testament, God promised He would refashion people by replacing their hearts of stone with hearts of flesh (Ezek. 36:26-27) and in the New Testament we find ourselves as *new creations* in Christ (2 Cor. 5:17). The creative work of God that wrought the world into existence is still at work in us through redemption, so that salvation is not merely an escape from a bad place but a work of re-creating the broken into the beautiful. "Christ did not come to make us Christians or to save our souls only but that He came to redeem us that we might be human in the full sense of the word."[31] God is creating a work of cosmos within us through Christ, transforming the chaos of void, meaninglessness, guilt, remorse, shame and death in us into a visionary work of art that bears the beautiful likenesses of His Son.

> "The Spirit of the Sovereign Lord is on me, because the Lord has anointed me to preach good news to the poor. He has sent me to bind up the brokenhearted, to proclaim freedom for the captive... to bestow on them a crown of beauty instead of ashes...They will be called oaks of righteousness, a planting of the Lord for the display of his splendor."[viii]
>
> [regarding Jesus]

Understanding our brokenness and our potential for beauty is like understanding "trash art". It takes us asking ourselves, "Am I worth redeeming?" Based on our brokenness, the answer honestly has to be no. But in the hands of the Maker of Beauty the answer is yes, because in His vision we are redefined.

Walk in Color

- Take five pieces of trash items from your home that would normally be discarded. How can you redeem them?
- Read Hosea 1:1-3:3. What is one aspect of your life you believe needs redeeming? How would redeeming it change you as an artist or creator?
- This week, what is one redeeming act you can commit in your community or to people around you?

_____

Notes: Chapter Eight

[1] H. W. Janson and Anthony F. Janson, History of Art, 5th ed. Revised (New York: Harry N. Abrams, Inc. Publishers, 1997), 863-4.

[2] Chad M. Wall, "Trashy Art or Artsy Trash?" in Eco-Footprint Solutions, May 1, 2009 (http://ecofootprintsolutions.com/2009/05/01/trashy-art-or-artsy-trash/).

[3] "Artist's Studio: John Chamberlain," interview by Arne Glimcher posted by Plum T.V., May 27, 2008. (http://www.youtube.com/watch?v=AHClgHdFvcY&feature=related).

[4] Janson, *History of Art*, 864.

[5] Leonid Ouspensky, "Icon and Art," in *Christian Spirituality: Origins to the Twelfth Century*, ed. Bernard McGinn, John Meyendorff, and Jean Leclercq (New York: Crossroad Publishing, 2000), 390.

[6] Makoto Fujimura, "Essence: That Final Dance" in *It Was Good: Making Art to the Glory of God*, ed. Ned Bustard, revised and expanded 2nd ed. (Baltimore: Square Halo Books, 2006), 300.

[7] Leonid Ouspensky, "Icon and Art," 388.

[8] Jeffrey F. Hamburger, "The Place of Theology" in *The Mind's Eye: Art and Theological Argument in the Middle Ages*, ed. Jeffrey F. Hamburger and Anne-Marie Bouche (Princeton: Department of Art and Archaeology, 2006), 24.

[9] Robin Margaret Jensen, *Face to Face: Portraits of the Divine in Early Christianity* (Minneapolis: Fortress Press, 2005), 52.

[10] Jensen, *Face to Face*, 58.

[11] Jensen, *Face to Face*, 16.

[12] Peter C. Craigie, *The Book of Deuteronomy* in The New International Commentary on the Old Testament (Grand Rapids: William B Eerdmans Publishing, 1976), 134.

[13] Bonaventure, "The Soul's Journey into God" in *Bonaventure: The Soul's Journey into God, The Tree of Life, The Life of St. Francis*, trans. Ewert Cousins (Mahwah: Paulist Press, 1978).

[14] John O'Donnell, "The logic of Divine Glory" from *The Beauty of Christ: An Introduction to the Theology of Hans Urs Von Balthasar*, ed. Bede McGregor and Thomas Norris (Edinburgh: T&T Clark, 1994), 164.

[15] Leon Morris, *The Gospel According to John*, The New International Commentary on the New Testament, rev. ed. (Grand Rapids: William B. Eerdmans Publishing, 1995), 66.

[16] D.H. Johnson, "Logos," in *Dictionary of Jesus and the Gospels*, ed. Joel B. Green, Scot McKnight, & I. Howard Marshall (Downers Grove: Intervarsity Press, 1992), 481.

[17] D.A. Carson, *The Gospel According to John*, The Pillar New Testament Commentary, gen. ed. D. A. Carson (Grand Rapids: William B. Eerdmans Publishing, 1991), 116.

[18] Trevor Hart, "Through the Arts: Hearing, Seeing and Touching the Truth" in *Beholding the Glory: Incarnation Through the Arts*, ed. Jeremy S. Begbie (Grand Rapids: Baker Academic, 2001), 17.

[19] John Piper, *What Jesus Demands from the World* (Wheaton: Crossway Books, 2006), 19.

[20] *Theological Dictionary of the New Testament*, 2003 abridged ed., s. v. "arkeo," by Geoffrey W. Bromiley.

[21] Carson, *The Gospel According to John*, 494.

[22] *Ibid.*

[23] Leon Morris, *The Gospel According to John*, The New International Commentary on the New Testament, revised ed. (Grand Rapids: Willliam B. Eerdmans, 1995), 571.

[24] Richard J. Foster and Kathryn A. Helmers, *Life with God: Reading the Bible for Spiritual Transformation* (New York: HarperCollins, 2008), 60.

[25] Bonaventure, "The Soul's Journey" in *Bonaventure: The Soul's Journey into God, The Tree of Life, the Life of St. Francis*, transl. Ewert Cousins (Mahwah: Paulist Press, 1978), 62.

[26] Bonaventure, *The Soul's Journey into God*, 89.

[27] *Dictionary of Biblical Imagery: An Encyclopedic Exploration of the Images, Symbols, Motifs, Metaphors, Figures of Speech and Literary Patterns of the Bible*, s. v. "Darkness," edited by Leland Ryken, James C. Wilhoit, Tremper Longman III.

[28] Craig S. Keener, *The IVP Bible Background Commentary: New Testament* (Downers Grove: InterVarsity Press, 1993), 255.

[29] Makoto Fujimura, *Refractions: A Journey of Faith, Art, and Culture* (Colorado Springs: NavPress, 2009), 54.

[30] Fujimura, *Refractions*, 48.

[31] Hans Rookmaaker, *Art Needs No Justification*. Chapter 2 (Downer's Grove: InterVarsity Press, 1978), http://www.dickstaub.com/culturewatch.php?record_id=912.

Pull Out Quotes:

[i] Anselm, "An Address (Proslogion)" from *A Scholastic Miscellany: Anselm to Ockham*, ed. Eugene R. Fairweather, Ichthus ed. (Philadelphia: The Westminster Press, 1982), 84-86. [ii] Hans Urs Von Balthasar, *The Glory of the Lord: A Theological Aesthetics – Seeing the Form*, transl. Erasmo Leiva-Merikakis, ed. Joseph Fessio S. J. and John Riches, vol. 1 (San Francisco: Ignatius Press, 1982), 327.

[iii] N. T. Wright, *The Challenge of Jesus: Rediscovering Who Jesus Was and Is* (Downers Grove: InterVarsity Press, 1999), 15.

[iv] Balthasar, *The Glory of the Lord*, 327.

[v] Cited in Dale Salvidge, "Acting and (the) Incarnation" in *It Was Good: Making Art to the Glory of God*, ed. Ned Bustard, second ed. (Baltimore: Square Halo Books, 2006), 177.

[vi] A. W. Tozer, *The Purpose of Man: Designed to Worship*, ed. James L. Snyder (Ventura: Regal, 2009), 35.

[vii] John Piper, *What Jesus Demands from the World* (Wheaton: Crossway Books, 2006), 82.

[viii] Isaiah 61:1-3

Chapter Nine

ARTISTRY

No one wants to feel futile. The passing of time without the bearing of fruit conveys a sense of futility. So the big question people – artists, writers, engineers, bankers, custodians, fathers and wives – ask is: how do I produce significant, beautiful fruit in my life? We have the idea that if what I do or create means something, then perhaps my ideas and my life will mean something. We long to create beauty, because beauty exudes worth, captures a sense of the infinite and embraces a view of redemption. We, therefore, desire to create things with harmony, order, perfection, virtue, honor, dignity, love and truth – whether in our stories, songs, paintings, portfolios, careers or homes. The secret to producing things of significance and beauty is to understand God as *the* producer. A hero of mine illustrated the nature of God's productivity well.

Mr. Incredible in Disney/Pixar's 2003 hit animated film, "The Incredibles", possessed an insight about why some people do what they do better than anyone else. In a scene with Mr. Incredible and Frozone, their dialogue revealed a profound concept that I dare to say we all need to grasp. While they were supposed to be out bowling, living normal, average, everyday lives, they were instead sitting in an alley at night listening to a police scanner. Different reports of crime and disasters came in, and Mr. Incredible was sifting out which crises they should respond to. But Frozone, who didn't have Mr. Incredible's clairvoyance towards their non-average activity, said, "I'd rather go bowling." Shaking his head at Mr. Incredible's apparent unwillingness to surrender the glory days of heroism, Frozone asked, "What are we doing here, Bob?"

Mr. Incredible replied with a manner of obviousness, "We're protecting people."

"But no one asked us to," Frozone logically rebutted.

Mr. Incredible, who saw themselves as heroes, responded with a surprised expression and a sense of absurdity to his friend's rebuttal: "You need an invitation?"

That was the difference between Mr. Incredible and his superhero colleagues. He didn't save people because someone asked him to or because he was rewarded for it. He did it because that's what superheroes do. Even when he was forced to assume a normal, non-superhero lifestyle as an agent in an insurance company, he was still helping his clients by granting them insurance money or by providing them with insider information to circumvent the bureaucratic system and get the help they needed. "We're supposed to help people," he said to his boss who was the opposite of Mr. Incredible's benevolent virtue. No matter what context Mr. Incredible was in, he was in the business of helping people. Mr. Incredible was always trying to save the day, because that's what superheroes do. It was in their nature.

Do we comprehend the concept of doing out of being where motivation and operation flow seamlessly together? Do we find the activities of our lives incarnationally joined with the identity of our salvation? Do we create beauty because beauty was created in us? Are we daily aware of God's redemptive artistry in us?

Relating to the Creator

The Bible could've introduced God in a number of ways—as a loving father figure, a supreme judge or a conquering ruler. But instead, God is first off introduced as the Creator. His role as the absolute Creator is inseparably related to His other roles as judge, king and Lord of the universe. Genesis 1 and 2 portrayed God's creatorship as a core characteristic of His. God was under no compulsions or practical needs to create. He created because it was in His nature. A creator sees something wrong with an empty, chaotic mass lacking beauty and has to do something creative with it, like a superhero has to do something about victims trapped inside a burning building. God created because it's what a creator does in creation and in redemption.

How we relate to someone is determined by the role that person plays in our lives. Some of us grew up relating to God as a father figure while others as a judge. It's fascinating that the Bible's introduction of God calls us to first and foremost relate to Him as our Creator. Our Author. Our Artist. Since humans bearing the *imago Dei* naturally create as well – cities, homes, portfolios, careers, art, music, stories – it is paramount that we comprehend what it means to relate to God as Creator. What we create is indispensably linked to what He creates in us.

A principle of artistry is relationship. The minute we choose to make something – a painting, an exquisite dish, a house – a relationship between the creator and the artifact is established. The relationship bears simple and yet profound implications.

1. An artist desires to form and transform an object(s) into an artwork.
2. An artwork yields to its artist's creativity and mastery; the more moldable the artwork is the more the artist will unleash his vision on it.
3. An artist envisions what no one else can see in the unformed artwork.
4. An artist enfleshes his ideas and inspiration in the artwork.
5. An artwork represents its artist's skill and mastery.
6. An artist is proud of his finished artwork and takes pleasure in it.
7. The artwork gives credit to the artist and not to another, including itself.

When I say it is paramount that we know what it means to relate to God as the Creator, I'm not only referring to the Creator in Genesis 1 and 2, though that was where it began. I'm also referring to His creative work in us today in salvation and sanctification.

The phrase *in the beginning* (Gen. 1:1), in its Hebrew grammatical structure, denoted not a singular point in time but the entire process and the end result.[1] In Genesis 1:1, the process most immediately referred to the six days of creation, but it also foreshadowed God's ongoing creative process until Revelation. The phrase *In the beginning was the Word* used in John 1:1 to introduce Jesus showed the continuity between God's creativity in creation and in redemption. Redemption is re-creation. Redemption is an act of love and sacrifice that gives dignity, honor and beauty to people who lost it to sin and death. Re-creation is about transforming the redeemed. For God, redemption does not happen without the intention of re-creation. God, an artist, creates even in salvation.

A second principle of artistry is change. It is a matter of not leaving something the way you found it. A painter changes the paint on a canvas. A sculptor changes a mound of clay. A writer changes the words on a screen. An actor changes himself or herself before a camera. God changes the world and us. The same God who formed and filled the lifeless, chaotic mass in the beginning of creation transforms our sinful, broken nature in redemption. This Divine Craftsman who took delight in molding the universe into a masterwork of beauty is the same God who desires to re-fashion our brokenness into beauty through sanctification, changing our state of chaos into a form of cosmos.

Ephesians 2:10 is a powerful verse that reveals a theology of God's artistry. The verse reads: *For we are God's workmanship, created in Christ Jesus to do good works, which God prepared in advance for us to do.*

First off, it refers to those who have been saved by grace through faith in Christ as God's artistry (Eph. 2:8-9). This verse reads, *For we are God's workmanship....* The term *workmanship* comes from the Greek term, *poieima,* that literally means something that is made with craftsmanship, like an artwork. This term occurs in only one other place in the New Testament, Romans 1:20, that describes God's creation of the universe. *Poieima* could easily denote "a work of art or a masterpiece".[2]

Our challenge lies in defining ourselves by what is being done in us, not in what we do. Until I know what it means to be God's craftsmanship, I cannot fully comprehend what it means to be a maker. My identity as a producer is based in the reality that I am produced. My ability to create beauty exists because I am being fashioned into beauty.

> "It appears then that art has to do first and foremost with God's activity in and through the artist which enables him to create works which display beauty."[ii]
>
> —Jeremy S. Begbie

So, the question is not only what is God doing in my life, but what is He making me into? It means grasping that we are not autonomous beings functioning with God's assistance. We are not merely seeking God's help to complete our projects. We *are* the project. We are the product. We are an ongoing work of art. So, discovering who I am as a person requires discovering who my Artist is and interacting with His creativity in me. Since He is my Artist, He has established a relationship with me as an artist to an artwork. Being truly human, then, has everything to do with discovering this artistic relationship.

New Creation

Revolutionary and award-winning comic artist Alex Ross and writer Paul Dini told a remarkable story about Superman who tried to deliver the world from suffering in the graphic novel *Superman: Peace on Earth*. But even Superman discovered in the end that he could not save the world in spite of his powers, because he ran into one problem he couldn't cure. It was the selfishness of men. Unless he could change human nature, he could never succeed in bringing peace on earth, for people didn't just need answers to their problems; they needed transformation. God's redemptive work does just that — it changes people's nature. The remarkable work of God's grace on the cross not only saves us from damnation but transforms us from brokenness to beauty.

A third principle of artistry is art is a process of composing loose parts into a visionary whole. God's creativity is a matter of taking the fragmented pieces of our souls and forming a harmonious, glorious whole. Throughout the Bible, the idea of new creation is coupled with deliverance. The language portrays God as not merely a fireman saving people from hell's fire, but as the Creator refashioning people into new creatures.

Oftentimes we fall short in grasping the gravity of being re-created. We are relieved to know that our afterlife is secured in a better place, but it doesn't end there. We have to develop a daily awareness of the re-creative process that began in us at the moment we accepted Jesus. Once we're saved, Ephesians 2:10 tells us that we are *created in Christ.* 2 Corinthians 5:17 and Galatians 6:15 call us new creations in Christ. The Bible is emphatic about our old nature being replaced by a new nature (Ro. 6:4-6). Titus 3:5 emphasizes the reality of a new beginning in the redeemed life,[3] echoing the force of newness as in Genesis 1:1 and John 1:1. Paul the apostle grasped this newness in himself when he wrote, *By the grace of God I am what I am, and his grace to me was not without effect* (1 Cor. 15:10).

Our transformation is drastic. We are salvaged from the *dominion of darkness* and transferred into the *kingdom of light* (Col. 1:12-14). Salvation is a kind of refashioning from chaos to cosmos. It is a divine work of changing a person from *tohuwebohu* (formless and empty) into *tob* (good). The same power that transformed the universe into a masterpiece is transforming us. Upon having faith in Jesus, God enters us into a sanctifying process of taking the ugliness of our hopeless and fragmented natures and refashioning us into a harmonious beauty. Not recognizing the immensity of change that God desires to work in us means missing the work of artistry He is unfurling in us.

While change can be one of the most redeeming experiences of life, it is also frequently the most frightening. Our human nature is adverse to change. It is no wonder Paul repeatedly reminds us to embrace change, foregoing the old nature and taking on the new (Eph. 5:8, Col. 3:5-10). Paul compels us to heed his words, for without change there is no pursuit of beauty. What then is this new creation we're being changed into?

New Image

I wondered why God chose to make people in His image. Why the change from the pattern of creating things without His image to creating beings who bore it? Why take the extra step of creating something to specially represent the character, personhood and heart of God? The only reason revealed in the Bible was the same as why He made everything else – He thought it was *good.* It was for His pleasure and glory.

God used His own image to be the model for our very essence. Since sin entered us through Adam, God's image in us was marred and fragmented. God's desire is to restore His beauty in us through Christ, the second Adam – the second model. Colossians 3:10 tells us that our *new self* is being renewed in *the image of its Creator.* Since Adam introduced to us a broken humanity with sin, Jesus Christ, who was the only human without sin and was the very image of God (Col. 1:15), introduced a new model for humanity that is beautiful and perfect (Ro. 5:17, 19). Christ became one of us in order to make a way for us to become like Him. So the goal of God's artistry in us is to refashion us into the image of His Son Jesus Christ (Ro. 8:29).

The early church father Gregory of Nyssa echoed Colossians 1:15 by calling Jesus the "image of the invisible God" and therefore also a "Prototype" for a brand new humanity.[4] In a world of brokenness, the discovery of beauty in ourselves will be about the model we choose to follow, whether continuing along the pattern set out by Adam's first disobedience or the one set by Christ who reveals absolute beauty in human form. Since beauty presents to us a form of the ideal, achieving beauty becomes a process of change. If in creation we were made in the image of God the Creator, in redemption we are remade into the image of Christ the Savior.

Beauty by Imitation

Gregory of Nyssa wrote that when we've come to recognize Jesus as the prototype for a renewed humanity, He is like a model for a painter. The painter must make every effort to follow the nuances and intricacies of the model in order to capture the essence of the model in his painting.

The "paints" and "brushes" that we work with are choices and actions that demonstrate the virtues of Christ-likeness. Gregory said, "every person is the painter of his own life and choice is the craftsman of the work, and the virtues are the paints for executing the image."[5] Though God is ultimately the artist who shapes who we are by His Word and Holy Spirit, we are participants in His process of creating beauty in us by our choices. The choices we make are not about satisfying a moral checklist but about mirroring Christ so that we become like Him as a person. As our choices and actions conform to Christ's character, we participate in God's work of re-creating beauty within us. By conforming to Christ-likeness we realize that a transformation from brokenness to beauty is only fulfilled by imitation.

People are by nature imitators, according to Aristotle. He called our activity of imitating, "*mimesis*". All art is an imitation of something.[6] From childhood, *mimesis* is how we learn about reality, process principles and grow.[7] Humans are impressionable beings. We're always imitating something. If we're not being transformed into the blueprint of Christ, then we're conforming to the patterns of the world.

For Aristotle, imitation did not mean to simply replicate or "copy" without creative thought, but it meant to reproduce the "universal truths" of the object imitated.[8] It was a matter of mirroring a reality or beauty we saw. It's not unlike our understanding of the Pharisees, who meticulously guarded every factual nuance of their religious lives but failed to reproduce the universal truths that generated real spirituality. Without the truths that are the essence of the facts, our imitation is empty.

The fact is imitation is key to discipleship. God calls us to be imitators of Him (Eph. 5:1). Jesus commanded us to be perfect as our heavenly Father is perfect, that is to be beautiful in character like God (Matt. 5:48), whole and without blemish. The basis for why God calls us to a life of holiness is because holiness is one of His essential qualities (Lev. 11:44, 1 Pet. 1:16). Similarly, Jesus called us to imitate Him in the way He loved others (Jn. 13:15). Paul exhorts us to be humble towards one another like Jesus when He forsook heaven, embraced humanity and died on the cross (Phi. 2:1-11). We're called to suffer like Jesus in 1 Peter 2:21; the Greek term in this verse for the word "example" comes from the imagery of a teacher's copper-plate that was used to teach children how to write by imitation.[9] The life of faith in Jesus is a life of *mimesis*. We can't know true discipleship without experiencing transformation and transformation is based on imitation.

What About Individuality?

It's true that by becoming like someone else we become less like who we were. Are we then losing our individuality? Imitation probably sounds awful to a generation that savors and guards their individuality for fear of losing themselves. But the irony is that to become more like Jesus is to discover more greatly our true humanity, since He is the model of a redeemed humanity. While we are our old selves, we bear an alternate version of humanity that conforms to brokenness. Transformation into Christ-likeness means being freed from brokenness to become who we're meant to be. It means embracing a beauty and a glory that's unavailable to us apart from being transformed. So, genuine individuality is found in imitating Christ and in the elegant work of God's artistry in our lives, where achieving true individuality is no longer a matter of mere self-discovery but of triumph over brokenness and chaos in ourselves.

I believe theater sheds much light on understanding the theology of transformation. I recall the night my wife and I saw the musical "Hairspray" in New York. We waited outside the theater to greet the cast. When George Wendt who played the drag Edna Turnblad came out, someone screamed, "Hey, Norm! You were great!" Norm? That was his character name in "Cheers" that ended back in 1993. Yes, it was an award-winning sitcom, but that was years ago! I wondered if George liked being identified as Norm since that was not his name. Or, perhaps he transformed into that character so well during "Cheers" that Norm's character became his iconic identity.

To be refashioned into Christ's likeness means to adopt a whole new identity. By crucifying our old selves and becoming new persons, we lose ourselves in order to find ourselves in Christ (Gal. 2:20). I believe that is partly why Jesus said that if anyone wants to save his life, he must first lose it (Luke 9:24). The discovery of beauty is only achieved through this paradox of losing one's self. The person refusing to yield to God's artistry with Christ as the model finds himself clinging to brokenness. It's in the paradox of lost that we find true freedom and of imitation that we discover a true identity. It's in self-denial that we embrace beauty because of the grace offered to us to become a beauty we could not achieve on our own.

So what kind of people do we become if we are changed into Christlikeness? There isn't one quality that says it all because the goal of the transformation by imitation is to embrace the totality of Christ's beauty in ourselves. But there is one quality that may stand out about Jesus – He genuinely loved God even unto dying on the cross. Jesus loved God the Father with His devotion and faithfulness. He sought to bring God glory (John 17:1, 4) and He chose God's desires above His own (Matt. 26:38-39). It was always God's desire to change people's hearts to love Him with a love that Jesus defined with obedience (Ezek. 36:27, John 14:21). Sinners who knew only ugliness could not love God, but sinners transformed by grace could. By changing us into Christ's image, it is to help us more greatly fulfill the greatest commandment to love God with all of our hearts, souls, minds and strength. If you wondered what we would become as a result of becoming Christ-like, it is to be greater lovers of God. It is in knowing what it means to passionately love God as Christ did that we discover a beauty in being and living.

Process in Triumph

A fourth principle of artistry is the process. Creating is a journey from unfashioned material to realized vision. Paul wrote, *We, who with unveiled faces all reflect the Lord's glory, are being transformed into his likeness with ever-increasing glory, which comes from the Lord, who is the Spirit* (2 Cor. 3:18). In light of God's artistry in our lives, the Christian progress is more than moral improvement. It is a daily pursuit and experience of this *ever-increasing glory*. It is an artistic venture of God to challenge the sins in our lives, forgive the sins done to us, resolve our regrets and erase our shame. As it was *in the beginning*, every creative step towards beauty is a triumph.

Beauty and spirituality should not be separated. When beauty is about change in Christ, the concept of self-beauty is not about decoration or cosmetics. It is a reality far more powerful. Beauty is about triumph. The struggle of being transformed from ugliness to beauty is a venture of conquest; it is a creative project set against tremendous odds, even impossible odds. It is a test of our faith and a testimony of God's faithfulness to see this process through. As a masterful painting created out of paint squirted onto a palette seems like a miracle, so is the work of God in our lives. Beauty is found in the results and in the process that details the interplay between the artist and His artwork. The process of making beauty is a dance between the maker and the clay, where an interweaving of authority, acceptance, skillfulness and submission takes place. When we yield to God's sculpting of our lives, we may say at the end of the day,

> "For myself what I need is something that speaks of the remaking, not the disappearance, of my bodily condition. And the Spirit that I believe in does not just leave the world behind, like an anxious babysitter who cannot cope, but joins in to sort the mess out."[i]
>
> —David Thistlethwaite

> Yet, O Lord, you are our Father.
> We are the clay, you are the potter;
> we are all the work of your hand
> (Isaiah 64:8).

Interacting with the Artist and His Artistry

In the 1800s, there developed a cultural mindset where people sought to produce beauty not only in objects but in themselves. The achievement of beauty in one's self became a conquest over the horrible and frail aspects of life. It was "a spirit of Art for Art's Sake", where "life itself ought to be lived as a work of art".[10] A view of beauty applied to self emerged. An example of such a movement of creating beauty on one's self was dandyism, where its followers saw the transformation of themselves as a "triumphant example of Beauty".[11] It was about life lived as art.

In Christian discipleship, the artistry of one's self is based in our inter-action with God. Unlike the dandies, the believer doesn't look to himself to complete the artistry but to someone outside of him – God. The process of beauty-making is a venture of how we relate to our Creator. Relating to our Artist entails three important aspects.

Trust & Surrender. Artistry requires surrender, where the materials being formed have to yield to the vision and craftsmanship of the artist. Hardened clay or paint is difficult, if not impossible, to work with. God de-sires us to have this kind of soft spirit, that is a heart of flesh and not of stone (Ezek. 36:26). The more we're willing to surrender to God's artistic work, the more we'll experience transformation. But since surrendering requires relinquishing our preferences, rights and desires, we are left vul-nerable. That is why trust must precede surrender.

Trust is difficult to come by when we have been broken. Guardedness and control is the natural response to anyone who has experienced bro-kenness. But God is the kind of artist who specializes in working with dis-carded and broken materials (Jer. 18:4).[12] His artistry *is* creating beauty out of brokenness.

The story of the "David" statue illustrates the art of making beauty from brokenness well. It began with the rulers of Florence wanting to cre-ate a statue to be a symbol of Florence's pride. They excavated a large marble block from Carrara for the statue to be made out of. In 1464, the rulers commissioned Agostino di Duccio for the project, but the contract was never fulfilled for unknown reasons. Then in 1475, they made a second attempt and commissioned Antonio Rossellino, "who roughed out a statue but did not finish it". After such a disappointment, the fine marble block that was now marred was abandoned in a warehouse.[13] The defaced mar-ble block was forsaken, and the hope of creating something monumentally beautiful was forgotten.

Until Michelangelo took up the task in 1501 – 37 years after the initial dream of creating this statue. Michelangelo used the same marble block that had been marred, abandoned and forgotten. After three years of working alone, never leaving his work and sleeping in the laboratory, he sculpted the "David" statue. This colossal, two-story-high statue with a

Greek god-like frame earned a place in "the center of the city's political life" and has remained one of the world's renowned and iconic masterpieces of all times. [14] Despite the failures, discouragement, loss of hope and defacing, the marble block simply needed to find itself in the hands of the right visionary and capable master.

Surrender and trust happen easily when we know we're in the hands of a master, regardless of the scars, disappointments and regrets we've incurred. A part of faith in God is to know that He is an artist who is an expert at working with broken, discarded material. He chooses to work with imperfection, and He is capable of succeeding where all others would fail. And like Michelangelo, He would not rest or cease until the work of beauty in us is complete (Phi. 1:6).

Offering & Pleasure. What would we smell like to God? Have you ever wondered that? In Romans 12:1, Paul exhorted us to *offer ourselves as living sacrifices, holy and pleasing to God*. In this verse, he drew upon the imageries of the sacrificial system portrayed in the Old Testament, [15] creating a visceral depiction of what it means for a believer to worship God. The Levitical sacrifices had a strong aesthetic concept. When the offerings were burned on the altar, they were *an aroma pleasing to the Lord* (Lev. 2:9, 3:5, 4:31, 6:15). As the people watched the smoke rise to the sky and smelled the burnt grain and grilled meat, the descriptive words of *an aroma pleasing to God* evoked an imagery of God smiling and enjoying the people's worship of Him. [16] This aesthetic experience of worship conveyed to the people that God does not simply choose to tolerate people. No, in fact, He desires to delight in them. God who makes and enjoys beauty cannot simply tolerate anything; He has to take pleasure in them.

In Exodus 30:34-38, God gave a unique recipe for making incense that would be offered to Him. It was a recipe that could not be used for any other purposes and was enjoyed by God alone (Exod. 30:38). God forbade anyone from enjoying this incense. This specific incense was *holy* to God (cf. Lev. 6:17). Things that are holy to God are set apart for God's enjoyment alone. They are meant for God's pleasure alone. Being an offering that's holy to God states the truth that our lives are foremost for the audience of one. If we achieve pleasing everyone in the world but God, we've missed what it means to be beautiful. If God isn't taking pleasure in us, we've yet to achieve beauty.

How do we become *living sacrifices, holy and pleasing to God?* It begins with our faith in God's grace enacted on us through Christ. It is God's mercy (explained in Romans 1-11) that empowers us to become such sacrifices (Ro. 12:1). Becoming a beautiful fragrance to God is first based on Christ's life in us and second on the work of the Holy Spirit in renewing our minds (Rom. 12:2). While God the Father is the Artist and Jesus is the Model, the Holy Spirit is the Means that carries out our transformation (2 Thess. 2:13). The shaping of our thoughts, perspectives and values that conform not to the patterns of the world but to the principles and philosophies of Christ is part of the process of transformation that takes place in the mind and not just in behavior. What we think reveals who we are and dictates what we do.

> "But beauty, true and most lovely, which can be contemplated by him alone who has purified his mind, is that of the divine and blessed nature. He who gazes steadfastly at the splendour and graces of it, receives some share from it, as if from an immersion, tingeing his own face with a sort of brilliant radiance."[iii]
>
> —Basil the Great

The physical side of being an offering to God is in what we do with our bodies — hands, eyes, mouth, feet, etc.; we could offer our bodies as instruments of wickedness or righteousness (Ro. 6:13). By *instruments,* Paul refers to our actions as something that tears down or builds up God's kingdom. We make choices daily that contribute to the work of corruption or creation. Which side do we find ourselves on?

For those He created in Christ Jesus, God finds pleasure in seeing His beauty reflected in them (Psa. 104:31).[17] The question of artistry is whom will we aim to please?

Walking & Abiding. Fellowshipping with God is key to imitating Him. The more time you spend with God, the more you become like Him. After Moses was "face-to-face" with God for days and nights, his face glowed with radiance like the glory of God (Exod. 34:29-30). God's beauty was contagious. So, the key is having close fellowship with God.

Jesus used a term to create an imagery of intimate fellowship with Him – abide. "Abide", from the Greek term *meno*, meant to reside in or "maintain unbroken fellowship" with someone.[18] Jesus called us to abide in Him and He would abide in us (Jn. 15:4). "To abide" cast a vivid imagery of living in Him and walking with Him, which was accomplished by following His teachings. But the problem is sin competes with our efforts to abide in Jesus.

I think "The Incredibles" got it right again when Mrs. Incredible told her children three mandates that would save their lives. They were hiding in a cave on an enemy island where their dad was held captive. Mrs. Incredible grabbed the children's attention because they didn't realize the severity of their situation. She explained that the bad guys were not like the ones in the cartoons. They were ruthless, they would show no mercy, and they would kill them. She told them three key mandates for their survival: 1) "be strong", 2) "run as fast as you can", and 3) "keep each other safe."

The mandates only carried a sense of urgency in light of the danger, just as the urgency to diligently fight for our fellowship with God makes sense in recognition of the ugliness that competes against it. There are realities of the flesh, the sin nature and Satan that oppose God and attempt to corrupt or redefine God's beauty. The monsters are real. God told Cain, *"If you do not do what is right, sin is crouching at your door; it desires to have you, but you must master it"* (Gen. 6:7b). Sin and Satan are not like the cartoons. They will not show mercy, and they will try to bring destruction on us if we allow it. We are to be strong, taking a stand in God's word with faithfulness (Isa. 7:9, Eph. 6:10, 1 Pet. 5:9, Jam. 4:7). We are to flee from sin (1 Tim. 6:11, 2 Tim. 2:22). And we are to bear with one another, holding each other accountable as well as grieving with one another when one falls (Gal. 6:1-2). We are each other's responsibility. Beauty in self, life and character must be fought for. It doesn't come easily.

When abiding takes place, fruit happens. Jesus said like a branch that produces fruit from abiding in the vine, we will produce fruit from abiding in Him (Jn. 15:5). Beauty in character and life is a result of our constant fellowship with God in Christ.

Beauty makes beauty

A common question I get asked is, "How can I make Christian art?" The nature of this question could be applied to anything we do in life not only to the profession or hobby of art-making. As creators, we are making and doing things all the time. So the question that applies to us all is: *how do I know what I'm making or doing in my life is 'Christian'?* It is a practical question. But it's the practical drive of the question that distracts us from the answer we need. The question seeks a behavioral answer, but the answer must be incarnational. What we make and do must come from who we are; who we are comes from what God does in us; the beauty we produce is found in the beauty God produces in us. In the end, we produce beauty because He makes us beautiful.

We have to grasp that God wants us to do significant things more than we want to. According to Ephesians 2:10, God intends for us do *good works*. God wants us to do significant things while on earth that reflect His glory and matter in eternity. We're meant to produce beauty. God's purpose in making us into a people of beauty is so that we would make beauty in the world. We are *created in Christ Jesus to do good works*.

When we engage the Creator, who did not leave the universe in chaos but formed cosmos out of it and is at work in our brokenness, we find a reservoir of goodness for our hopes, strengths and potential in doing good things that matter in eternity – whether it's creating a painting, writing a sonnet, helping an old lady cross the street or showing love to a co-worker when it is undeserved.[19] God's work in us becomes the basis for the good we create in the world.

Though many may not see Stephen King as a maker of beauty, he revealed a keen insight when he wrote, "You cannot hope to sweep someone else away by the force of your writing until it has been done to you."[20] I find this principle to be true to artistry and discipleship. Though God's common grace is at work in many who don't know Him, there's truth in knowing we can't hope to create good things in life until we've been radically swept by God's amazing artistry in us, an artistry that's waiting to happen if we'll yield to it or that's already happening and we need the faith to see it.

I believe the first most important question to ask ourselves is not "what have I done?" but "what has God done in me?" and it is not "what have I accomplished?" but "whom have I become before my Artist?" Whether we are artists, musicians, writers, engineers or accountants, we are driven by the desire to produce significant works, but we cannot forget we are first artworks meant to reveal beauty. "What is ultimate is that in our obedient lives God be displayed as the most beautiful reality in the world."[21] Our striving is to discover God's ultimate triumph over our brokenness through Christ while we struggle daily to achieve moments of beauty. As a result of God's artistry over us, we'll become more beautiful like Christ, greater lovers of God and makers of beauty in a seeking world. As God's artworks, we will begin to see ourselves in His greater story for restoring beauty. That story is where we turn to next.

Walk in Color

• Study these passages and write how these affect your relationship with the Artist.

> Isaiah 29:15-16, Jeremiah 18:1-12,
> Ezekiel 36:24-32, Colossians 3:1-10

• Describe something you would like to create or a project you are working on. Write in detail how God's Artistry in you can be the basis for what you do.

Notes: Chapter Nine

¹ Derek Kidner, *Genesis: An Introduction & Commentary*, Tyndale Old Testament Commentaries, ed. D. J. Wiseman (Downers Grove; InterVarsity Press, 1967), 43.

² Harold W. Hoehner, "Ephesians," in *The Bible Knowledge Commentary: An Exposition of the Scriptures by the Dallas Seminary Faculty*, New Testament ed., ed. John F. Walvoord and Roy B. Zuck (U.S.A: Scripture Press Publications, 1983), 624. Hoehner specifically distinguishes this kind of work from *ergon*, referring to the generic activity of doing or laboring. *Poiema* is a creation out of one's artistry.

³ The NIV translation of "rebirth" could be rendered "new beginning", marking an unprecedented start in the believer's life that is as crucial as a rebirth. George W. Knight, III, *The Pastoral Epistles*, The New International Greek Testament Commentary (Grand Rapids: William B. Eerdmans, 1992), 342.

⁴ Gregory of Nyssa, "On Perfection," *Theological Aesthetics: A Reader*, ed. Gesa Elsbeth Thiessen (Grand Rapids: William B. Eerdmans Publishing Co.. 2005), 40.

⁵ *Ibid.*

⁶ Aristotle, "Poetics" transl. Stephen Halliwell, *Aristotle: Poetics, Longinus: On the Sublime & Demetrius: On Style* (Cambridge: Harvard University Press, 1995), 29.

⁷ *Ibid.*, 37.

⁸ Max Harris, *Theater and Incarnation* (Grand Rapids: William B. Eerdmans, 1990), 41.

⁹ Sinclair B. Ferguson, *The Holy Spirit*, Contours of Christian Theology, ed. Gerald Bray (Downer's Grove: InterVarsity Press, 1996), 152-3.

¹⁰ Umberto Eco, *History of Beauty*, transl. Alastair McEwen (New York: Rizzoli, 2004), 330.

¹¹ *Ibid.*, 334.

¹² The term translated as *marred* in the NIV literally means "ruined" or "spoiled". Furthermore, the implication of the term is that the object is useless and meant to be thrown out. A significance of this imagery of God as a potter working with a ruined vessel is he does not discard it but chooses instead to refashion it.
http://net.bible.org/verse.php?book=Jer&chapter=18&verse=4&tab=commentaries

¹³ Enrica Crispino, *Michelangelo*, English ver. (Florence: Giunti, 2001), 40.

¹⁴ *Ibid.*, 40, 44.

¹⁵ The term *to present* or *offer paristemi*) is the technical term referring to the sacrifices of the Levitical system. Kenneth Wuest, *Wuest Word Studies from the Greek New Testament*, vol. 1 (Grand Rapids: William B. Eerdmans Publishing, 1973), 205. The offering of our "bodies" further reinforces the imagery of the burnt offerings of animals.

¹⁶ As Allen P. Ross clarifies, this language is anthropomorphic since God is spirit and not fleshly with a physical nose. But its meaning of God's pleasure is also clarified by this aesthetic wording. Allen P. Ross, *Holiness to the Lord: A Guide to the Exposition of the Book of Leviticus* (Grand Rapids: Baker Academic, 2002), 95.

¹⁷ John Piper, *The Pleasures of God: Meditations on God's Delight in Being God* (Portland: Multnomah Publishing, 1991), 83.

[18] R. V. Unmack, "Abide," *Evangelical Dictionary of Theology.*

[19] Jeremy S. Begbie noted from Abraham Kuyper's view that God is the inspiration of the artist. Begbie, however, specified that this doesn't mean inspiration for art and beauty only happens within the Church but can happen also by God's common grace in the world. The divine source of beauty and the credit to whom it is due however is the same. Jeremy S. Begbie, *Voicing Creation's Praise: Towards a Theology of the Arts* (London: T&T Clark, 1991), 97-98.

[20] Stephen King, *On Writing: A Memoir of the Craft* (New York: Pocket Books, 2002), 141.

[21] John Piper, *What Jesus Demands from the World* (Wheaton: Crossway Books, 2006), 18.

Pull Out Quotes

[i] Begbie, *Voicing Creation's Praise*, 98.

[ii] David Thistlethwaite, *The Art of God and the Religions of Art* (Carlisle: Solway, 1998), 100.

[iii] Basil, *On Psalm 29 (Homily 14)*, from *Theological Aesthetics: A Reader*, ed. Gesa Elsbeth Thiessen (Grand Rapids: William B. Eerdmans Publishing Company, 2004), 23.

Chapter Ten

STORY

Y ou know the dissatisfaction with something unfinished? It's like not finishing a good book. An unfinished story feels like a jigsaw puzzle with a missing piece. The incompletion is unsettling. It's the same with watching movies, where we're not content with stopping in the middle. Even if it's a bad film, we still find ourselves watching the rest of it only to wonder why we wasted our time. There's something about the need to get to the end. What is it that drives us to finish a story? It's the feeling of dissatisfaction over something unfinished. We hate the feeling of something incomplete. It's this dissatisfaction that drives us toward the end because we need to see the story through.

The Beauty of Story

Beauty resides in good stories that have the power to move us along in a journey. Stories speak to our imagination and cause us to find ourselves in the midst of a new world presented to us that mirrors in some fashion our own. We identify with the characters, their experiences and their challenges. The dilemmas they face are similar to ours in real life. In the end, stories not only provide entertainment but a spiritually and psychologically healthy way for the audience to resolve problems, process pain, consider choices and learn life-lessons. We can grow through stories. Christopher Vogler wrote in *A Writer's Journey*:

> Good stories make you feel you've been through a satisfying, complete experience. You've cried or laughed or both. You finish the story feeling you've learned something about life or about yourself. Perhaps you've picked up a new awareness, a new character or attitude to model your life on.[1]

When I watched Pixar's animated film "Up", I was surprised by my desire to cry throughout the film. I am not a crier for the record. One could think: "It's just an animation." But I kept asking myself, "What would I do if I were that character?" As I watched the film, I became the character Carl and I pondered on the value of my marriage and the dreams my wife and I share. I considered the pain of loss and evaluated the meaning of a fulfilled life. I was caught up in the real humanness of the story.

Caught Up in Story

By seeing ourselves in the stories, we are able to process our troubles and the themes occurring in our lives. Stories could even act as guides or sages at times as we observe how the characters resolve the conflicts that test their virtues and values. Perhaps that's why stories have remained a constant and powerful element of culture throughout human history in every civilization. They not only mirror or record life, they invite us to process and find resolutions to the issues of life. After reviewing over 10,000 screenplays for major motion picture studios, Vogler in *The Writer's Journey* observed the power of well-crafted stories. He wrote the "ancient tools of the storyteller's craft still have tremendous power to heal our people and make the world a better place."[2]

Stories have a unique place in expressing beauty, because a complete story helps us to achieve a sense of wholeness. A story is a micro cosmos with a beginning, middle and end, with a problem and resolution, or with a dilemma and conclusion. A story offers us a sense of wholeness and design in an unpredictable and often fragmented world where success is not guaranteed. They give us a sense of purposefulness with events in life that appear random. They offer us hope in a world where happiness needs to be fought for and the struggle between good and evil continues. Robert K. Johnston from Fuller Seminary commented that "stories are performative; they give meaning to facts. In the process they help answer questions concerning who we are and point us to that larger truth which lies beyond our grasp."[3] Stories help us make sense of life.

Stories develop in readers a hunger to be swallowed up by the magic of the tales, to be found in "liv[ing] their lives like a novel, carried away by the power of sentiments they were unable to resist."[4] Some of us are familiar with the fantasies of journeying with Frodo to Mount Doom in *The Lord of the Rings*, the feelings of despair and hopelessness and the small voice inside that tells us to go one step further – don't give up! Some of us

> "A story is not just a vehicle for an idea, such that the story can be discarded once one has the idea. Rather, our goal is to enhance the experience of the story as a story...For it is only in the reading and the hearing of the story itself that we experience its magic and its capacity to change us."
>
> —Rhoads, Dewey & Michie

have been the Samwise Gamgee, the faithful friend who never gave up on Frodo, while others of us realized we don't have a friend like Samwise in our lives but we need one. We find not only hope and courage but also healing as we process with the main characters through the pain of loss and the attempts to find peace, like in "P.S. I Love You". At other times, we're challenged to be more, like in "The Incredibles".

Is it surprising that we have this cry to be taken up into stories, when our own lives play out like a story? Life unfolds in chapters, like seasons, where our dreams are the goals of the stories, people are like characters who help or hinder us, and the obstacles we face test our quality and teach us lessons.

But there is a greater story playing out which is God's story, where our stories are wrapped up in His. We are presently living in His story of redemption, where the antagonist is sin, Satan and death whose goal is to thwart God's redemption of us. The main character of the story is God whose goal is to defeat the enemy and save people in order to bring glory to Himself through His Son Jesus. The beauty of the stories we see on screen and read in novels is they echo God's drama with humanity. J. R. R. Tolkien recalled one of C.S. Lewis' insights when he wrote to his son,

> Lewis recently wrote a most interesting essay (if published I don't know) showing of what great value the 'story-value' was, as mental nourishment – of the whole Chr[istian] story (NT especially). It was a defence of that kind of attitude which we tend to sneer at: the fainthearted that loses faith, but clings at least to the beauty of 'the story' as having some permanent value.

Some of the principal beauties of stories are the timeless elements that make up a good story. We'll see what one of these elements is and how it on a grander scale points us by general revelation to God's greater story for redeeming humanity.[5]

Beauty of the Hero's Journey

Every story is about a hero. Vogler observed certain structural elements that are consistently present in all tales, myths, legends and movies. These timeless elements of stories comprise 'The Hero's Journey'.[6] A story is about the journey the hero undergoes and the quest he/she must fulfill, whether it's Neo in "The Matrix" saving the last remnant of humans from the machines or Marlin finding Nemo. The story is about the hero's lessons learned, obstacles to

> "Stories invite us to invest part of our personal identity in the Hero for the duration of the experience."[vii]
>
> —Christopher Vogler

overcome and triumph in the end through this journey. We as the audience are meant to identify with the hero. The hero's universal "qualities, emotions, and motivations" draw us into his or her experiences, and therefore, his or her struggles, triumphs and lessons learned become ours during the quest.[7]

The prevalence of the hero's journey in all good stories through the ages serves to reveal the story of God's redemption of humanity. We see the hero's journey in the gospel story from Genesis to Revelation.

Kevin J. Vanhoozer from Trinity Evangelical Divinity School described the redemptive story of the Bible in five acts: Act 1 – creation, Act 2 – God's election, rejection and restoration of Israel, Act 3 – the pivotal and climactic event of Jesus, Act 4 – the acts of the Holy Spirit through the church, and Act 5 – the *eschaton* (biblical events of the last days) and final consummation of all things.[8] Dr. Reg Grant at Dallas Theological Seminary depicted the divine narrative in terms of seasons: Summer is paradise prior to The Fall, Fall is The Fall of man and the curse, Winter is the period of the prophets where God calls out to Israel but Israel struggles and fails to be faithful to God resulting in cycles of judgment and mercy, and Spring is the event of Christ's birth, crucifixion and resurrection. The church, thus, exists somewhere in between Spring and Summer, awaiting the season of paradise's return. God is the hero of His own story, which is about His journey to redeem people from sin, Satan and death.

The Bible is not merely a list of propositions to be memorized. The Bible is a story that invites us to experience its drama so that we may understand the theology it teaches and may develop faith in God. Max Harris, in *Theater and Incarnation*, offered a wise caution on how we read the Bible when he wrote, "Christians who pay attention only to the medium of the written word and resist imaginative reconstruction of the very palpable events to which it claims to bear witness will miss much of the fully sensual and even theatrical nature of God's self-revelation."[9] In the biblical story, the characters are God – the hero, people – the victims who need to be saved and turned into heroes, and Satan – the villain. The stakes are life and glory.

The obstacle is sin and Satan. Marlin's relentless love as a father propels him on a vigilant quest to find and retrieve his lost son Nemo who faced the threat of death at the hands of a selfish, destructive child. God pursues us relentlessly, even recklessly by sending His Son to die a brutal death, while we are faced with the threat of eternal punishment. By being caught up in God's story we understand our relationships as sinners with a holy God who loves us as a father and judges the universe as a ruler. God's Word is intended to evoke our imagination, but we must consciously choose to read it imaginatively

> "Theologies and cosmogonies have laid hold of imagination because they have been attended with solemn processions, incense, embroidered robes, music, the radiance of colored lights, with stories that stir wonder and induce hypnotic admiration. That is, they have come to man through a direct appeal to sense and to sensuous imagination."[viii]
>
> —John Dewey

and creatively in order to comprehend theological truths in an experiential way. In essence, reading God's Scriptures means we're required to exercise those qualities about us that are akin to the image of God in us, in order to dramatically believe in the theologically redemptive narrative He draws us into.

The Bible is the most profound story that we can readily find ourselves in, and it's through the visceral theatricality of this divine-human drama that God reveals whom He is to us, what He is doing in us and what He desires of us. Every time we read the Bible, we're invited to enter into God's story and learn by dramatic experience truths about Him, ourselves and the quest for glory. As we engage with God's story, we see our parts in it and we see God's. We engage an experiential education of theology. We're invited to consume theological truths, not mechanically, but dramatically. He invites us to enter into His story by faith. He invites us to know Him as the hero.

Looking for a Hero

Oprah Winfrey is a modern-day hero to more than 40 million viewers. I watched a show by CNBC explaining the "Oprah Effect", which described

Oprah's impact on anything she approved, whether a new book or a small start-up business. Insurmountable success was the result of the Oprah Effect. Basically if Oprah liked it, millions would buy into it. The Oprah Effect happens because millions of people look up to Oprah. She is a minority who bears the triumphant rags-to-riches story in her own life. She speaks of self-empowerment and demonstrates charity. They respect her values and are inspired by her messages. She is a hero to Christians and non-Christians alike.

Though Oprah is not a hero of the gospel, since her theology is not biblically sound and she does not believe in the gospel of Jesus Christ, she and others like her are social and spiritual heroes of society. Society perceives these heroes as the humanistic symbols of beauty because they represent ideal human qualities that we desire in ourselves. They inspire us to rise above the norm, the mundane and the evil. They challenge us to change and to create change. They offer hope. They give us a vision for a brighter tomorrow and they remind us we can be better than the limitations of our fears. Oprah does that for millions. Thus, we esteem them and their opinions. The scary thing is when the hero neither mirrors Jesus nor points people toward Jesus. In the end, the crucial question is, do society's heroes take us to absolute and redemptive beauty?

Even Jesus warned people against following the Pharisees who were society's heroes at the time. They exhibited a glow of holiness and moral perfection, a kind of godly beauty, when in actuality Jesus claimed they were the very opposite inside. Jesus cautioned against following Pharisaic heroes because it led people not to a life of faith in God that resulted in righteousness and salvation, but to a hypocritical life burdened with legalism, guilt and self-pride. Society's heroes take the people to a perceived ideal beauty. The question is whether that perception mirrors God's beauty.

The fact is our society needs heroes, whether in stories or in real life. We look for heroes because we are unconsciously aware of our brokenness. If we believed we lived in a perfect world we wouldn't need heroes (anymore than we need Disneyland). If we believed our lives were perfect, we wouldn't invent heroes in stories to save the day. Heroes would be meaningless to people who had perfection. Only an imperfect world with imperfect people need heroes. The presence of heroes testifies to our deep-seated desire for salvation, because that's what heroes do – they save us.

What is a Hero?

Throughout time and across cultures, people perceived heroes with varying qualities. For instance in the Renaissance period, one type of hero was someone who personified strength and power and portrayed himself to be at the world's center.[10] Visible wealth and musculature was the mark of power and the ideal. This view is not so different from our contemporary day when power is still seen as a heroic virtue. Because heroes represent the ideal human to us, whom we see as our heroes offers defining insights into the kind of people we are. Our choice of heroes indicates the values we esteem. Our heroes define our society, since heroes bear the virtues that we hope for in ourselves. They embody our dreams and we dream of becoming them.

When I ask my students, "What is a hero?", they list the characteristics of selflessness, readiness to sacrifice for others and ability to save others. They readily identify the 9/11 firefighters, teachers, soldiers or parents as examples. Someone who selflessly offers others salvation through some personal sacrifice is an archetypical perception of a hero. Vogler defined a hero as "someone who is willing to sacrifice his own needs on behalf of others, like a shepherd who will sacrifice to protect and serve his flock".[11] We can see this quality in our contemporary heroes in cinema –Spider-man, Harry Potter, Edward in "Twilight", Neo in "The Matrix", Robert Neville in "I Am Legend", William Wallace in "Braveheart", Chris Gardner in "The Pursuit of Happyness", or Woody in "Toy Story 3" to name a few. The beauty of stories is the hero triumphs over brokenness and evil by sacrificing himself.

Heroes lead, inspire and challenge us every day. They challenge us to be better than we are and to improve our present circumstances. They are the living semblance of beauty that rises above the common brokenness. Heroes lead us beyond the brokenness; they are the ones who tell us that death will not be our fate – they are the 9/11 firefighters running into the flaming mouths of a doomed building to be guides for people in peril. But these heroes of society are hints of the greatest hero in the drama of humanity.

A hero according to the Bible is someone who loves God by serving Him faithfully in the mission of redemption, while trusting Him against the odds and honoring Him above personal comforts. The Bible is full of heroes, such as Moses, Gideon, Ruth, David, Elijah and Hezekiah, but their heroic roles in the Bible foreshadowed the ultimate hero who fulfills the entire story of the Bible. They serve as symbols of hope of the greater one to come. Their imperfections, whether Moses' dishonor of God in the desert or David's fall with Bathsheba, leave us wanting and waiting for that perfect hero. Jesus completes *the* story of the God-human drama as that hero.

The Real Hero

While we see many heroes in many stories, the beauty of them is they point to the ultimate hero of humanity told in the biblical story, the one who epitomized the concept of selfless sacrifice for the salvation of others against earthly and supernatural odds – Jesus Christ. God Himself fulfills the climactic role of the hero in the divine-human drama when God the Son became man and entered into our struggle as one of us (John 1:14). Jesus Christ is the hero of heroes, who had the power to command angels, storms, demons, diseases and even life but chose to sacrificially die a criminal's death though he was innocent, in order to save countless people from the plight of sin and damnation.

The messiah-archetype modeled by Jesus is a familiar, stereotypical character type in our popular stories. The suffering, heroic figure, like Eli in "Book of Eli", mirrors the suffering messiah of God's story. The socially insignificant and weak or despised individual, like Peter Parker in "Spiderman" or Harry Potter, who unexpectedly rises up to save others reflects Jesus of Nazareth, who had no socially outward beauty (Isa. 53:2). Heroes in mainstream culture serve as icons of not only hopes and virtues but, by God's common grace, of the ultimate hero in His story. Heroes in the Bible and in our mainstream stories prophetically hint at the beauty of Jesus Christ as humanity's hero.

Why is Jesus the real hero? Christopher Vogler observed one common element in good stories is the hero duels with death. "At the heart of every story is a confrontation with death," and the hero must face "actual death" or the "threat of death".[12] In the end, "heroes show us how to deal with death".[13] That's what Jesus did. He dealt with death and showed us how to deal with it.

Jesus stared death in the face on the cross of Calvary when the sky darkened, the earth quaked and the Spirit of God was nowhere to be found (Matt. 27:45-51). God's wrath was poured out on Him; God was crushing Him for our sake (Isa. 53:10). He was sealed in the cold earth and visited the "souls in prison" (1 Pet. 3:19). He didn't just face death. Death claimed Him. But it would not keep Him. Jesus is the hero of humanity who tells us death shall not claim our eternity if we follow Him. He was the one foreshadowed to save us (Heb. 10:1-4, 10).

Heroes lead. They lead us to discover, even fight for, a reality we could not know otherwise. They are the firefighters who point the way toward the exit out of a collapsing building. Jesus is the second Adam who showed us the way to escape death and destruction (Ro. 5:12-21). When Jesus conquered death by coming out of the tomb, He presented a course for a new destiny, one that steered away from hell and eternal chaos and led to the artistic cosmos of God that is not formless and void but forever "good".

Heroes remain an inescapable element in our stories because we sense our lives need a hero to lead us out of our brokenness and God's common grace works in our stories to direct us to Jesus. When we see heroes in stories, like Spiderman who fights Dr. Octopus to save a city, Aslan who sacrifices himself to save a traitor and Frodo who relinquishes his comforts in the Shire to assume a burden not his to save the world, we are reminded of Jesus who left heaven to save His enemies (Phi. 2:6-11, Ro. 5:10).

But there's still a catch to the hero's journey in God's story. It isn't finished yet.

Unfinished

Many people know Leonardo da Vinci for his masterful artworks, such as "The Last Supper" and "The Mona Lisa", but few know about his numerous unfinished works. In one example, da Vinci was commissioned by the monks at Santissima Annunziata to create an altarpiece, a painting in a prominent place of viewing. His sketch of the Madonna and baby Jesus already drew an audience. The sketch was significantly admirable, according to the 16th century biographer Giorgio Vasari. The excitement burgeoned as the artist began painting a portrait of Ginerva. But to everyone's dismay, da Vinci abandoned the commissioned work, leaving it forever unfinished.[14]

Not finishing an art project was characteristic of da Vinci. Vasari explained,

> It is clearly evident that because of Leonardo's understanding of art, he began many projects but never finished any of them, feeling that his hand could not reach artistic perfection in the works he conceived, since he envisioned such subtle, marvelous, and difficult problems that his hands, while extremely skilful, were incapable of ever realizing them.[15]

Da Vinci often found that his visionary endeavors were too large for his craftsmanship to suffice. His larger than life visions were part of what made him a great master, no doubt, but what if his skills could've matched his level of vision?

Any kind of potential masterpiece left unfinished is unsatisfying. It feels like stopping in the middle of a good book. Paul described this dissatisfaction as a groaning. He wrote, "we groan, longing to be clothed with our heavenly dwelling" (2 Cor. 5:2). In fact, not only do we groan but, "the whole creation has been groaning as in the pains of childbirth", longing to be liberated from the bondage of decay (Ro. 8:21, 22). The groans are an extended sigh or an ache in our souls over the dissatisfaction of our present conditions. This groan is like a deep moaning that expresses our longing for a future where aging and decay disappear and suffering is gone.[16] It is a reality of cosmos without chaos, of glory without degradation. In this promised reality, the faithful are in perfect fellowship with Him. God's story is one of reconciliation with His children that ends in final reunion, where we see the reality of the Father's invitation, *"Come and share in your master's happiness"* (Matt. 25:21).

> *"Beauty itself was beheld no longer in the ephemeral aspect of creaturely existence but rather in the future trans-figuration of the creature and creation."[iv]*
>
> —Leonid Ouspensky

The future we yearn for is likened to our past. In the class I teach at Biola University, one of my student groups went out to the streets of Pasadena, CA, to ask people what they considered to be *absolutely* beautiful. My students were surprised by the frequent answer of "nature". Even for people living and working in the cities who don't know God, they still possess a fundamental perception that beauty is found in nature, in the things God created. Perhaps this latent perception echoes our hunger for a pre-Fall, Garden of Eden existence when beauty was untainted by brokenness, and this hunger rests at such a subconscious level we can't describe it with words but only with groans. It is as J. R. R. Tolkien wrote to his son Christopher,

> "But certainly there was an Eden on this very unhappy earth. We all long for it, and we are constantly glimpsing it: our whole nature at its best and least corrupted, its gentlest and most humane, is still soaked with the sense of 'exile'."[17]

If we didn't have such a reminiscence and yearning we would be fully content with the present state of the world. We desire to return to the season of summer. Our groaning is a yearning for the redemptive artistry of God to be completed in Christ through His Spirit. Our groaning expresses our longing for beauty.

But let's admit it. Most of us don't like feeling dissatisfied.

Dissatisfaction

It would be a sin to pacify our groaning with the niceties of this world or to silence it with the busyness of life. Most of us hate discomfort. We don't like feeling unsettled, and yet, it is the unsettledness that is vital for us to have a godly passion that's aligned with God's heart. The pursuit and achievement of the American Dream not only smothers a godly passion, it is a futile substitute for God's redemptive artistry. If we stop groaning, yearning and longing, we might settle to believe that this is as good as it gets. Sinfully, that's what the American Dream tells us. But there is no greater "dream" than the one God has envisioned at the end of His story. It's tragic to settle for making mud pies in the slums if there's an offer for building sand castles at the beach or to not go after the Kobe steak because someone gave us a fifty cent burger. The groaning within reminds us that God's work is not done yet and gives us the appetite for true beauty.

Unlike da Vinci and other great masters on earth, God is *the* master par excellence, where the perfection of His vision will be fully satisfied by His perfect craftsmanship, so we could be confident that He never leaves his work unfinished. The creative words He spoke into creation are the same words that will not return to Him empty (Isa. 55:10-11). He will continue to *bara* (create) as he did in the beginning as a craftsman until His people are wholly redeemed into beauty and glory (Isa. 65:18-19, Ro. 8:18). He is faithful in completing His story (Phi. 1:6). As He did in creation, He will transform chaos to cosmos in redemption. This will all be fulfilled in Christ's return, but until then we have a good reason to be dissatisfied.

Dissatisfaction might be a tough idea to swallow because it means: don't allow yourself to be completely happy. We are a people who have been taught to be obsessed with attaining maximum comfort and happiness. But if there is anything a Christian can understand when he or she has a grasp of true beauty, it's that final happiness will not be found here. Contrary to the American Dream that offers a temporal, fading beauty, until God's kingdom comes ultimate happiness still awaits us. Telling ourselves that we are fully happy because we have a big home, stable income, glamorous lifestyle and the latest gadgets is a cover-up for our brokenness and a sales pitch for low expectations. There is no greater passion-killer than to settle for the small beauties of the world when a masterpiece is promised. The desire to see the end of the story is part of the holy drive for us in carrying out God's mission of the gospel. Until we see the end, we have not experienced the final beauty that God wrote about.

But how do we reconcile the biblical principle that Christians are supposed to experience complete contentment in Christ, especially when joy is one of the Christian virtues? (Gal. 5:22, Phi. 3:1, 4:11). We resolve this by learning to live in a biblical paradox. The paradox lies in the joy of knowing God and being known by Him and in the honest ugliness we see in ourselves and the world. Because we've tasted absolute beauty in God, we can perceive ugliness and have the desire to change it. Our desire for the perfect beauty God envisions at the end of the story fuels a godly passion to strive in this life for His glory.

So until this story is complete we exist in the reality of ugliness and beauty. We exist in a godly paradox between the two and see our own journey captured in God's. Our present contentment is therefore in the hope of a renewed beauty God has in store, a future reality that we can taste by faith (Heb. 11:1). And because we can taste this beauty God has in mind, our groaning should grow louder. When we stop groaning, it's an indicator that we have settled for this world. Living in the tension of dissatisfaction is key to faithful living and to attaining genuine contentment. We see our dissatisfaction when the unfinished story of God becomes our hunger for His mission.

What's the point?

What's the point of the story anyway? Every story has a point, a goal needs to be achieved, whether it's getting the one ring to Mount Doom, saving Private Ryan, learning to let go after your loved one dies or rescuing some damsel in distress so that all can be well again in the kingdom. What's the point of the biblical story?

I loved the film, "Book of Eli", but I disagree with its conclusion about the point of the Bible. Eli said to Solara that after having read the Bible repeatedly, the point of the story is to "do for others what you do for yourself." This morally sounds great, but it's not the point of the story. It's these superficial conclusions about religions that permit people to stereotypically lump all religions together as communicating the same message: be good to others (which is like saying all Asians are basically the same!). Yes, the Bible emphasizes our need to show mercy, love and kindness to others. But that's not the point of the story any more than concluding that *The Lord of the Rings* is about not trusting orcs. So then, what is the point, that final beauty, which God is trying to get to? How is this story supposed to end? And how does the ending define our lives?

That's what we turn to next.

Walk in Color

- Who was one of your heroes in stories? Why was this person a hero to you?
- How content are you right now with life and who you are?
- What's been your primary understanding of what Christianity is about?
- Try reading these passages as story. Let the narrator guide you, experience the drama and see yourself as one of the characters: 2 Kings 5 & Mark 4-5.

Notes: Chapter Ten

[1] Christopher Vogler, *The Writer's Journey: Mythic Structure for Writers*, second ed. (Studio City: Michael Wiese Productions, 1998), 2.

[2] *Ibid.*, 1.

[3] Robert K. Johnston, *Reel Spirituality: Theology and Film in Dialogue*, Engaging Culture (Grand Rapids: Baker Academic, 2000), 79.

[4] Umberto Eco, *History of Beauty*, transl. Alastair McEwen (New York: Rizzoli, 2005), 314.

[5] General revelation can be defined as "that divine disclosure to all persons at all times and places by which one comes to know that God is, and what he is like". B.A. Demarest, "Revelation, General" in *Evangelical Dictionary of Theology*, ed. Walter A. Elwell (Grand Rapids: Baker Books, 1984), 944. General revelation is significant to us in the discussion of stories because the timeless elements of stories show us the greater biblical truth of the presence of God and His redemptive activity. General revelation only offers us a hint of the reality of God but special revelation (i.e. the gospel) offers a clear knowledge of Jesus to have saving faith. But general revelation in stories is vital in suggesting the greater design of God for humanity and the active story He is unfolding to redeem humanity.

[6] Vogler, *The Writer's Journey*, 1.

[7] *Ibid.*, 36.

[8] Kevin J. Vanhoozer, *The Drama of Doctrine: A Canonical Linguistic Approach to Christian Theology*, first ed. (Louisville: Westminster John Knox Press, 2005), 2-3.

[9] Max Harris, *Theater and Incarnation* (Grand Rapids: William B. Eerdmans Publishing Company, 1990), 7.

[10] Eco, *History of Beauty*, 200.

[11] Vogler, *The Writer's Journey*, 35.

[12] *Ibid.*, 38.

[13] *Ibid.*

[14] Sherwin B. Nuland, *Leonardo da Vinci* (New York: Penguin Group, 2000), 66-7.

[15] Giorgio Vasari, *The Lives of the Artists*, intro. and transl. Julia Conaway Bondanella and Peter Bondanella (Oxford: Oxford University Press, 1998), 286-7.

[16] *Groaning* is a key term that communicates the "cry of agony and travail", where this painful cry is not out of tragedy but out of an anticipation of new life as in childbirth. Grant R. Osborne, *Romans*, The IVP New Testament Commentary Series, consulting ed. D. Stuart Briscoe and Haddon Robinson (Downers Grove: InterVarsity, 2004), 213.

[17] J.R.R. Tolkien, *The Letters of J.R.R. Tolkien*, ed. Humphrey Carpenter with assistance by Christopher Tolkien (New York: Houghton Mifflin Co., 1981), 110.

Pull Out Quotes
[1] David Rhoads, Joanna Dewey & Donald Michie, *Mark as Story: An Introduction to the Narrative of a Gospel*, 2nd ed. (Minneapolis: Fortress Press, 1999), 7.

ⁱⁱ Vogler, *The Writer's Journey*, 36.

ⁱⁱⁱ John Dewey, *Art as Experience* (New York: Penguin Group, 2005), 31.

ⁱᵛ Leonid Ouspensky, "Icon and Art" in *Christian Spirituality: Origins to the Twelfth Century*, ed. Bernard McGinn, John Meyendorff and Jean Leclercq (New York: Crossroad Publishing, 2000), 384.

Chapter Eleven

MISSION

I was eleven-years old when the man locked me in the van with him. I didn't have a choice in the matter. All the kids eventually went through it. I knew I was next. Nervousness crept over me because I didn't know what to expect.

The van space inside was small, forcing us to sit close together. As he faced me, he reached in his pocket and pulled out a little booklet with colored pages but no words. He called it the "wordless book". Using the colors of the pages, he explained the gospel to me. He explained how my sin warranted death and punishment in hell but Christ died for me and if I accept Him as my savior I could escape hell and go to heaven. "So, do you want to accept Jesus into your heart?" he asked me.

Well, honestly, I didn't think he was going to let me out of the van unless I did. I was a Buddhist. I didn't get how someone else's death on the cross relieved my punishment as a sinner. But I didn't want to look at the blank booklet and be trapped in the stuffy van with this man any more, so I said, "Yes." He led me in prayer and I was declared saved that day. He said I should feel happy now.

I came out of the van, breathed in the fresh air and felt confused.

As the eldest boy raised in a Buddhist family, Christianity was a foreign concept. In Buddhism, there was no sin nature, no one God and no savior's sacrifice on the cross.

What was Christianity about? I remembered hearing a lot about *me*, what God did for me and for the many poor lost souls in the world who need saving. What is the point of the story? Was it about us? Or was it about the hero of the story?

The Point of the Story

We all sense there's a purpose for being alive. In other words, there's a point to being here, whether in the back of our minds we believe that point is to achieve happiness, provide for our families, accomplish something significant or amass as much wealth as we can before we die. But there is only one God-ordained point to our lives, and His greater story for humanity determines the point of our personal lives. The point of the story defines the mission God has for us, and the mission defines the purpose of our lives. Therefore, the purpose of our lives is tied to the point of God's story.

I know. You want me to finally get to that point.

The point of God's story is to create lovers of Him through Jesus and the Spirit.

Therefore, the purpose of our lives is to love God with our entire being. The point of God's story is the great commandment: *"Love the Lord your God with all your heart and with all your soul and with all your mind"* (Matt. 22:37). The objective of the story then is not to love ourselves. It's to love God. The problem is the point of God's story runs counterintuitive with our nature and the messages of our culture.

In our romanticized age, we'd like to think of the point of the gospel message as being "me". Particularly in our present day where the perception of beauty is shaped by the mass media[1] that caters to our desires and appetites, we are easily led to believe that our interests are central. We live in a culture where beauty is defined by consumption, as Umberto Eco observed,[2] where everything from fashion magazines, television shows, internet ads and pop music to the latest health diets appeal to our appetites. In a consumerist culture, what's beautiful to us is whatever we consume. Beauty may not be about encountering truth and goodness. It may not be about discovering the Absolute Divine. It may not be about something that reveals my brokenness. Consumerist beauty is about my appetite. And what feeds me and serves me will be beautiful to me. Under this mentality, the gospel becomes something for us to consume. If it satisfies my needs or my appetite, then it is beautiful to me. The gospel can fall prey to this perception. Jesus died for me, offers me eternal life for free and I'll take it. End of story?

If beauty is not defined by an outside "canon" – that is an objective standard that comes from an authoritative source outside of myself – but rather is defined by my personal tastes, then the sense of the ideal and perfect does revolve around my happiness, my likings and my desires. Perfection is defined in our eyes as when all my needs are satisfied. The ultimate pursuit is for my good.

Why Not Me?

In the 1980s, Whitney Houston sang a number one hit song that expressed a modern ideal with the lyrics, "Learning to love yourself, it is the greatest love of all." This iconic song in the history of pop culture verbalized the ideal beauty of human life. Interestingly, Linda Creed (along with Michael Masser) wrote the song during her years of coping with an impending death due to breast cancer.[3] People echoed her cry that in the face of brokenness, loving oneself was the point to all of our stories. The sentiment is that loving yourself is perhaps the best thing to do in the fading frailty of life. Simply love yourself and seek your own happiness as the highest goal in an existence where death could claim you at any moment. The American Dream of pursuing your own happiness is the greatest beauty one could attain. My mentor, Martin Hironaga, once said to me that people have to learn how to deal with death. For many seeking the American Dream is a way of coping with death. But the American Dream is self-idolatry.

If loving yourself is the highest end for living then you must see the fulfillment of your own desires as the greatest beauty. Ultimately, we pursue what we find most beautiful. If loving ourselves is the highest end, we have to deny or diminish the beauty of God. In order to focus on ourselves, we have to ignore the glory, nature and character of God, which define God's beauty. By centralizing our subjective appetites we have to dismiss God's absolute beauty. In order to make the point of our stories to be about us, we have to ignore the point of God's story as being about Him. By doing so, we deny that God is truly worthy to be God since He is not worthy of our highest pursuits.

But God didn't write the story to be about us. He didn't design creation, the universe and the human story to be about us. Every Christian initially comes to faith in Jesus Christ because they love themselves enough to want to preserve their lives eternally. But when we discover the glory and mission of God, we ultimately should learn that salvation has a much higher end than us. We should eventually discover that being saved invited us into a vision for life that's grander than our personal goals.

Did Jesus die and resurrect just so we may be saved? Or did he die and resurrect so we may fulfill the great commandment as a people of God? Take a look at the prophetic words of God that laid the path for Christ's coming.

Jeremiah 31:33-34

> *"This is the covenant I will make with*
> *the house of Israel*
> *after that time," declares the Lord.*
> *"I will put my law in their minds*
> *and write it on their hearts.*
> *I will be their God,*
> *and they will be my people.*
> *No longer will a man teach his neighbor,*
> *or a man his brother, saying, 'Know the Lord,'*
> *because they will all know me,*
> *from the least of them to the*

> greatest," declares the Lord.
> "For I will forgive their wickedness
> and will remember their sins no more."

And…

Ezekiel 36:26-27

> "I will give you a new heart and put a new spirit in
> you; I will remove from you your heart of stone and
> give you a heart of flesh. And I will put my Spirit in you
> and move you to follow my decrees and be careful to
> keep my laws."

When God led Israel out of bondage in Egypt, it was to make a people with one goal. Following the great *shema*, the Hebrew's distinctive declaration of there being one God, He commanded them: "*Love the Lord your God with all your heart and with all your soul and with all your strength*" (Deut. 6:5). God said the point of delivering the Hebrews out of Egypt was "*so that they may worship me in the desert*" (Exod. 7:16). God's purpose for redeeming people from slavery was not merely for humanitarian reasons. There was a greater purpose in mind that aligned with the point of God's story. Redemption was not only about freeing us from sin and death. Redemption was about reclaiming enemies of God to becoming lovers of God at the cost of the Son of God!

A Lesson and a Bit of Whipping From Jesus

When Jesus was asked 1,500 years later what the greatest commandment was, He didn't say, be a good person, donate to the poor or be happy. He said, "*Love the Lord your God with all your heart and with all your soul and with all your mind*" (Matt. 22:37). Jesus knew the point of God's story and He knew the outcome of His sacrifice – to create passionate, furious lovers of God.

Our love for God defines our genuineness as a people of God. Jesus' declaration of the great commandment to love God (Matt. 21:23-22:46) was a response to the Pharisees' attempt to discredit him with a challenging question. This attempt was one of three attempts by three different groups of authorities to trap Jesus. Prior to these trapping attempts, Jesus told three convicting parables. So, the biblical context for the great commandment enlightens our understanding of the meaning of loving God.

Jesus' first parable about a father and his two sons stated that the kingdom of God is for those who are repentant and believing in God's Son (21:28-32). The second parable about the landowner and his servants stated that the kingdom of God was for those who produced fruit for the kingdom and not just for themselves (21:33-46). The third parable about the king and his wedding guests stated that the kingdom of heaven was for the "chosen" (22:1-14). The "chosen" indicated the *true, genuine* people of God – those who belonged in God's house. Everyone is invited into God's kingdom but not everyone is truly God's people. Those who aren't will be cast out from His kingdom. The question was: how are the chosen identified? The first two parables gave some indications. They were people who were repentant and believing and they were those who sought to produce fruit for the kingdom and not just for themselves. That's not all.

The following three trapping attempts opened opportunities for Jesus to define the meaning of genuine faith. When asked about paying taxes (22:15-22), Jesus referred to an artistic principle that expressed a spiritual truth. When you make something with your image, literally *artistic expression*, on it, that object belongs to you. Since Caesar's portrait was molded onto his coins, give the coins to him. But the greater principle is God fashioned us in His image, so we should devote ourselves wholly to Him!

When Jesus was asked about the resurrection, He stated that God is the God of those who are eternally living. The people of God will have eternal life.

And finally, when asked about what was the greatest commandment, He stated it was to love God with our entire being.

After three parables and three trapping attempts, Jesus refined the characteristics for the true people of God. They are the repentant and believing (not the stubborn), the fruitful for God's kingdom (versus for them-selves), the chosen (not the hypocrites), the devoted to God (and not themselves), the eternally living (not the dead) and the lovers of God (and not lovers of themselves). Jesus clarified that being a lover of God summed up the rest of the requirements when He said that all the other writings in Scripture hinge on our love for God and for others (Matt. 22:40). But that's not all.

Jesus' teachings call us to evaluate the sincerity of our faith. Are we still in it for ourselves? Or have we encountered the greater beauty that calls us to love someone greater than ourselves? This can be a tricky question.

The Difference Between Saul and David

Sometimes we unknowingly miss the point. The difference between someone who gets it and someone who doesn't is well illustrated by Is-rael's first two kings – Saul and David.

Saul was the tragic hero figure, the one we had a lot of hope for but turned out to be a disappointment. What was Saul's fatal flaw? God gave him a mission to carry out His justice by conquering the Amalekites. Saul followed God's command and bravely triumphed over their enemies. But he didn't fully carry out God's command to destroy all the cattle (1 Sam 15:9). He killed the weak cattle but saved the good ones. When Samuel the prophet challenged him about his lack of faithfulness to God, Saul re-butted and said, "But I did obey the Lord" (1 Sam 15:20). Saul claimed his intention was to sacrifice the animals to God. Whether Saul's intentions were genuine or not, Samuel clarified for Saul that obedience was better than sacrifices because obedience meant love and faithfulness to God. But disobedience was arrogance. Even disobedience with good intentions says you're doing it your way and you think you know better than God.

I think the matter stemmed from Saul's heart. It was his heart that in-evitably defined his actions. After his great victory against the Amalekites, he went and did something that revealed that he did not wholly love God. He built a monument in his own honor (1 Sam. 15:12).[4] After the victory, Saul's act of creativity expressed not God's glory but his own. To a public audience, it was a sculpture to honor Saul (1 Sam. 15:12). Saul testified to others that he was about his own glory. Not God's. The ultimate beauty he pursued to manifest in the end was his own. Not God's.

I think however that Saul was not consciously being defiant. I bet in his own mind, he really thought he was right with God. But the lack of complete faithfulness to obeying God's command was connected to his lack of fully loving God. I think the problem for Saul was the misplacement of his love, which he might not have been consciously aware of. His heart wasn't fully devoted to God.

How many of us are like Saul? We help out in Sunday school classes or as ushers. We joined a small group Bible study. We attend church services regularly. We might even tithe a full ten percent of our income. We seem to be doing all the right things. But in the grand scheme of our lives, we're really building monuments for ourselves represented by the worldly things that satisfy our appetites, feed our pride and secure our comforts. We're building our dreams, pursuing our happiness and seeking our own kingdoms. Church is a side thing. God is an addition. But our main thing is our kingdoms. Really, we love ourselves. And, we love loving ourselves. At best, all the good and right religious things we do are partial obediences, but our hearts are not *fully* devoted to Him. We live such lives perhaps unknowingly and may find ourselves saying to God in the end with a breath of confusion, "But I *did* obey you." How many of us follow the tragedy of Saul? But then there's David.

After David won a few significant wars, his first creative pursuit was not to make a monument for himself; it was to reclaim and celebrate an artistic monument that magnified God – the ark of the covenant (2 Sam. 6). This elaborate chest testified to God's character, promises and presence; it was an artistic expression of God's absolute beauty. David retrieved the ark from enemy hands. While it was being transported back to Jerusalem, he led the people to celebrate *with all their might before the Lord* with music and all kinds of instruments (2 Sam. 6:5). David celebrated God's glory. Not his own. And he led others to celebrate God's glory with him.

David's first artistic act as king was to create a dance! He danced his heart out as he and his people paraded God's ark into the city (2 Sam.

6:14). He didn't care how foolish he looked. He wasn't concerned about his own glory. He defined his reputation by his love for God's glory. When his wife accused him of publicly embarrassing himself, he replied confidently, "*I will celebrate before the Lord. I will become even more undignified than this, and I will be humiliated in my own eyes*" (2 Sam. 6:21-22). David was too busy enjoying God's beauty and glory to be worried about his own. This is the same David who could not take his gaze off of God's beauty (Psa. 27:4). He wasn't a perfect man, by any means. The Bible frankly displayed his mistakes and sins, like his incident with Uriah and Bathsheba (2 Sam. 11-12). But God knew David's heart (1 Sam. 16:7) and proudly declared him as "*a man after my own heart*" (Acts 13:22).

There are Sauls and there are Davids in the world. The Sauls are professed believers, but they have not encountered a beauty greater than themselves. They see themselves as living good, Christian lives, but their hearts are not fully devoted to God. The Davids can't take their eyes off of God's beauty. Their hearts follow God's heart and their actions are a relentless pursuit after God's glory. Davids are imperfect people who love God wholly. Which are you? I have to ask myself regularly, which am I? The wonder of the Christian life is Jesus shows us absolute beauty every day in His face if we choose to interact with Him. We are being redeemed into a vision of beauty modeled by Christ. And now we have the opportunity to pursue God relentlessly.

My experience in the stuffy van with the man with the wordless book, as strange as it seemed, was my first exposure to the gospel. In the following years of wrestling with the meaning of the gospel, I came to understand the unfathomable love of God for me displayed in the redeeming work of Christ on the cross, only to learn God had a greater vision in mind that involved His glory. It was liberating and inspiring to discover the end of the gospel message was not me. Though I find myself tending towards a Saul-like Christianity, God's beauty pulls me towards having a David-like heart.

The gospel is an expression of His love for us but it is also an invitation for us to love Him.

Our first and foremost mission in life is to love God. It is to fulfill what Jesus called *"the first and greatest commandment"*.

However, the first great commandment does not stand without the support of the second great commandment and the great commission, both of which help to drive the mission home.

Loving God Cannot be Private

A great, contemporary misconception about our relationship with God is it is private. Loving God cannot be purely private. Loving God has to become communal. This doesn't mean that our love for God is done out of conformity, institutionalization or social pressure. Contemporary society's disenchantment with institutionalized religion has tainted for us the communal aspect of loving God. But rediscovering a genuine love for God requires a communal expression.

John the apostle wrote: *If anyone says, "I love God," yet hates his brother, he is a liar. For anyone who does not love his brother, whom he has seen cannot love God, whom he has not seen. And he has given us this command: Whoever loves God must also love his brother* (1 Jn. 4:20-21).

Loving others is the second greatest commandment. Jesus said that the Law and Prophets hang on the first and second greatest commandments. If being a Christian doesn't focus us on loving God as our main passion and pursuit and loving others as the most important means to fulfilling the first commandment, then we've missed the point of the story.

Loving others is essentially connected to our love for God. As discussed in Chapter 6, loving others is the evidence that we have God's love and remain in His love (1 Jn 4:11). It shows that we are empowered by God's love (1 Jn. 4:19). So, how we love others doesn't only reveal the kind of relationship we have with others but ultimately the kind of relationship we have with Him. Loving others is a means to loving God. Even as Jesus said, *"I tell you the truth, whatever you did for one of the least of these brothers of mine, you did for me"* (Matt. 25:40). So loving God should mean we love our wives, neighbors, co-workers, bosses, children, local homeless people, bus drivers, grocery baggers, babysitters and dentists better.

A Radical Love

I bet we've heard the command to love others before. But I bet we've yet to grasp the gravity of the command.

God called us to love others as radically as He loved us. Consider how God loves and how we're called to love. God sent His Son to die for His enemies (Ro. 5:10), and Jesus told us to love our enemies (Matt. 6:43-48). Jesus came as a humble servant to serve us (Matt. 20:28), and Jesus told us to serve each other (Jn. 13:14). As Jesus loved the church sacrificially, husbands are meant to love their wives in the same way (Eph. 5:25). Jesus prayed for the forgiveness of those who crucified Him (Luke 23:34), and He told us to bless those who curse us and pray for those who mistreat us (Luke 6:28). God forgave us of our sins, and we are supposed to endlessly forgive others who offend us (Matt. 18:21-35, Col. 3:13). Jesus surrendered His privileges as God to love us, and we're supposed to surrender our own interests in order to serve others (Phi. 2:1-11). In the same way Jesus loved us, He commanded us to love others (Jn. 13:34).

The kind of love God commands His people to exercise is not like the popular notions of love that call us to love when it is deserved. Our love for others is unprecedented, requires no cause or reason and is undeserved by others. We are to love those who are socially estranged from us at our own expense, like in the parable of the Good Samaritan. We are to love those who are uncomfortable to us. We are to gladly love the enemies who hurt us. We are to love during suffering. We are to love in such a way that causes the world to think we are crazy. But that's the kind of love the world needs to experience from us in order to catch a glimpse of God's absolute beauty and Christ's redemption of brokenness, because the love we model is God's. We show the world the reality of God's love by loving them in the way He loves us. As lovers of God who love others as God loves us, we are agents of God's beauty to a hurting world.

Make no mistake. The call to love others is not an optional quality to develop, like how we tend to think loving others is a nice notion. Loving others as Jesus did is a *command* (Jn. 13:34). Every time we fail to love, we sin. Of course, we can't perfectly love as Jesus did. But do we honestly try? Then again, some of our shortcomings in loving others as Jesus did stem from our lack of knowing how much Jesus loved us. We may realize we need to go back to the basics of not taking for granted Christ's love for us and needing to discover daily the depth and height of His love (Eph. 3:17-19). We can't dilute the command to love each other into a humanitarian ideal. It is a serious mandate because it is a way in which we accomplish the greatest commandment. When we strive by God's grace to radically love others as Jesus loved us, we present to the world a *je ne sais quoi* kind of beauty. We cause people to ask, "What is that?"

So while world peace is not the goal of Christianity, Christianity does produce peacemakers. For when we genuinely, rightly and passionately love God, we automatically bring greater peace into a broken world.

What's more is our love is our testimony because Jesus said, "*By this all men will know that you are my disciples, if you love one another*" (Jn. 13:35). Our love ultimately points to our hero. When we think that our love for others has to do with fulfilling the great commission, we realize the paramount necessity of this radical love.

The Great Commission

The more we love God, the more we realize He is worthy not only of our love but of everyone's love. Loving God is not merely private and only communal. Loving God must become global. The great commission fulfills the great commandment globally.

Jesus said in Matthew 28:19-20:

> "All authority in heaven and on earth has been given
> to me. Therefore go and make disciples of all nations,
> baptizing them in the name of the Father and of the
> Son and of the Holy Spirit, and teaching them to obey
> everything I have commanded you. And surely I am
> with you always, to the very end of the age."

The great commission is also not a nice option. It is a command. The words "*make disciples*" were written in a particular Greek grammar tense that explicitly expresses a commandment.[5] The command is not to fill church seats. It is not to make converts. It is to *make* disciples. The act of "making" means the great commission involves a level of joining God in the ongoing quest of creativity. It implies a gradual process of creating by schooling, educating and mentoring[6] with the effect of transformation, faith development and life change. The results of this making-process are "*disciples*" — followers, learners and lovers of Jesus.

The great commission is essential to fulfilling the point of God's story. The beauty of the great commission is the once enemies of God who became lovers of God are now commissioned to create more love for God. The once broken who are redeemed and refashioned into the beauty of Christ are called to create further beauty among broken people. The people of God become creators of beauty. Creators of

> "Resurrection doesn't mean escaping from the world; it means mission to the world based on Jesus' lordship over the world."[ii]
>
> —N. T. Wright

beauty do not run from brokenness. As Jesus commanded us to "*Go*", we are called to run *into* brokenness and fashion beauty in it by building a kingdom of lovers of God.

Kingdom Come

You can tell a lot about a person's pursuits by their prayers. What people lift up to God is usually what people most desire. When the disciples asked Jesus about how they should pray to God, Jesus gave us this prayer (Matt. 6:9-13):

> "Our Father in heaven
> hallowed be your name,
> your kingdom come,
> your will be done
> on earth as it is in heaven.
> Give us today our daily bread.
> Forgive us our debts,
> as we also have forgiven our debtors.

*And lead us not into temptation
but deliver us from the evil one."*

This prescribed prayer has been popularly known as the Lord's Prayer, recited in masses and services for ages. However, the Lord's Prayer is not only a prescription for liturgy but for our deepest desire. The Lord's Prayer should be the cry of our hearts, where our greatest desire is not to build our own kingdoms but His. *Your* kingdom come. *Your* will be done. Not our American Dream. Not our wills. Above our homes, 401ks, mutual funds and career advancements, our desire should be for God's kingdom.

> "For what did he mean when he said, in the words of the prophet, 'I shall be their God, and they will be my people'? Did he not mean, 'I shall be the source of their satisfaction; I shall be everything that men can honourably desire: life, health, food, wealth, glory, honour, peace and every blessing'? For that is also the correct interpretation of the Apostle's words, 'so that God may be all in all'. He will be the goal of all our longings; and we shall see him for ever; we shall love him without satiety; we shall praise him without wearying. This will be the duty, the delight, the activity of all, shared by all who share the life of eternity."[ii]
>
> —Augustine

The Bible provides us a vision of the end result of God's kingdom established on earth in Revelation 21:3-27. In the vision, the city of God is renewed in beauty, radiating like perfectly clear, precious gems and shining with the glory of God. It reflects God's perfect beauty. Its massive walls, decorated with every precious stone, mark off the perimeter of this enormous city. It is a city with streets of gold and gates of pearl. These beautiful elements may be a metaphor for the perfect beauty of God, that it will be a city with the beauty of God's holiness where there will be no sin and impurity (21:27), the beauty of His creativity where there will be no brokenness or sorrow (21:4) and the beauty of His love where He and His people will live in harmony (21:3). The final outcome of God's story is a reality of beauty without brokenness, where beauty is clearly more than a cosmetic but a new state of being.

In the middle of this beauty is a perfect reconciliation between God and His people. God said: "*Now the dwelling of God is with men, and he will live with them. They will be his people, and God himself will be with them and be their God*" (21:3). The end reality, which is just the beginning of God's new kingdom, is people are in right relationships with Him. This is the final chapter of the story. Through the great commission, we have the honor of pursuing this end.

Follow the Hero Towards the Kingdom

How ready are we to make the great commandment our purpose in life? How ready are we to see the great commandment fulfilled on this earth through fulfilling the second greatest commandment and the great commission? How sincere are we about wanting to see God's kingdom come and His will be done in place of our kingdom and wills? It's honestly a scary thought – the whole idea of letting go of our wants and rights. Truly embracing the Lord's Prayer, which often has been so casually re-hearsed, would change our lives and the world.

Jesus himself championed this prayer at the Garden of Gethsemane when He struggled with taking the final steps to the cross where He would be tortured, humiliated and brutally killed. On that cold, dreary night, Jesus agonized as he said to God, "*Father if you are willing, take this cup from me*" (Luke 22:42a). The cup represented the suffering he had to endure at the wrath of God in order to atone for our sins. Jesus knew He was heading into the fire and like any human being who doesn't like pain, Jesus was distraught (Matt. 26:38). But He lived up to the Lord's Prayer as He said, "*Yet not my will, but yours be done*" (Luke 22:42b).

Why is Jesus our hero, besides that He died for us, resurrected, reigns with the Father and redeems us? It is because He perfectly loved God. Holding nothing back, not even His own life and forsaking whatever kingdoms He could've had (Luke 4:5-8), He loved God the Father with His entire being and fought only for God's kingdom. He fulfilled perfectly the point of God's story. And He wants to lead us toward that same end. Where did you think Jesus was going when He said, "Follow me"?

Some of the greatest heroes in stories will not only save people from danger but inspire them to run straight into it. Like William Wallace in "Braveheart" or Captain Miller in "Saving Private Ryan", heroes sometimes lead others into the fire in order to triumph over brokenness and achieve beauty. So, when Jesus said, *"Deny yourself, take up your cross and follow me"* (Luke 9:23), he calls us to let go of ourselves enough to pursue with faithfulness, courage and passion the quest of redemption to bring about the beauty of God. He has not said to us, "I saved you. Now, stay here and be safe." The comforting thing is Jesus did not say, "You go." He said, *"Follow me"*, meaning we run into danger in the company of Christ with Him in the lead. He leads us to be a kind of hero to others as kingdom builders, relationship makers, beauty creators and God lovers.

Only when we follow our hero towards building a kingdom of God lovers will we see the meaning of the purple curtain.

Walk in Color

- What, honestly, are your greatest loves right now?
- How would you evaluate your pursuit of living out the great commandment?
- What can you do to respond to the great commission tomorrow and in the future?
- Read Isaiah 61. How are we called to be beauty partakers and beauty makers?

Notes: Chapter Eleven

[1] Eco, *History of Beauty*, 418.

[2] *Ibid.*

[3] http://www.lindacreed.org/linda_bio.php

[4] It was customary for kings in the ancient Mesopotamia to construct monuments after a victory that gave credit to themselves as well as to God. John H. Walton, Victor H. Matthews and Mark W. Chavalas, *The IVP Bible Background Commentary: Old Testament* (Downers Grove: InterVarsity Press, 2000), 303. But in this case, a third party viewer clearly reported the monument was built to honor only Saul.

[5] The verb is an imperative.

[6] Frederick Dale Bruner, *Matthew, a Commentary: Matthew 13-28*, The Churchbook, vol. 2, revised and expanded ed. (Grand Rapids: William B. Eerdmans Publishing Company, 2007), 815-6.

Pull Out Quotes

[i] Nicholas Thomas Wright, *Surprised by Hope: Rethinking Heaven, the Resurrection, and the Mission of the Church* (New York: HarperCollins Publishers, 2008), 235.

[ii] Augustine, *Concerning the City of God Against the Pagans*, transl. Henry Bettenson (London: Penguin Books, 1984), 1088.

Chapter Twelve

MAKE

A curtain heightens our hope for something great.

Do you recall the exhilarating feeling of walking into an auditorium before the start of a show? People are checking their tickets and meandering to their seats while the orchestra tunes their instruments. Chatter fills the auditorium as everyone waits with excitement over what's behind the curtain.

The curtain creates anticipation by separating us from the stage, so that both physically and emotionally we are disconnected from the artistry behind the curtain. The curtain cuts off our experience of the beauty it's meant to reveal and creates an insurmountable distance between us and what we hope to see. The curtain fosters hope, because it always introduces something great. We can't wait until the curtain opens.

Hiding Beauty

An extraordinarily beautiful curtain separated people from the beauty of God in the Tabernacle and Temple. This curtain made of fine linen was blue, scarlet and purple (Exod. 26:31, 2 Chron. 3:14). The color blue conveyed God's heavenliness, transcendence and prestige.[1] Scarlet (or red) symbolized blood sacrifices, which expressed God's mercy, grace and forgiveness.[2] Purple symbolized God's power, majesty and royalty.[3] Purple is unique because it is formed from combining blue and red, which are two colors on the extreme opposite ends of the color spectrum. Purple is created out of the mixture of two opposing colors, similar to the harmony of God's perfect character.

Purple symbolizes the sum of the color spectrum. It is the color of perfection, wholeness and completion. It expresses the vast array of God's attributes, from His transcendent majesty that makes Him lofty and distant to His atoning mercy that makes Him near and intimate – from the justice God exercises in the heavenly realm to the gracious mercy God shows on the earthly plane. Pulling in blue from one end and red from the other, it expresses "the Alpha and Omega" of God (two Greek letters on the opposite ends of the alphabet), the totality and infinity of absolute beauty. Purple is the color that lacks nothing and is without fault. It is the color that cries out, "I AM." This purple curtain introduced the absolute beauty of God. But it separated people from Him.

This curtain made by an expert artist divided the Holy Place from the Holy of Holies. Behind this curtain lay the Ark of the Covenant that represented God's presence. This curtain of beauty fittingly indicated that a divine and most beautiful presence lay in the room beyond it. But this beautiful curtain was a barrier. People could not pass through this curtain into the Holy of Holies to experience God's presence, except once a year on the Day of Atonement the high priest may enter (Lev. 16). This fabric created a vast distance between the perfect God and broken people.

However, the purple curtain was a necessary barrier. Passing the curtain on a non-atonement day meant death. Surprisingly, you wouldn't die by a sword, lion or cruel torture device. You would die by God's beauty. God's presence would appear in a radiating cloud (Lev. 16:2), known as His *shekinah glory*, the manifestation of all His brilliance and beauty. His beauty would be too overwhelming for a broken sinner and death would be the result. The distance between beauty and brokenness was vast.

The purple curtain reminded people of a desperate problem. Pure brokenness could not experience pure beauty. But brokenness without beauty is without hope. If there's one thing brokenness yearns for, it's beauty. We live in a consumerist's world where media has sold people the notion that if you buy a certain product you will be happy. Or, if you attain this, you will achieve a level of beauty that will satisfy your longing. What people fail to see in the consumerist mentality is the utter depth of our brokenness can only be satiated by the perfection of absolute beauty. Everything else is a pacifier. Without true beauty that surpasses this fading world, there is no future and there is no present. There is no future because we haven't discovered a destiny beyond what's perishing and there is no present because we haven't found our God-given dignity. A life without destiny and dignity is a life without beauty.

A. W. Tozer wrote: "The world is perishing for lack of the knowledge of God and the Church is famishing for want of His Presence. The instant cure of most of our religious ills would be to enter the Presence in spiritual experience…"[4]. The anchor for our souls lay beyond the purple curtain – where God's beauty is found (Heb. 6:19). Fortunately, curtains are meant to be open.

Opening the Curtain

The purple curtain was ripped open at the death of Christ (Matt. 27:51). It was not torn during His miracles, flogging or crucifixion. It was torn at the moment of His death. Nothing but the complete destruction of Christ could open the curtain. Our paradoxical situation had to be resolved by another paradox – *Jesus who was the absolute beauty of God had to be broken in order for broken people to enter into absolute beauty.* Faith in Jesus is necessary because it is by His blood we may pass the curtain (Heb. 9:7). Without blood, there is no entering into beauty and brokenness remains hopeless. The key to opening the curtain was a sacrifice. Grace.

There is no discovery of beauty without an understanding of grace. Our culture teaches us to work hard and not depend upon others. Work hard for your education, career, money and family plans. Society teaches us a worldview that our success and significance is dependent on our work. Paul wrote that many are veiled by the curtain of the "old covenant", which is the legalistic way of achieving your own beauty by working hard

> "Grace means that God already loves us as much as an infinite God can possibly love."
>
> —Philip Yancey

at obeying the law. He wrote: "the same veil remains when the old covenant is read. It has not been removed, because only in Christ is it taken away" (2 Cor. 3:14). Only faith in Christ removes the curtain that blocks us from having fellowship with God. When we embrace grace as the means to beauty, we're reminded of God's work of redemption in us and in the world.

The Other Curtain

There is another curtain at play.

The Apostle Paul wrote, "*And even if our gospel is veiled, it is veiled to those who are perishing. The god of this age has blinded the minds of unbelievers, so that they cannot see the light of the gospel of the glory of Christ, who is the image of God*" (2 Cor. 4:3-4). Like the curtain of the Tabernacle and Temple, our personal curtains (veils) separate us from God. A.W. Tozer called this curtain, "Self". He wrote that by self he referred to all the self-sins, including "self-righteousness, self-pity, self-confidence, self-sufficiency, self-admiration, self-love and a host of others like them"[5]. Legalism and self are intimate partners — it's about what *I* do. *Self* is a big obstacle to pursuing genuine beauty in life and in the world. Our infatuations with our opinions keep us from truly listening or seeing; our pride keeps us from seeking a beauty greater than ourselves; our focus on self-love prevents us from seeing how much God loves us; our self-centeredness towards satisfying our own happiness keeps us from seeing a greater purpose for which to live. While self-gratification feels like a great reward, it actually is our greatest enemy. According to Paul, the "*god of this age*" (a.k.a. the Devil) wants to keep us blinded by self and veiled to God's beauty. If we're too busy with ourselves, we won't notice God.

Our mission in God's story requires overcoming the obstacle of *self*. How do we tear down the veil of self? The answer is similar to how Jesus tore down the purple curtain – *die*.

Curtain Removers, Beauty Unveilers

Our consumerist culture teaches the principle that what satisfies me is most important. It is a context that allows for *self* to be god, where our betterment and gratification are our highest ends. Consumerism is about the nice house *I* want, the nice school *I* want for *my* children, and the happiness *I* want to achieve for *myself*. *I* want media, ads and businesses to cater to *my* tastes.[6] And what's more, *I* can achieve all this.

Consumerist thinking allows us to settle for a sentiment of beauty and forsake absolute beauty. Sentimentality offers us good feelings without truth or transformation that absolute beauty offers. Our *self* loves sentiments, because we can stay the way we are and feel good about it. When we say beauty is in "the eye of the beholder", we mean whatever pleases *me* is beautiful and ideal. The concept of relativity simply becomes an excuse for self-godhood. To reclaim a definition of absolute beauty in the world we must begin with ourselves, and dying to self is the first step.

Jesus said, "*If anyone would come after me, he must deny himself and take up his cross daily and follow me*" (Luke 9:23). But He also said, "*What good is it for a man to gain the whole world, and yet lose or forfeit his very self?*" (Luke 9:25) Hear the irony: Jesus called us to deny our *self* in order to save our *self*. Jesus is not eradicating individuality or disdaining life. In fact, it is the very opposite. He's trying to save ourselves from ourselves. By following Jesus, we entrust ourselves to the one through whom the universe was made (Col. 1:16) and to the Creator's intent for *self*,

> "Self is the opaque veil that hides the Face of God from us. It can be removed only in spiritual experience, never by mere instruction."[ii]
>
> —A. W. Tozer

one that is not diminished to the sum of our appetites. It is a self that embraces true beauty. But the reality is we can't cling to our broken selves and attempt to follow Jesus into beauty.

To deny our selves fundamentally means to be *selfless*.[7] It means think-ing that we are not the most important persons and our appetites are not what matter most. To be a Christian requires us to be selfless towards God. Self-denial is a prerequisite to following the savior.[8] Dietrich Bonho-effer, who was a minister and martyr of Jesus Christ while Bonheoffer was an inmate in the Nazi prisons, wrote:

> Self-denial is never just a series of isolated acts of mortification or asceticism…To deny oneself is to be aware only of Christ and no more of self, to see only him who goes before and no more the road which is too hard for us. Once more, all that self-denial can say is: 'He leads the way, keep close to him.'[9]

Self-denial sounds ridiculous, because it is a radical move of faith. But then again, broken people attempting to achieve beauty is radical. As Jesus died to open the curtain, we're called to die in order to rend the curtain of self that blinds us to God's beauty.

I know it's not easy. Relinquishing ourselves is a painful process. A.W. Tozer honestly admitted, a dying of *self*-will is not pleasant. "In human ex-perience that veil is made of living spiritual tissue; it is composed of the sentient, quivering stuff of which our whole beings consist, and to touch it is to touch us where we feel pain. To tear it away is to injure us, to hurt us and make us bleed."[10] It is not simple. It requires extreme courage and sur-render.

But self-denial does not equate to depression, low self-esteem or lack of ambition. It is, in fact, the very opposite of these. We don't deny our-selves because we have nothing to live for. It is because we've discovered the reason for living that we passionately and joyfully abandon ourselves to attain that which is greater than ourselves. Don't be afraid of letting go of yourself. Be afraid of not having realized the reason that's worth letting go of yourself for. For beauty-lovers and glory-seekers, self-denial is met with a passionate pursuit. For we know that what lies on the other side of the curtain is far better than the side we're on.

In the practical, daily experience of self-denial, we may identify with Paul's struggle in Romans 7:7-25. We don't do the good we know we should do, and the wrong we know we shouldn't do, that we do. The urge to do what we shouldn't comes from the *self*. Paul calls it the *old self* or *flesh*. How many of us know this struggle too well? It's an excruciating roller coaster ride, which we get tired of and at times want to give in to or give up on. But there is a surprising beauty we may not realize from this struggle.

In the moments we do good, we are creating beauty. Part way through this passage of Romans 7, Paul introduces a different Greek term for "good". He doesn't just call the good *agathos*, which means "noble". He calls it *kalos* (v. 16ff), which means "beautiful"[ii]. When we struggle to live out God's laws, we attempt to mirror God's character. Obedience to God is not only a moral matter but one of reflecting God's absolute beauty in ourselves. Our moral struggle is tied to an aesthetic pursuit, where our quest to do good is a fight for beauty to triumph in us. Even in the very wrestling of denying ourselves,

> "The cross is laid on every Christian. The first Christ-suffering which every man must experience is the call to abandon the attachments of this world. It is that dying of the old man which is the result of his encounter with Christ. As we embark upon discipleship we surrender ourselves to Christ in union with his death...the cross is not the terrible end to an otherwise godfearing and happy life, but it meets us at the beginning of our communion with Christ. When Christ calls a man, he bids him come and die."[iii]
>
> —Dietrich Bonhoeffer

we're creating beauty by fighting for the beauty of God to take hold of us. Our motivation to stay in this fight is an indicator that we still know something of real beauty and want it. We know that settling for self is too short-sighted. Without the struggle against *self*, we cannot create beauty.

Be

In a postmodern culture that has something for everyone, people long for something real. Postmodernism accommodates everyone's tastes in the name of tolerance and it is compromising at its core.[12] It deletes the notion of objective definitions. Beauty is purely subjective, and the self becomes the authority. But even in the *self*-culture, there is a cry for experiencing and witnessing something real. There is a desire to experience something that is not driven by what sells or whatever conforms to popular media. Postmodernism yearns for authenticity, or what I call a kind of truthfulness. Postmodernism doesn't subscribe to absolute truth, but it seeks truthfulness, which is equated to real-ness. That is, our world wants to see real people, real values and real relationships. And Jesus commissioned us to show the world something real.

Jesus' final words to us before He ascended to heaven were, *"But you will receive power when the Holy Spirit comes on you; and you will be my witnesses in Jerusalem, and in all Judea and Samaria, and to the ends of the earth"* (Acts 1:8). This is part of the great commission. I like how definitive Jesus was. In Matthew 28:19-20, He commanded us to go and make disciples, giving us the choice

> *"A role which is built of truth will grow, whereas one built on stereotype will shrivel."*[iv]
>
> —Constantin Stanislavski

to obey or not. But in Acts 1:8, he plainly said, *"you will receive"* and *"you will be."* He stated it as a reality that will happen to us. Basically, the Spirit of God *will* enter, transform and empower you, and then you *will* be His witnesses. No buts or ifs. Being a witness of Jesus is part of the reality of being a believer of Jesus.

I like the action word Jesus chose: *be*. He did not say we will testify, proclaim or evangelize. The action is incarnational. We will *be*. The call was not to do something, but to *be* something. When we complete a task, the task ends. But there is no start or stop to *being*. Being means it is a part of who we are. As long as we exist, the being continues. The quality of a task is evaluated on performance. The quality of being is evaluated on life change, identity embracement, personal transformation and, most of all, fellowship with God. When we *are*, it assumes we will *do*. We aren't simply carrying a message. The message is a part of who we are and an expression of our identity.

I also like Jesus' selective word choice in what we become – *witnesses*. The concept of a witness stemmed from the Old Testament understanding of someone who observed or encountered something firsthand and testified to the truth of it (Deut. 17-19; Prov. 14:5). In the book of Acts, we see that personal experiences were necessary for being a witness. The replacement for Judas as the twelfth apostle had to have had direct encounters with Jesus (Acts 1:22), so that he could testify to what he personally experienced. The Bible emphasized personal experiences were part of what defined a witness. Therefore, to be a "witness" meant having experienced Jesus.[13]

Experiences are not just about things that happen to us but about the things we personally choose to engage. Do we engage God's Word by knowing and obeying it? Do we welcome the Holy Spirit (Gal. 5:25) to transform our minds (Ro. 12:2), guide us (Jn. 16:7-9), produce fruit in us (Gal. 5:22) and intoxicate us (Eph. 5:18)? Do we choose to mentally dwell in the beauties of God? Philippians 4:8 invites us to bask in the things that reflect God's beauty. For instance, it tells us to think about truth, which is a core element of absolute beauty. To think about "whatever is noble" means to ponder on things that echo God's majesty, splendor and magnificence. "Whatever is lovely" means enjoy the pleasures and delights of God. The list includes whatever is right, pure, admirable, excellent and praiseworthy. We have to choose to be in absolute beauty. On a practical level, it won't just happen.

When we are a people who authentically know beauty, we may be able to rightly create beauty in a broken world that longs for beauty but is skeptical of its authenticity. I find truth in one of Constantin Stanislavski's principles of good acting. He wrote, "Never allow yourself externally to portray anything that you have not inwardly experienced..."[14]. Show the world something real. Whenever someone asks me, "Can you teach a class on evangelism?" I tell them, "I can show you instead how to walk with Jesus." Our witness has to be based on our discipleship. How we witness

Jesus and how we walk with Him are inseparable. Give people a firsthand exposure to the beauty we've experienced as broken people.

Expression

To be a witness means to express one's self. A witness is meant to be heard and seen. You cannot be a Christian and not be noticed, because we're light. Jesus said we're *"the light of the world"* (Matt. 5:14). Jesus gave a painfully obvious explanation about lamps, when He said no one lights a lamp and puts it under a bowl. Of course not! That would be absurd. It is just as absurd for Christians to remain hidden and silent. Light is meant to be seen. It's interesting the beauty of God is typically described with intense light, as we saw in chapter 3. Rays of light, brilliant light, rainbows of light and fiery light were all iconic characteristics of God's imagery. God is light (1 Jn. 1:5). Jesus is the light of the world (Jn. 8:12). And, He called us the *"light of the world"*. We are meant to express God's beauty in a darkened world. If we didn't, it would be absurd.

> *"That God is the Master Craftsman and we are the extension of His creative model compels us to contemplate His lavish endowments."*
>
> —Howard G. Hendricks

As witnesses described with the imagery of light, creativity in expressing the gospel is a must. Why creativity? God's image in us equipped every person with the capacity to communicate and relate creatively.

When we see God in Genesis 1 forming a masterpiece out of loose parts, we see the premise for our creative expressions. As image bearers, we too can take parts to form a whole that bear godly delight. We can create poems and songs, like David; clothing, like the designers of the priestly garments; interior design, like the artists of the Tabernacle; drawings and models, like Ezekiel; and dances, like Miriam and David. Creative expression for God's glory can be an act of faith and worship towards God.

Expressing the gospel creatively creates different levels of understanding God's redeeming work. God used creative imagery to convey messages of salvation. Take for example, Jesus' reference to His atoning work on the cross to the imagery of Moses' sculpture of a snake (Jn. 3:14). Jesus likened himself to one of Moses' artworks. During one of the Israelites' rebellious incidences, God punished them with venomous snakes. When the people cried out to God, He created a way for their salvation by commanding Moses to fashion a bronze snake and post it on a stake. If an Israelite looked up at this art piece, he was healed (Num. 21:4-9).

Moses sculpted a snake to mirror the snakes that bit the people. It was made of bronze so it had a brilliant sheen that represented the attributes of divinity and honor. When bronze was polished enough, it could be as shiny as a mirror. The bronze snake foreshadowed a crucial truth about Jesus – He would be the man on the cross with God's divine beauty bearing God's wrath upon himself (Jn. 3:14-15). The creativity of the Bible formed deep understandings of truth. As God's image-bearers and Jesus' witnesses, the charge for us to be creative in our expressions of the gospel is both faithful and responsible.

This example of the bronze snake and Jesus speaks of an important principle, especially in our image-oriented culture. I've come across people who fear certain images because the images were used in pagan traditions or at one time represented something ungodly. It's the same issue with other types of creative expressions, like music. Is it okay to use images that expressed something pagan? A lady once rebuked me for wearing a shirt with a Chinese dragon on it because it looked like a snake and the snake was the image of the devil in Genesis 3.

Images, however, in the Bible are interchangeable as we see Moses and Jesus using the bronze snake on a stake as an image for God's atoning work of salvation. God's use of images also function relevantly within culture. For example, cherubim are not unique to the Bible. Cherubim can be found in Egyptian and other Ancient Mesopotamian cultures and religions. Cherubim were un-

> "the creative Christian spirit in art should be pointing the way forward and upward..."[vi]
>
> —Frank E. Gaebelein

derstood to be angelic, unearthly creatures that highlight the heavenliness of the deity they represented. God didn't invent a new image but used an image that was understood by the surrounding cultures even if the image was associated with pagan gods. But God does something more. He redeems the image. Other pagan cultures generally posed the cherubim as guards for their deities. In the Bible however, the cherubim worship God, not guard Him, as in Isaiah 6, Ezekiel 1, Exodus 25 and Revelation 4. God doesn't merely borrow images; He redeems them.

Images are condemned when they lead people away from the truth and glory of God or when they become idols, as the bronze snake eventually became. People started worshipping the bronze snake and as a result it had to be destroyed (2 Kgs. 18:4). Interestingly, though, the original intent of the bronze snake was preserved by Jesus' reference to it several hundred years later. This shows the fluidity of images.

The creative use of images teaches us that most everything in the world can be redeemed. We can't be too fearful about culture. Culture will always have a mixture of sinfulness and brokenness with God's goodness and the potential for redemption. When we see the power of God's grace in redeeming elements of culture, we gain the freedom to express His truth creatively as long as we think biblically. We're called to think theologically, relevantly and creatively in order to show a broken world the beauty of God. As witnesses, we're much like the avant-garde artists whose aim was "to teach us to interpret the world through different eyes…"[15]. I like what Steve Turner wrote about the best kinds of art. "The best art doesn't tell people what to believe but enables them, for a short while, to see things differently, and the Christian can enable people to momentarily glimpse the world through eyes that have been touched by Christ."[16] Our creative expressions allow people to see, hear, taste, smell, touch, feel and experience a reality of God's truth that may lead them one step further to fostering faith in Christ.

Creative Thinking

Creative expression forces us to be incarnational, where our very lives can be powerful expressions of the gospel. I love what Francis Schaeffer wrote: "Christian art is the expression of the whole life of the whole person who is a Christian."[17] This is the sort of artistic expression that no evangelism class can teach us. It comes from discipleship.

Creative thinking causes us to consider the matters of our hearts, thoughts and attitudes. Creativity forces us to act beyond mere intellectualism. Creativity forces us to think deeper about truth and more analytically about our culture. In order to be creative, we can't be trite. We can't gloss over an idea or be lazy about our communication. We have to think about what a truth means in order to express it creatively. We have to consider critically and sensitively what our culture is about in order to express ourselves relevantly. Our assumptions are challenged when we think creatively. We learn that being creative doesn't allow us to be complacent. Thinking creatively as the Bible models for us keeps us spiritually in tune, inspired and challenged.

John Dewey gave this insight: "The enemies of the [a]esthetic are neither the practical nor the intellectual. They are the humdrum; slackness of loose ends; submission to convention in practice and intellectual procedure."[18] Putting it into a spiritual perspective, complacency, assumptions and lazy thinking dull creativity. I heard a great piece of philosophy once from Remy, the rat in "Ratatouille", who said, "Change is nature." Being creative forces us to be brave with the possibilities of change. When we aren't afraid of change, we aren't afraid to grow and engage the world.

Beauty-Makers

A prostitute approached me in Vegas, and I wished I had responded differently. She bypassed my friends and came straight for me. She introduced herself very pleasantly and highlighted her body with her hands. My friend and I knew instantly what she was trying to sell to me. I instinctively waved my hands in front of her and said politely, "No, thanks." I walked away quickly as I heard her say, "OK." She must've been no more than 18 years old. Some might say I averted evil and triumphed over temptation. But as I replayed that incident in my mind minutes afterwards, I only saw the face of a broken girl who had a story to her. I wish I could redo that moment where instead of avoiding her, I gave her my attention, listened to her and spoke with her about God's love. I had an opportunity to show some level of grace, goodness and redeeming beauty to a broken person. Instead, I naturally avoided the brokenness. I think we avoid brokenness because we're afraid it will drag us down or because it resonates with a brokenness within us we haven't resolved.

But in God's story brokenness is the context for making beauty. Jesus called us to be witnesses "*in Jerusalem, Judea and Samaria and to the ends of the earth*". We're not called to send an email or testify from afar. We're called to be in broken places, interacting with culture, ideologies and lives.

> "The message of new creation, of the beauty of the present world taken up and transcended in the beauty of the world that is yet to be – with part of that beauty being precisely the healing of the present anguish – comes as a surprising hope. Part of the role of the church in the past was – and could and should be again – to foster and sustain lives of beauty and aesthetic meaning at every level, from music making in the village pub to drama in local primary school..."[vii]
>
> —N. T. Wright

When we see we're on a mission as witnesses to create beauty, we have to seek out brokenness and engage it. God is not trying to create beauty out of beauty – it is beauty out of brokenness. He wants to create life from the dead, dignity out of shame, peace out of pain, hope out of helplessness and lovers of Him out of His enemies. Too often we seek the Disneylands when God has called us to the slums. Beauty is created when we bring grace into brokenness. And sometimes, brokenness comes right to us. It came to me. The task of the great commission to fulfill the great commandment calls us to make beauty in a broken world that God has not given up on. Sometimes we think the brokenness and ugliness of the world that comes knocking on our doors are from the devil. Sometimes I think they're from God. What if God is bringing brokenness and ugliness to us because He has called us to be light to darkness?

We are sculptors when we pay attention to the fragments of our community and try to bring wholeness to it. We are architects when we build families on the foundation of God's Word. We are writers when we daily live out God's redeeming story in our workplaces. We are actors when we authentically show Jesus to our neighbors. We are poets when we speak the gospel to others. We are musicians when we offer comfort to the hurting. We are dancers when we persevere in pain. We are painters when we offer a vision of hope for the weary. We are heroes when we bring beauty to the broken.

The End

When is the work finished? I like what John Chamberlain, the artist who made sculptures out of trash, said when he was asked the same question. He said he's finished "when there are no more holes to fill". When *cosmos* is once more achieved, we are done. The completed work of God's artistry is nothing short of perfection. When there is wholeness in creation and in our human nature and when our glory is nothing less than a clear reflection of Christ, then the work of God through the Holy Spirit in the name of Jesus is done. Our hope is in a time when all the holes are filled. When the broken pieces in ourselves and in our world are made whole. When we find ourselves dancing with God and see Him rejoicing over a people who love Him (Isa. 65:17-19). That's the reaction we would expect over pure beauty.

When God's vision is realized, we'll see a radiant city of pure gold adorned with clear jewels, where its foundations are made of jasper, sapphire, chalcedony, emerald, sardonyx, carnelian, chrysolite, beryl, topaz, chrysoprase, jacinth and amethyst, its gates are pearls and its streets are gold (Rev. 21:11-21). It is a vision of beauty. Whether these materials of the city are actual or metaphorical, the description of its outer beauty expresses its inner beauty, because it will be a city where sin is no more (Rev. 21:7-8), where the thirsty are satisfied (Rev. 21:6), where sorrow is gone (Rev. 21:4), and, above all, where God's presence and beauty resides (Rev. 21:22). It will be beautiful because it will perfectly shine with God's glory (Rev. 21:23). This city will be the community of God who are in perfect fellowship with Him. It will be the reality the Hero of the story strives to bring. It will be the kingdom the lovers of God pray to come. It will be the beauty the broken long for. It is the vision God will create.

Until then, let's follow Christ past the purple curtain to know absolute beauty daily and to make beauty in brokenness as lovers of God and witnesses of Jesus.

Walk in Color

- What is one area of *self* you have not denied that keeps you from God's beauty?
- How do you feel about engaging brokenness? How can you engage it more?
- How can you be a creative witness in making beauty in brokenness tomorrow, next week and this year?

Notes: Chapter Twelve

[1] Dictionary of Biblical Imagery, 1998 ed., s.v. "Colors".

[2] *Ibid.*

[3] *Ibid.*

[4] A.W. Tozer, *The Pursuit of God*, intro. by Samuel M. Zwemer (Lexington: Soho Books, 2010), 20.

[5] *Ibid.*, 24.

[6] From another point of view, Robert Williams argued that the consumerist culture leads to a destruction of a true self because we are being reduced to our appetites devoid of creative and inventive thought. Consumerism fosters conformity for the sake of self-satisfaction that erases individual identity. (Robert Williams, *Art Theory: An Historical Introduction* (Malden: Blackwell Publishing, 2004), 226 & 261). Thus, while consumerism focuses on the self (consumer), it is a self that is redefined as wants and needs versus a self that is inspired, enlightened or aware. In the end, it is a self that is still blind.

[7] "arneomai", *A Greek-English Lexicon of the New testament and Other Early Christian Literature*, 3rd ed., 133.

[8] As Dr. Darrell Bock pointed out, the first two imperatival commands – deny yourself and take up your cross – are in the aorist tense while the last command – follow Jesus – is in the present tense. The first two commands have to be done before the third can be accomplished. One cannot hang on to self and follow Jesus. Darrell L. Bock, *Luke*, Baker Exegetical Commentary on the New Testament, vol. 1: 1:1-9:50 (Grand Rapids: Baker Books, 2004), 852.

[9] Dietrich Bonhoeffer, *The Cost of Discipleship*, translated from the German *Nachfolge* (New York: Simon and Schuster, 1995), 88.

[10] A.W. Tozer, *The Pursuit of God*, 25.

[11] Leon Morris, *The Epistle to the Romans*, The Pillar New Testament Commentary (Grand Rapids: William B. Eerdmans Publishing Company, 1988), 292.

[12] Fred S. Kleiner and Christin J. Mamiya, *Gardner's Art Through the Ages*, 12th ed. (Belmont: Wadsworth/Thomson Learning, 2005), 1034.

[13] Darrell L. Bock, *Acts*, Baker Exegetical Commentary on the New Testament (Grand Rapids: Baker Academic, 2007), 64.

[14] Constantin Stanislavski, *An Actor Prepares*, transl. Elizabeth Reynolds Hapgood (New York: Routledge, 2003), 31.

[15] Janson, *History of Beauty*, 415.

[16] Steve Turner, *Imagine: A Vision for Christians in the Arts* (Downers Grove: InterVarsity Press, 2001), 115-116.

[17] Francis A. Schaeffer, *Art and the Bible*, foreword by Michael Card (Downers Grove: InterVarsity Press, 2006), 90.

[18] John Dewey, *Art as Experience* (New York: The Berkeley Publishing Group, 2005), 42.

The Purple Curtain

Pull Out Quotes

[i] Philip D. Yancey, *What's So Amazing About Grace?* (Grand Rapids: Zondervan, 1997), 70.

[ii] A.W. Tozer, *The Pursuit of God*, 24-25.

[iii] Dietrich Bonhoeffer, *The Cost of Discipleship*, transl. from *Nachfolge* by R. H. Fuller (New York: Simon & Schuster, 1995), 89.

[iv] Constantin Stanislavski, *An Actor Prepares* (New York: Routledge, 2003), 31.

[v] Howard G. Hendricks, *Color Outside the Lines*, Swindoll Leadership Library, ed. by Charles R. Swindoll (Nashville: Word Publishing, 1998), 33.

[vi] Frank E. Gaebelein, *The Christian, The Arts, and Truth: Regaining the Vision of Greatness*, ed. by D. Bruce Lockerbie (Portland: Multnomah Press, 1985), 57.

[vii] N.T. Wright, *Surprised by Hope: Rethinking Heaven, the Resurrection, and the Mission of the Church* (New York: Harper One, 2008), 231-232.

Final Thought

If you're not sure where to begin in making beauty, perhaps start with enjoying His beauty. Immerse in His character, words, works and desires. Then start creating.

> "I make a sacrifice of praise to him who sanctifies me, for the beauty which flows through men's minds into their skilful hands comes from the Beauty which is above their souls and for which my soul sighs all day and night."[i]
>
> —Augustine

[i] Augustine, *Confessions*, transl. R. S. Pine-Coffin (New York: Penguin Group, 1961), 241.